Library of
Davidson College

OTHER PEOPLE'S MONEY

OTHER PEOPLE'S MONEY

The Rise and Fall of OPM Leasing Services

STEPHEN FENICHELL

Anchor Press/Doubleday
Garden City, New York
1985

364.16
F3330

85-9048

Library of Congress Cataloging in Publication Data
Fenichell, Stephen
Other people's money
1. OPM Leasing Services. 2. Computer leases—United States—Corrupt practices—Case studies. I. Title.
HF5548.6.F46   1985   364.1'68'0973
ISBN: 0-385-19368-8
Library of Congress Catalog Card Number: 84-24256
COPYRIGHT © 1985 BY STEPHEN FENICHELL
ALL RIGHTS RESERVED
PRINTED IN THE UNITED STATES OF AMERICA
FIRST EDITION

ACKNOWLEDGMENTS

The author would like to thank James P. Hassett, the OPM trustee, for his help and cooperation during the researching of this book. Without the dedication of the trustee and his staff, and the trustee's special counsel, Wilmer Cutler & Pickering, to their full-scale investigation of the fraud at OPM, an accurate portrayal of the events set forth in this book would have been practically impossible. Robert Bennett and Alan Rothman were particularly generous with their time and assistance, as were numerous other members of the trustee's staff I encountered during my time at OPM.

I would like to thank my editor, Peyton Moss, for his generous editorial attention, and my agent, Julian Bach, for his advice and support.

1

New Year's Day 1979.

Two thirty-three-year-old businessmen from New York are flying first-class to Los Angeles. Myron Goodman, on the aisle, tall, thin-haired, in the wide-rimmed glasses and custom-cut pin-striped suit, is supposed to be some sort of financial genius. Mordecai Weissman, at the window, heavyset, sideburned, mod haircut, in the louder-patterned salesman's suit, is a reputed marketing whiz. These are bright young men on the move. Out in front, up and up. One look at them, you'd have to say they've got it made. Made, if you like, out of money.

Myron and Mordy are partners eight years. Partners in business, partners for life. They grew up in Brooklyn together, were wheeled in baby carriages through the streets of Williamsburg together, attended Yeshiva Torah Vodaath Mesivta together, graduated from Brooklyn College together. Even in marriage, they wound up together, marrying a set of sisters right out of college. They went into business together, made it big together, moved out to Long Island together. Now they are stuck together. Together for life: a life sentence.

Going into the leasing business was Mordy's idea. Mordy always had the ideas. Ever since grade school, Mordy was quick. Myron: "What he had in his little pinky I didn't have in my entire head." Whereas Myron was always a little bit slow. "I was a very slow learner. A slow reader. I had to review things many times."

Even in college, Myron got by more on memory: "I do have a knack to remember things. People have accused me of having a

photographic memory. I tend to think they are not accurate."
Mordy got by on his wits, and all kinds of ploys. At Brooklyn College, while Myron was studying eight hours a day with an additional four devoted to Hebrew, Mordy was horsing around. Senior year they took a course together. The grade was based on a midterm, a paper, and a final exam. While Myron plugged away at the paper, struggled his way through the final, Mordy was wheeling and dealing his way out of the paper and the exam with a whole song and dance about getting married. Mordy aced the course on the midterm. Myron was lucky to pass.

After a stint of teaching, Mordy found a job more to his liking in the leasing business. He was exceedingly moved by how easy it was to make twice a teacher's salary on sales commissions alone. In July of 1970, he went into business on his own. He borrowed ten thousand dollars from his parents and rented a one-room office over a candy store on Church Avenue in Brooklyn. The name of the company was LSD: Leasing Services Division.

A name like that was supposed to give a good impression. Equipment users were supposed to think LSD was a division of the company selling the equipment, not an independent concern. But the state of New York turned the name down. Not, as Mordy later liked to claim, because it sounded like a certain illegal drug. It was already the name of a subsidiary of the Control Data Corporation, a large computer manufacturer.

Mordy found a better name in a book, a biography of Aristotle Onassis. According to Ari, the only way to become rich these days was off Other People's Money, OPM for short. Which also happened to sound like another illegal drug: opium. Clever Mordy at twenty-three had a fatal fondness for cheap puns.

OPM Leasing was the perfect name. It described the leasing business at its easy best. A leasing company gets an equipment user to sign a lease, committing him to rent a piece of equipment over a specified period of time at a specified rent. Once the user signs a lease, he becomes a "lessee." The leasing company becomes the "lessor." The lessor takes the lease to a bank and gets it financed; the bank lends the lessor the money to buy the equipment. The loan is paid back over time out of rent payments from the lessee.

The lessor makes money in three ways. First, he might be able to finance the lease for a little something above the equipment cost. Second, the first couple of rent payments are usually kept as a commission. Third, after the lease has run out, the leasing company is free to rent the equipment again. This "residual value" is pure profit. Very little, and more likely nothing at all, has been invested by the leasing company itself. Nothing risked and something gained. OPM, pure and simple.

Myron, meanwhile, found himself a job at Chase. He lusted after a plum position with the elite International Investment Group. He had an interview with a Chase International vice president late on a Friday afternoon.

IVP: "If you had to go to Paris for a meeting on a Saturday morning, could you leave on a Friday night?"

Myron: "Someone else would have to go. I could go on a Saturday night or Sunday morning, but not on a Friday night."

Myron was an Orthodox Jew, and a Sabbath observer. Monday morning Myron was called into his supervisor's office. He had been turned down for the job. A friend of his in Personnel told him he'd seen it right in his file: "Sabbath Observer."

Myron: "I wasn't very happy about it. I'm still not happy about it. A lot of things would have been different if I'd gotten that job."

Myron went to a group called COPRA which handled cases of this kind. But his lawsuit "never fell off the ground" because he took a year's job at Chase's main London branch instead.

When Myron returned in the spring of 1970, Mordy came to him with one hell of a partnership pitch.

"We're brothers-in-law. We're friends for twenty-three years. Our mothers wheeled us together in baby carriages together. Etcetera, etcetera."

Myron, meanwhile, said to himself:

"I'm twenty-three. I'm young enough to take this chance. This is an opportunity for me to try to do something on my own. To do it with Mordy versus security. Besides, if it doesn't work out, at my age I can always go back and do something else."

January 1, 1971: Myron started work at OPM.

Business was slow at first. But they were resourceful. Whatever anyone wanted to lease, they would lease. A chicken fryer. A burglar alarm system. A tractor.

Their very first deal was for air conditioners for the San Carlos Hotel in Manhattan. Which was a very rich deal, comparatively. Mordy bought the equipment from his brother, Herbert, in the furniture business. Three thousand, wholesale. But he marked it up to its full retail value, eight thousand. He was able to finance the lease at the bank for the full eight thousand.

Myron: "Mordy did the ultimate thing. He bought wholesale and leased retail."

Herbert got himself a commission, and 5 percent of OPM. Myron and Mordy got five thousand more OPM to play with. OPM was in business.

Their next customer was the Cryonics Society.

Myron: "They froze bodies. They got a copying machine."

Things just evolved from there. In 1971 they moved into larger offices, two small rooms above a bar, down the street from the candy store. By 1972 Mordy had made contacts at a few office equipment companies, like Burroughs, Olivetti, and Basic Four Information Systems. Robert Davis, Mordy's man at Olivetti, became New York area manager for Basic Four. Mordy paid Davis and his salesmen substantial finder's fees for persuading customers to lease office equipment from OPM instead of buying outright. It didn't make any difference to Basic Four; they still booked the lease as a sale. But OPM got its lease and stayed in business.

OPM, courtesy of Robert Davis and friends, obtained a virtual monopoly on Basic Four leases. Basic Four became one of the bestselling minicomputer makers in the country. Basic Four business grew. OPM business grew. By April 1972, OPM had set up shop at 99 Wall Street. The offices were no better than the ones in Brooklyn. But the Wall Street address said it all: OPM was here to stay. To enhance their burgeoning national image, Myron and Mordy opened a string of branch offices in Los Angeles, Atlanta, Chicago, and Boston, even though they had fewer than six people working the New York operation. The branch offices sounded good, but they ate up capital. They were a fiasco. They had to be closed down.

But the boys continued to do well for themselves. Myron attributed their success to three essential "inducements":

1. We sold ourselves on service.
2. Our rates were a little lower.
3. We paid the salesmen off.

Mordy was the marketing man, the outside man, always on the road. Myron was the inside man, the back office man, minding the store. But they split weeks half-and-half between New York and the Coast. They liked the Coast. Especially Mordy, who appreciated the freewheeling life-style. Myron appreciated being treated like a big-deal exec from New York. On their way back from doing deals in L.A., they'd stop off in Vegas for rest and relaxation. Both men liked to gamble.

By 1975 Mordy met a man at Montefiore Hospital in the Bronx. Henry Weiss happened to be a Hasid. Mordy handed him his business card. They found they had a lot in common. Mordy leased him an IBM 370 mainframe, and the ball game just took off from there. Mainframe leasing, big-ticket leasing. Before long they had broken into American Express, Fireman's Fund, General Motors, AT&T, RCA, Revlon, Lockheed, Hertz, McDonnell Douglas, Merrill Lynch, Southern California Edison, and Rockwell International. To obtain the complex financing needed for these big deals, OPM went first to Goldman Sachs, then to Lehman Brothers. Big banks like Bankers Life, Manufacturers Hanover, National Bank of North America, Marine Midland lent OPM the small fortunes they needed to finance these lucrative leases.

By 1978, OPM had reopened branch offices in thirteen major cities across the country, in addition to a costly "international presence" headquartered in London, serving OPM subsidiaries in France, Germany, and the United Kingdom. Myron and Mordy personally owned a bank outside New Orleans worth well over $10 million. Headquarters in New York filled three plush floors of the stately old U.S. Steel headquarters building at 71 Broadway, near the corner of Broadway and Wall. Myron and Mordy reclined, when in town, in suitable comfort in custom-cabineted, deep-carpeted, indirectly lit, blond-wood-and-marble offices, complete with kitchen, dining room, bathrooms with showers and steam baths, pull-out beds, television sets, and a conference room with enough electronic features to look like Hollywood's idea of a war room.

A company kitchen was lavishly outfitted with two sets of plumbing and double dishwashers for preparing kosher meals. Every office door had sprouted its own mezuzah. Afternoon mincha services were held daily at four in the oak-paneled circular library, with the faithful summoned by loudspeaker by chairman of the board Myron S. Goodman himself. The only time the office was closed was on Saturdays and Jewish holidays.

By the end of 1978, business has gone through the roof. Closings chaotic, always delayed, salesmen calling in fresh accounts before old transactions could be recorded. Consultants call this "back office confusion" and OPM is turning full speed into a textbook case. Myron and Mordy are being driven in diverging fast lanes, so frantically crisscrossing the continent that the only way to meet privately is on airplanes.

Myron: "Mordy always kept in touch . . . Just to meet with me he would travel."

Myron and Mordy have long since moved from Brooklyn to Lawrence, Long Island, where Myron lives in something approaching baronial splendor at The Castle, the former property of the Wardwell who founded one of New York's more blue-chip law firms, Davis Polk & Wardwell. Myron and Mordy have literally sunk millions in hard-earned OPM into both places. Myron's palatial estate, with its sprawling French-style manor house, swimming pool, and separate greenhouse, has been extensively renovated in a lushly romantic Empire style, with a basement finished to the tune of a half million plus change, complete with disco, movie theater, and ballet room for his daughters. Myron keeps a hundred pairs of shoes in his walk-in closet which he bought one day on a whim from a mail-order catalogue he found in an airplane seat pocket. He has learned to indulge in expensive wines, has amassed a substantial fortune in antique clocks, and likes to fly to work before daybreak in a helicopter. Mordy's place, much more modest, is still nothing to sneeze at, furnished throughout with rare Oriental antiques and countless costly exotic knickknacks.

Today is New Year's Day 1979. The close of another landmark year. The subject of this morning's, afternoon's, and evening's meeting is broad: full-scale, in-depth, year-end review. Salary and personnel review, future planning, survey of all transactions on the books at this time. Myron is just zeroing in on a few dry, operational details when Mordy cuts him off, midsentence.

"So how are you feeling?"

That Myron is dying at age thirty-four usually goes without saying. His rare condition is called sarcoidosis. A mysterious disease involving the progressive generation of excess tissue in a given part of the body. Myron's was first detected while he was studying for exams in college: a painful, persistent ringing and buzzing in the left ear resulting in time in virtual deafness.

December 6, 1971: Myron and Mordy went in for a routine chest X ray. Mordy's was normal but Myron exhibited excess granulated tissue in his left lung. September 28, 1972: lung biopsy performed at Downstate Medical Center. Diagnosis: active sarcoid. Left ear deafness caused by an auditory nerve severed by the spread of the sarcoid. By July 7, 1977, the sarcoid had spread to the heart. A pacemaker was surgically implanted. More recently, the sarcoid has begun to affect the optic nerves, resulting in severe tunnel vision.

Myron: "I live constantly with the fear of death . . . A disease that 99 percent of the time is arrested in one part of an individual's body is purported to have spread to three or four parts of my body . . . When it is going to stop, I don't know . . . At that meeting, I was very scared of dying . . . I didn't know when I was going to die. I could only assume it wouldn't be a long time."

Myron is in constant pain from his pacemaker. He takes massive quantities of drugs to counteract it, from codeine to steroids to antidepressants to tranquilizers. He has become a habitual pill popper, who occasionally passes out during business conferences and forgets decisions arrived at the day before.

Myron: "When I had problems, no matter what they were, all

I had to do was pop some pills and the feeling of the problem would just go away."

Unfortunately for Myron, getting rid of the feeling of the problem was never quite so easy as getting rid of the problem itself.

Rather than force him into semiretirement, Myron's sickness has caused him to focus, obsessively, on the day-to-day operations of the business. He works fourteen-hour days, at a minimum, starting out at 4 A.M. with a dark predawn drive into Wall Street in a chauffeur-driven limousine. Every night, his assistants gather up the foot-high mound of papers from his eight-foot-long trapezoidal desk, painstakingly pack them in document carrier bags, and load them into an OPM limo to be driven out to Long Island. Every morning at four those same documents are shuttled back into the city and arranged on Myron's desk in precisely the places where they had been the night before.

Now Mordy suggests a practical advantage to a very sad situation: taking out additional life insurance on Myron, making Mordy the sole beneficiary. There they are, soberly discussing estate planning, when Myron begins to realize that Mordy is acting nervous, edgy, ashamed, disturbed. Which strikes Myron, even in his distressed state, as more than a little bit odd.

Myron: "Mordy is the type of guy who is always very sharp and cool. Nothing ever fazes him much. He never gets excited. And if there is ever any problem he always tries to maintain his cool."

Here Mordy, mister cool, is not even trying to maintain. In fact, Mordy had dropped his guard so far as to be actually crying. Myron, with all his problems, has a problem calming Mordy down. And though the tears do dry in time, Myron still isn't hearing any confessions. Usually it is Myron who has done things wrong and has to confess to Mordy. Now it is Mordy's turn in the booth, and Mordy isn't opening up. Mordy, the consummate gregarious outgoing salesman, is a very withdrawn person in person.

Finally, Mordy blurts most of it out: he wants out of OPM. He is sick and tired of OPM. He talks about family, about time, about outside interests, about priorities. While Myron has turned into a workaholic, Mordy has grown into a hippie.

Mordy's millions have largely gone into financing a life of leisurely adventure: safaris in Africa, mountain climbing in the Himalayas, beachcombing in Hawaii. His dream is to retire by thirty-five, a deadline coming due in two years.

Myron: "He wanted to live with one or two million off on some island and not get involved with all this anymore . . . And the only way to do that was to have his two million in the bank and not have to worry about anything."

Mordy is sick of the worry. Myron thrives on the pressure. They close the first phase of their midair marathon partnership conference by coming to terms with the separation, in principle. Mordy needs his two million, whereas Myron is looking forward to finding it.

Myron: "At this point my ego is very high. I see me becoming President of OPM." Myron, master of a multimillion-dollar financial empire. The emperor of OPM.

As the plane lands at LAX, the OPM entourage springs into action. Myron and Mordy employ a string of young assistants whose general title of "vice president" does not exactly constitute a precise job description. Steve Lichtman and Mannes Friedman are Myron's chief aides, assigned to the august duties of relaying phone messages from New York, ferrying documents back and forth from New York to California, and handling the mountains of luggage Myron insists on taking with him everywhere he goes.

Myron and Mordy fly first-class, but the entourage always travels coach. Steve and Mannes are up and running as soon as the plane taxis toward the terminal, claim tickets clutched firmly in hand, to round up the several dozen document carrier bags, attaché cases, suitcases, transfiles, and other assorted luggage at the baggage area. Myron is notorious with airlines for taking his entire office on the plane, including adding machines, calculators, copying equipment, as well as every file, document, paper, relevant or not, from the office in New York.

An endless black stretch limo, rented from Starlite in Beverly Hills, is waiting for them at the gate. Mannes and Steve load twelve large black document bags into the back, as the OPM team is whisked off to the Beverly Wilshire, their home away from home in the Los Angeles area. Myron and Mordy are booked into a magnificent suite in the older main section of the hotel, while Mannes and Steve are stuck in a smaller room in the more modern annex. While the entourage roams in and out, fetching and carrying, handling details, making arrangements, Myron and Mordy continue their partnership conference in their living room.

The question, as always, is the same: how and where to raise more cash. They need two million to buy Mordy out, but if that were all, they wouldn't be worrying. Endless obligations, commitments, agreements, contractual arrangements have yet to be fulfilled, for which the numbers Myron is sitting on are not terribly pretty. The constant cash crunch, never comfy, has become all too dire of late. But Myron and Mordy are confident, bullish, still sure of themselves. Haven't they always pulled the rabbit out of the hat before, at the last possible minute? Wasn't the motto We Shall Overcome practically engraved over the massive front doors at 71 Broadway? There are always ways to generate cash, all sorts of ways. After eight risky years in the leasing business, Myron and Mordy know them all. The other, less official but more appropriate motto, more commonly swept under the mat than set up in bold letters, is Do What You Have to Do. The brothers-in-law, childhood chums, business geniuses, saviors of their families, pillars of their community, are anxiously agitating over ways to lay hands on large lumps of liquid assets when the earthquake hits L.A.

Mordy runs for the door. Myron stays behind, gathering up all the papers. In three or four minutes Myron would have run after him, but Mordy is standing in the doorway yelling, "Why don't you come? Hurry up, let's get out of here!" Myron has at least a dozen document bags and half a dozen attaché cases stuffed with precious documents, and he is not about to let them out of his sight for even one minute. Mordy runs back into the room as an aftershock rocks the building. He turns around and runs back out, yelling for Myron to follow.

But everything is in those bags, the whole sad story up to now.

Myron would rather die in that earthquake than leave his papers to fall into unauthorized hands to, horror of horrors, be found someday in the rubble of the Beverly Wilshire. He doesn't have long to live anyhow. So Myron stays bravely behind securing the secrets while his fast friend, brother-in-law, and cradle companion, runs safely off down the hall.

2

In 1961 Saul Steinberg, the twenty-two-year-old son of a Brooklyn rubber goods manufacturer, founded the computer leasing industry on twenty-five thousand dollars borrowed from his father. Steinberg was straight out of Wharton Business School when he started asking banks to lend him money to buy computers so he could lease them out to various businesses. As the bright young man brightly explained to innumerable wary loan officers, IBM would gladly offer its customers the option of leasing as opposed to buying one of its enormously costly mainframe computers outright. But IBM's leases were structured with very short terms and very high monthly rates, reflecting the giant company's somewhat conservative view of the useful life of its products.

Steinberg was asking the banks to put their money on a simple bet: that IBM was being just a bit stodgy in evaluating the staying power of its equipment. By offering customers longer leases at lower rates, Steinberg was gambling he could recoup the initial equipment cost over time and still have a useful, valuable piece of machinery to rent out once the first lease was up. In this "window" period, set some years down the road, lay an opportunity for considerable profit. If Steinberg was right.

Steinberg was right. In five years he was pulling in profits of eight million a year, enough to take his company public. Computers remained in high demand. Steinberg kept beating IBM on its rates. Profits soared, the stock shot up, and Leasco Data Processing Equipment Corp. began slowly buying up other companies, first little ones related to leasing, and then a big one that was not: the Reliance Insurance Company, an old-line Philadelphia fire-and-casualty company ten times little Leasco's size. As John Brooks of *The New Yorker* described it in his classic account of Steinberg's rise to fame and fortune, "it was a case of the minnow swallowing the whale." At takeover's end Steinberg was worth well over fifty million dollars on paper, having just made more money on his own than any other American of his generation.

Fortunately for Steinberg, his Reliance group was only marginally involved in the leasing business when the market finally collapsed. In 1970, IBM aggressively reasserted its dominance over the field when it introduced a new line of mainframe computers to replace its bestselling 360 Series: the 370. Leasing companies had been basing their projections of the "residual" value of the 360—the value a computer should have once its first lease is terminated—on a useful life of about ten years. By radically slashing prices on the 360 to pave the way for the 370, leasing companies were left holding title to hundreds of outmoded machines very few major companies still wanted, and nobody wanted at the old prices. The leasing business was shaken down. Smaller companies simply folded. IBM jumped back into the driver's seat, the undisputed master of the game.

But third-party leasing was in fact only damaged, and far from dead. A handful of reeling survivors were left to dispose of their old machines as best they could, hoping to regain their former advantage by enthusiastically embracing the new technological generation. Leasing companies continued to set rates on the new machines well below those offered by IBM; customers still preferred not having to expend their own capital on costly computer acquisitions; paying rent on leases could still be relegated to obscure footnotes on financial statements, resulting in a popular practice known as "off the books" financing. Computer leasing remained still little more than a clever accounting trick, an industry without a product, an enterprise that even its savvy young founder found to be little more than "a way of getting free computers."

The seventies ushered in a number of bold new wrinkles in the pure paper magic of leasing: the "leveraged," "wraparound," or "equity" sale, in which the lease itself is treated as primarily a transfer of tax benefits, such as equipment depreciation, investment tax credits, and the like, to a third party. Leasing companies were able to raise additional capital, and thus offer more competitive rates, by "selling" their computers to investors, who in turn leased them back to the leasing company, which then simply leased the computer out to the lessee, just as before. The whole "sale-leaseback" transaction being basically just a paper shuffle in which nearly everyone involved comes out a winner, with the usual exception of the United States Treasury.

The primary effect of these new "leveraged" leases was to avoid some of the risk of ownership. The leasing company could raise about 20 percent of its equipment cost by "selling the deal into equity." The rest of the money would come from a bank just as before, or from some other financing source. At the end of a lease, the leasing company and the equity group would share in any residual value. If the computer could not be leased out at a profit, the equity investors would be still around to help shoulder any losses. Equity money helped revive a faltering industry, but the essence of leasing remained much the same: a crapshoot. Even with the new tax advantages, residual values were still the only real key to profits. But these so-called values remained merely projections at best, about as accurate as a weather forecast.

Leasing continued as a cutthroat industry operating on profit margins nobody could ever quite figure. Volume depended on competitive rates; rates, based on dubious values, were little more than a guessing game; actual profits, ostensibly racked up years down the road, became little more than convenient fictions. Financial health really depended on cash flow: how much cash the company could get in to meet current obligations, and how much cash the company had left over to invest in new equipment. Or in timely acquisitions of other companies, as Saul Steinberg had so brilliantly done. The deals themselves became simply a way to generate current cash, to spend on operating expenses, to put into other more stable businesses, or to save for a rainy day. Which in the leasing industry was bound to come before not very long.

3

OPM did its first equity participation transaction (EPT) in late 1972. Kent Klineman, a prominent promoter of tax-favored securities, was introduced to OPM by a mutual friend. Klineman had graduated from Harvard Law School in 1959 and practiced a few years with a firm in New York before setting himself up on his own as a broker-dealer. He approached Myron with the mutually beneficial concept of selling the tax benefits on machines where the accelerated depreciation allowance, investment tax credit, and other lucrative breaks could not be taken advantage of by the lessee, often because profits were sufficiently low to make the tax break virtually useless.

Klineman proposed setting up a limited partnership, restricted to twenty-five individuals in compliance with the SEC's rules for a private offering. He called the first such group Lark Associates and formed a second "intermediary" company called Alphanumeric to satisfy certain "at-risk" provisions of the tax code. How the mere insertion of a paper entity into a paper transaction constituted an element of risk would be left up to the IRS to decide.

A major question with these equity deals was whether or not they constituted a sale of securities under SEC rules. Klineman followed the less restrictive rules required for a private offering of partnership interests, by which he could avoid registering the transaction under the Securities Act of 1933. But he did believe a certain obligation of "due diligence" to his investors obliged him to provide his investors with financial statements.

According to Myron, Klineman asked Myron for financials,

commenting that leasing companies he worked with tended to have a positive net worth. Myron was sadly forced to admit that OPM had a negative net worth. OPM had suffered a loss for 1972 of nearly $125,000 and was operating under a "stockholder's deficiency" of nearly $140,000. Myron hardly had to look twice at his Touche Ross report with its ominous "going concern qualification" to realize such an impression would hardly satisfy Klineman's justifiably edgy investors. Myron recalls a certain exchange.

Klineman: "You have to show me a positive net worth."

Goodman: "The only way I can do that is to make up the financials . . . I will put on top of them 'For Internal Management Use Only.' "

Klineman insists he told Myron he needed the statements to show to his investors. That all he ever said concerning OPM's financial status was "the better the leasing company, the better it would be . . ." Myron claims Klineman "swore he wouldn't show them to anybody . . . that he'd keep them in a desk drawer." (Klineman denies advising Myron to falsify his financials.)

All the same the "Internal Management Use" financials Myron gave Klineman told a very different story from the Touche Ross report. OPM now had an annual income of $71,000 and a comfortable stockholder's equity of $56,000. Not bad for such a fledgling outfit, and just possibly one of those "interesting little situations" so beloved by creative investors.

And if fake financials were not enough, the appraisals on which the equity deals were based were equally bogus, according to Myron. To support the accelerated depreciation deductions so essential to the life of the deal, Klineman would have an appraisal performed to determine the fair market value of the equipment. Klineman had his equipment appraisals performed by a certain Anthony DiMarco.

Myron: "Between myself, Kent, and Andy Reinhard [OPM's outside lawyer] we would come up with a number and [DiMarco] would, for a fee, type out the appraisal . . . once or twice we held up closings trying to find DiMarco at midnight . . . because the numbers were all shifting around."

The numbers kept shifting around because, Myron maintains, Klineman had developed the dubious habit of working backward from the money he had available from investors to calculate the value of the computer he was arranging to sell them.

Myron: "Klineman was directing the whole thing because we didn't know what we were doing . . . So if [Klineman] had a dollar and the number on top should be two dollars, he would say the number should be two dollars because he only had a dollar. But if he had two dollars and he said the number should be three dollars, he would tell us the number should be three dollars and DiMarco would make it a three because [Klineman] had a two."

In other words, the appraisal was exactly what Klineman told DiMarco it should be. To Myron, this made perfect sense. "DiMarco was paid by a percentage of the appraised value, so he didn't care . . . The higher the appraisal, the more money he made." After DiMarco, another appraiser came along, Harvey Berlent. Berlent turned out to be cut from much the same cloth.

Myron: "Mordy was more in touch with [Berlent] because he was one of [his] cronies . . . Mordy would be telling him what the appraisal should be . . . DiMarco was Klineman's 'boy.' What Klineman said, DiMarco did. What we said, Berlent did . . . Eventually Klineman and Berlent got to know one another . . . and then what Klineman said, Berlent did."

A fair market value indeed.

Myron: "Klineman would be in his office and have to run down [here] because they had changed the figures around . . . We have to change the papers around! Where is DiMarco? Get him on the phone! Tell him we need two dollars instead of three! . . . And put it all together right now because we only have until six in the morning to close the deal."

DiMarco denies ever having been "Klineman's boy": "I wouldn't know [Klineman] if I fell over him."

The equity closings, held in a conference room at OPM's lawyers' offices, usually at peculiar hours, were even more frenetic than most other OPM deals. Equity financings would pile one on top of the other toward the end of the year, and OPM was forced to start naming practically everyone in the company above the level of maintenance man officers so they could sign papers for the endless paper companies set up to keep the IRS happy.

The IRS finally questioned one of DiMarco's evaluations for a Klineman setup between OPM and a group calling itself Wyatt Associates. The case is still pending before the U.S. Tax Court.

In December of 1974, Kent Klineman was indicted by a federal grand jury for alleged illegal activities in promoting oil-drilling tax shelters for the Home Stake Production Company, a shady Ponzi scheme dreamed up by a shyster named Trippet in Oklahoma. The Justice Department dropped the charges against Klineman in February of 1977, commenting only that "it appears unlikely that the prosecution would be successful . . ."

And if phoney financials and bogus appraisals were still not enough, Myron would occasionally give Klineman phoney title documentation. On the very first equity deal Myron could not find the title material for the equipment. "As usual, the files were all messed up." So he had one of his secretaries white out the numbers on a genuine equipment invoice and type in the numbers Klineman gave him to close the deal.

According to Myron, Klineman, "an extremely sharp individual," caught him at it. He took one look at Myron's badly botched title material.

Klineman: "This is not real."

Myron: "Well, the equipment is there. We just didn't have the documentation and we had to take care of it."

Myron claims he even challenged Klineman to call up the vendor to make sure the deal was real. "But that would have held up the closing, and that was one thing Kent Klineman did not like to do." Klineman has no recollection of ever having had such a discussion with Myron.

No one was even quite sure the equity deals as structured by OPM would wash with the IRS. Because so little money actually changed hands for any legitimate business purpose, the IRS could easily challenge the investments as not intrinsically worthwhile. OPM even went so far as to admit in a memorandum to investors that its treatment of these "tax-advantaged" leases was "at variance" with IRS guidelines. But the equity deals meant big money for OPM. Over the next seven years, Kent Klineman arranged for over $160 million in equity deals with OPM, of which OPM received $30 million in cash, and Kent Klineman Associates $5 million in fees.

Another equity promoter, Joel Mallin, had graduated from Columbia Law School in 1961 and practiced tax law until pleading guilty to aiding and abetting a violation of the Federal Reserve Board's Regulation U, involving the extension of credit by banks to purchase securities, when managing discretionary accounts for the Mercantile Bank and Trust Company. Mallin became a tax shelter promoter. He arranged equity deals for OPM worth nearly $300 million, from which OPM realized $60 million in cash and Mallin nearly $13 million in fees.

The EPT was very good to OPM.

4

Late 1972: a company called Sig Smith agreed to sign an OPM lease. Chase agreed to finance it. But there were problems. Software problems. Sig Smith refused to accept the machine. Chase needed to see a blue "equipment acceptance form" before they would give OPM its money. Myron had been counting on that cash from Chase to meet current obligations.

Myron: "We had been expanding a little bit. Maybe too fast. And we needed cash." The solution was, as usual, Mordy's idea.

Myron: "He approached me on the entire concept. In my office. I personally didn't think we should do it. He didn't think we should do it. But we went ahead and did it."

They forged the form.

Myron had a big glass table in his living room. Myron crouched under the table holding a flashlight. Mordy traced the Sig Smith signature on a blank blue form. They sent Chase the phoney blue form and Chase sent OPM its money.

Chase followed standard procedure and sent Sig Smith a coupon book to keep track of its lease payments. Sig Smith was confused. They hadn't even signed a lease yet. They called Mordy to find out what was going on.

Mordy handled this one like a pro. He said, quite casually, that Chase must have been in error. If they would just send him the coupon book, he'd take care of the whole thing. Mordy did just what he had promised: he took care of the whole thing. Mordy might have had the book back, but Chase still expected its payments. So OPM made the payments and kept the bank's money.

The equipment problem was straightened out. Sig Smith signed its lease. OPM spent the money from Chase to pay for the Sig Smith computer. But OPM still needed the cash. Now Mordy had an even better idea, a true burst of amoral inspiration. They took the new lease to a different bank and got a second loan. Magic: double the money, double the OPM. Effortlessly increasing the power of the OPM purse. Thereby sliding into a whole new realm of shady dealing: "double hocking," "double discounting," or to those really in the know, "dipsy doodles." Hocking because getting money from a bank to buy a computer is a bit like pawning the machine. Discounting because banks rarely forked over the full cost of the machine, usually more like 80 percent.

Double hocking would never work if banks started calling up lessees to see if the machines were actually there. Neither could you have your lessees knowingly making payments to more than one bank. Myron and Mordy solved this problem neatly: Chemical, Chase, and Tilden Commercial Alliance, their three major financing sources in the early days, were persuaded to let OPM arrange "nonnotification" financing. Which meant that the lessees were not told where the lease was financed, or even if it had been financed. Which made things simple for the lessees, because they just had to send OPM a single monthly payment for any and all leases they had, and OPM could pay the bank one lump sum on all its leases at that bank.

Myron: "The idea was to make the lessee think OPM was a big company and we could hold the paper on our own."

Double hocking was easy money. They fell into bad habits.

Myron: "I would go to Mordy and tell him we needed cash. Mordy would come up with a lessee he could control . . . So if anything fouled up he would be able to talk his way out of it . . . Mordy controlled a lot of these lessees . . . He knew them very well and they would do a lot that he would say."

"Control" meant having someone on the inside. Someone to call for favors: returning a coupon book or two, signing a few extra blue forms now and then. Someone who wouldn't ask difficult questions. Mordy made sure to maintain at least one such "control" inside nearly every lessee.

By the summer of 1974, Mordy was down on OPM. He confided to Myron: "The essence of OPM's business is not good." Mordy was genuinely depressed by the whole business: the double hocking, the fear of discovery, the shady payoffs to salesmen in parking lots with unmarked envelopes stuffed with cash. They talked about selling the business, about buying another business. They talked about filing for bankruptcy. But they were scared to file Chapter Eleven because then all their bad deals would come out in court. They had to clean up OPM.

They needed help.

Myron: "I needed someone from outside, someone to put discipline on me. Someone I had total confidence in to help me, to watch over me, to make sure the deals were bought out, to make sure the cash coming into the company was not diverted to anything else but buying out the bad deals."

Myron's first thought was Andy Reinhard.

June 3, 1969: Myron married Carol Ganz. That night, "just going through the wedding presents," they heard a broom angrily knocking from downstairs, at four or five in the morning. Someone shouting about how they were making too much noise. On their wedding night, no less! A summons was eventually presented for disturbing the peace. Myron was clearly being persecuted. He went to call on the law.

Myron's closest friend as a kid had been Michael Reinhard. Myron: "I almost lived in the Reinhard house, as Michael lived in my house." Michael had an older brother, Andy, four years older than Myron. Andy would take Mike and Myron to baseball games, basketball games. Myron was a serious sports fan.

Andy Reinhard went on to Columbia and Harvard Law School. When Myron received his summons the first person he called was Andy. Who took care of the problem "one, two, three." And, very nicely, charged no fee.

When it came time for OPM to take a lawyer, Andy was the obvious choice. In 1967 Andy had joined a small firm which would become known as Singer Hutner Levine & Seeman. For a small retainer Andy advised OPM on structuring its early lease deals, on suing lessees who failed to meet their monthly payments, on general legal principles governing their business.

Andy Reinhard became OPM's first independent disciplinarian. A post somebody desperately needed to fill. Myron and Mordy above all else lacked financial discipline.

Myron could have tried to talk to Mordy about stopping this double hocking, but Mordy was just not the man for the job. "Mordy's not a methodical individual. His head wouldn't have been into it. He couldn't hold a hatchet over myself. He wasn't an independent third party." So Myron went to have a talk with Andy.

Myron: "I have a problem. I need someone to be on top of me . . . to watch over me . . . Mordy is just not that individual . . . I want you to help me."

He told Andy what was going on.

Myron: "Andy and I were very close. Closer than brothers could have been. He emphasized to me what was wrong. He was extremely upset."

He used language.

Andy: "How the fuck could you do something like this?"

Myron "handed Andy one of my famous lines, unfortunately. I won't do it again."

Andy: "Get rid of them period."

Myron: "I played the little boy to him, in effect. The big brother, little brother bit."

Andy was four years older than Myron.

Myron: "I know, Andy, you're right. But this is done and this is it."

Andy might have been a little older, but he wasn't much wiser.

Myron: "He took my word that we were going to buy them out, proceed on schedule."

Andy's only practical suggestion was tell Mendy Weissman. Mendy was OPM's independent outside auditor. A partner in the small New York accounting firm of Rashba & Pokart, and Mordy's first cousin. This suggestion made sense to Myron, for several reasons:

1. Mendy was going to find out sooner or later.
2. Myron was close to Mendy.

3. If anyone was going to discipline Myron, it was going to be Mendy.
4. Mendy was probably going to get angry, and start yelling, and so on.

Myron and Mordy had first run into Mendy the summer of 1973 at Taub's Bungalow Colony in the Catskills. Mordy hadn't seen Mendy in years. One evening Myron started complaining to Mendy about his accountants, Touche Ross. Now it was summer and he hadn't even seen his last year's numbers yet. And there were other things Touche was up to Myron didn't like.

Touche had placed the company under a "going concern" qualification. This implied that the company would not stay in business very much longer unless business improved. Touche had insisted on sticking to standard industry practice of assigning low residual values, the value of a computer when it came off lease, adamantly refusing to go over 10 percent of cost. Myron had kept pushing for 15 percent, which would have vastly improved OPM's balance sheet. But Touche Ross just wouldn't budge. Touche then refused to expense Mordy's shady payoffs, largely unrecorded, as "Direct Lease Acquisition Costs." They refused to accept an "assumption of collectibility" on an alarming number of lessees who had defaulted on their monthly payments, forcing OPM to make the payments itself. Finally, they had had the nerve to offer Myron a list of specific recommendations on how to improve OPM's anarchic accounting systems. Rather than adopt stricter procedures, Myron fired them. He hired cousin Mendy.

Myron thought his accounting problems were over when he hired Mendy. Mendy was family; family could usually be controlled. But Mendy turned out to be his own man. When he first came down to OPM, he found the company records in sorry shape. And he quickly realized that Myron's problems with Touche Ross had more to do with OPM's problems than with any failing on Touche Ross's part. He refused to go along with many of Myron's fiscal whims.

Which was why Myron was scared to tell Mendy about the double hocking.

Myron: "Andy doesn't yell at me. He doesn't yell that often. I was more afraid of Mendy because he yelled at me a lot."

Myron claims he told Mendy the whole sad story before Labor Day, that hectic summer of 1974. At Taub's Bungalow Colony, where the Myron Goodmans and the Marvin Weissmans were spending the summer. He places the meeting before Labor Day 1974 because the next summer he and Mordy went to Jacoby's, forsaking Taub's. Myron says he asked Mendy to meet with him at OPM's offices. He had prepared a list of all the double discounts in blue ink on a yellow piece of paper, which he carried around on his person. There was a blue ink line on that paper, and below that a number. A total. The total amount of bad deals at that time stood at about three quarters of a million dollars.

Myron was deathly afraid Mendy was going to get upset. He did get upset. But Myron was finally able to calm Mendy down on the spurious grounds that he was planning to stop. Mendy said they should meet once a week to go over the bad deals, to see whether or not they'd been bought out.

Mendy: "No matter what is going on, we should always have a meeting. Come hell or high water, we should meet."

In the end, Myron was glad he told Mendy. Now Mendy had agreed to "sit on" him.

Mendy remembers Myron's confession somewhat differently. Myron didn't come to him. He went to Myron. Mendy claims he knew nothing about the double discounts until late 1975, when Marshall Zieses, an accountant working for Mendy on the engagement, came across some ledger cards that appeared to indicate "there were certain leases financed at more than one bank." Zieses had been trying to put together a master lease schedule for OPM. Lessees on the left, banks on the right. He found the same lease corresponding to more than one loan. When Zieses showed the evidence to Mendy, he seemed "stunned."

Mendy: "When Marshall showed me the list I knew something was happening that should not have been happening . . . I was so upset, annoyed, disgusted at the gross fact of it . . . that I didn't even take care to look over each transaction."

No confession in the Catskills, no tears at Taub's.

Mendy says he stormed into Myron's office brandishing a lease schedule prepared for the occasion: "OPM Leasing Services Leases with Multiple Notes Payable." Intending to force a confrontation, Mendy instead found himself quietly pacified.

Mendy: "His comments were relatively nonchalant. He was not at all upset. His comment was in effect, 'What are you guys getting so upset about? It's no big deal. I'll pay it off. I can take care of it.'"

Mendy had expected a noisy fight culminating in his own resignation. But he ended up agreeing to help Myron make restitution to the banks. He extracted a solemn promise from Myron to pay back the loans. Marshall Zieses was given the thankless job of monitoring the payments, of keeping Myron honest.

Whether Mendy knew in 1974 or 1975 about the double discounts only matters if you look at the Rashba & Pokart financial statements for 1973. Mendy showed Myron some pencil-draft statements in August of 1974, well after Myron claims he told Mendy about the double hocking. The pencil draft contained a footnote marked "Claims Receivable" for some $700,000, which Myron took as a virtual disclosure of the double discounts. Myron was extremely upset.

Myron: "I was more than upset. I was ill. I was livid."

To Myron, the draft statements just about broadcast "a number of bad deals that should have been bought out." He had warned Mendy already he didn't want any surprises. Not only did Mendy have the double discounts in there, he had also brazenly included half a million dollars in "Officer's Loans" made since the end of the year, money that had gone to buying the officers expensive houses on Long Island. Mendy had even gone so far as to add, "no provision has been made . . . for repayment . . ." Myron hit the roof.

He fired Mendy. As far as Myron was concerned, he had more than sufficient cause.

Myron: "Mendy, and I have used the expression before, but it certainly applies to him more than anyone else that I dealt with, was to the right of fascist. He was ultra-conservative in what he did, certainly in what he put down in writing."

Myron told Mordy first. "It was his cousin." Mordy's response was typical.

Mordy: "You do what you have to do, how you have to do it. And go ahead and do it."

Myron and Mordy did what they had to do with Mendy's audit. They took it down to the office on a Sunday afternoon, the only day the company closed, and used it as inspiration for forging some fine fake financials. Mordy did the typing, and the forging. Myron finally learned to forge, but he never did learn how to type.

The offending "Claims Receivable" was changed to a far more innocuous "Equipment Lease Receivable," which implied that OPM expected to get the money back. The disclosure of the half million officer's loans was simply excised. Because both items were not only in the statements themselves, but were included in the accompanying Rashba & Pokart report as well, Mordy had to type up a new report. He made a fair copy of the R&P letterhead and retyped the report, making such a botch of the job that the body of the text was visibly slanted beneath the letterhead.

Nobody noticed at Chase. They did ask a naïve question or two about certain leases listed as "warehoused"; they weren't too sure what that meant. Myron wasn't exactly clear on it either: he had assumed "this was a fancy way of discussing double discounts without telling them it was double discounts." In any case, the operation was such a roaring success Myron couldn't help staging an encore a few months later, when Chemical was pushing to see some numbers and he didn't feel like showing them real ones.

Myron: "Anytime you give financials to banks they usually cause more problems." At least with fake ones, they didn't ask so many questions.

Fascist or not, Mendy ended up being rehired by Myron. Mendy, for his part, agreed to a major change: he reduced the total loss from $200,000 to $100,000, by miraculously finding an extra $100,000 in equity income which had appeared toward the end of the year. But on the other issues that bothered Myron, Mendy still wouldn't budge. Myron accepted Rashba & Pokart's audit for 1973 pretty much as originally submitted, though he continued to give out fake versions to most everyone who asked to see one. Mendy never did another audit for OPM. Myron never asked him. Myron knew Mendy would never release unqualified financials as long as the double discounts were still not bought out.

Mendy's first condition for taking on the OPM audit had been that Myron hire a young accountant from the disgraced Touche audit staff to fill a new job: controller. John Clifton became Myron's third senior disciplinarian. John Clifton was not a member of the family. He was not a member of the Orthodox "community." He was not even Jewish. Clifton was black.

This gave Clifton a certain degree of immunity to Myron's incessant personal pressure. When Myron first offered him the job, his reaction was simple: "They sure could use somebody like me to go in and straighten them out." He liked the fact that "Myron and Mordy were young guys . . . about my own age . . . and it was an opportunity to get in on the ground floor of a company that was growing rapidly." Myron clinched the deal by offering Clifton $30,000, which was considerably better than he had been doing at Touche.

Myron told Clifton he wanted to take the company public someday. Clifton told Myron straight out that OPM was not the sort of company you could easily take public, because OPM was "not used to operating in the mode in which a controlled company reporting to the SEC has to operate." Which meant keeping decent records, keeping its postings up-to-date, and generally not fooling around too much with its money. Touche's "going concern qualification" was largely due to the fact that OPM was in a continual deficit position. This situation was not helped by management's habit of taking large sums of money out of the company for their own personal use and giving large sums of money they really didn't have to charity. Charitable contributions did not even offer them usable tax breaks. Without income on the books, about the last thing OPM needed was a tax break.

Clifton was equally alarmed by the officer's loans, which had doubled in 1973 from just under $10,000 to more than $20,000, while the annual deficit had leapt from $15,000 to nearly $150,000. As Clifton saw it, "If you looked at the receivables from officers and at the capital stock section, you knew they had no money in that company." But business volume was expanding rapidly. "As long as they were expanding . . . they were able to generate enough cash to sustain themselves, even though they were in fact generating losses, not profits."

OPM suffered a net loss of over $100,000 in 1973, resulting in a negative net worth close to $250,000 by year's end. But volume had indeed shot up, to close to $12 million, out of which approximately $1 million could be expected to show up as eventual profit, and another $1 million could be attributed to double discounts.

Clifton discovered the existence of the double discounts in 1975, when he instituted an "exchange" account system to replace Myron's outmoded "ledger card" system to keep track of leases. Theoretically, when you took all the cards together at the end of the month, they should have balanced out. They didn't. Instead, significant balances kept building up in various accounts, indicating money going in and out not directly traceable to the lease records. Clifton studied these accounts for some time. He could see "where there were two and sometimes three leases completed around the same time, around the same size, around the same cost, but only one payment would be coming in from the lessee." And when he went to see if the equipment had ever been paid for, he found "you had no equipment paid for, which made the transaction stand out somewhat." Because the equipment he was looking for didn't exist.

This problem remained "a gray area" to Clifton for about a year. He mentioned the subject a few times to Myron, who would become suddenly vague, and mumbling. "Well, yes, that transaction may exist. We may have inadvertently financed that one twice . . . it may have happened by accident . . . we have permission from the lessees . . ."

Clifton never quite screwed up the courage to ask, "Okay, Myron, I know they exist. But why do they exist? Why do you do them?" He assumed Mendy knew, and that Myron and Mendy had to be handling it together.

About a year later, OPM was moving into leasing mainframe computers. There were lawyers for banks and lessees all over the place, coming to closings, looking at lease documentation, talking to the investment bankers, supposedly keeping an eye on things. John Clifton got it straight from Mendy Weissman: "Myron is turning over a new leaf. From now on, everything is going to be according to Hoyle."

So Clifton was more than a little surprised to get a call from National Bank of North America about a check bouncing at some account he'd never even heard of. He called Mendy Weissman, who knew nothing about it. He called Myron. Myron knew something about it. Myron told Clifton to come up to his office right away.

Mordy was sitting right there. But Myron did all the talking.

Myron: "Look, I've got two choices: either I give you the books, or I fire you. So here are the books."

Myron handed Clifton the books and told him to go and record all the transactions and close down the account. At this point, it was all too clear to Clifton that Myron wasn't talking about legitimate transactions. Or accidents either. Here they had opened up this secret account and were making secret payments through it.

Myron had been playing a shell game with Mendy. To wriggle out of his sworn promise to pay the banks back on the bad loans, he was making monthly lease payments instead to the banks through his secret account. He would tell Marshall Zieses to write out checks to buy out the bad loans. Zieses would record the buy outs and tell Mendy that the "clean up" campaign was proceeding according to plan. Clifton had even seen those checks at various times; he had seen Zieses cut them. But Myron would take the checks and simply hold on to them. He kept them in his desk drawer.

Mendy soon found out about this.

Myron: "We were alone . . . [Mendy] took out a list, a list I believe prepared by Marshall Zieses . . . and I went over my list with him . . . and he found other double discounts which were not on his list. Which did not make him happy."

Mendy: "I thought you stopped."

Myron: "Well, we did more, we had to do more."

According to Myron, Andy Reinhard wasn't happy either to learn the double discounting had never been stopped.

Myron: "Andy, we had to do them. Or else we'd get into a lot of trouble . . . We had to get the money in."

Andy: "You said you weren't going to do them anymore. You told me the company was going to write a lot of good transactions."

Myron: "We are and everything, fine. Except we still have this cash problem."

Myron viewed Andy as an earnest but ineffective disciplinarian.

Myron: "He always told me that I shouldn't do any more. He always told me everything I shouldn't do any more."

Sometime after the first of the year, 1976, John Clifton ran into Myron running down the hall. Clifton asked him if the buy outs were going ahead according to schedule. Myron was in a terrible hurry. But he confided to Clifton, just as he was about to rush off, "We're not buying them out after all. We decided we needed a cushion instead."

5

OPM broke into mainframe leasing in 1975. Mordy did most of his breaking in through the good offices of one George Prussin. George was a salesman who specialized in peripheral equipment, attachments to mainframe computers, made by Electronic Magnetics and Memory (EM&M). George had plenty of contacts in the field: data-processing managers at the sorts of corporations able to afford an IBM mainframe, retailing at that time for up to five million dollars. Marketing mainframe leases was not like marketing minicomputer leases. With the minis, Mordy could go to the vendor salesmen themselves and get them to steer customers his way. With mainframes, you had to get in with the people in charge of hardware acquisition at the lessees themselves. Mordy didn't know any of these people. George Prussin did.

George and Mordy had lunch and cut themselves a nice deal: Mordy agreed to buy EM&M equipment from George and pay George a finder's fee for persuading his contacts to lease equipment from OPM rather than buy direct from EM&M. George still got his sale, but now OPM had its lease. And OPM had what it needed most: a contact with a data-processing manager at an established company.

George had valuable ins at The Bank of New York, American Express, Merrill Lynch, Woolworth's, Blue Cross and Blue Shield of Greater New York, and many others. To do his deals with OPM, George set up a corporation called Sha-Li Leasing, which operated out of a spare room in his house. Prussin would write Sha-Li leases for memory, and OPM leases for the mainframe itself. On some mainframe deals George went into partnership with OPM, sharing in the profits and losses on deals he brought in. Prussin eventually became OPM's top salesman, at a base salary of $100,000 a year, but with profit-sharing commissions totaling over $7,000,000 over the next several years. Which was a great deal more than Myron and Mordy combined ever earned over the same period.

Not to say George didn't work for a living. He introduced Mordy to people Mordy needed to meet. He put Mordy onto Henry Weiss, head of data processing at the Montefiore Hospital & Medical Center in the Bronx. George knew Weiss was interested in expanding the hospital's computer capacity, and suggested that Weiss talk to Weissman. Henry was a Hasid, and when Mordy handed him a business card with the name "Mordecai Weissman," Myron recalls, "They got to talking and found out they had a lot in common." George arranged with Henry and Mordy to lease an IBM 370 for Montefiore from OPM. On the date of the closing, August 29, 1974, Mordy was sick in the Catskills and Myron had to come down from the mountains to sign on the deal.

Henry didn't work for free. His father, Ephraim, ran a diamond business on Forty-seventh Street. Mordy would ask Myron for money to send to Henry's father, a rabbi, in checks made payable to various charities. Ephraim would contribute the money to the charities, and some of it would actually go to the charities. But much of it ended up as kickbacks lining Henry's pocket, because a few months after the checks went to the charities part of the amount came back in cash. Over the years, OPM laundered upward of half a million through Ephraim Weiss, of which about four hundred thousand actually went to Congregation Beth David in Monsey, New York.

Myron: "On that first big main-frame deal, a lot of that money went to the yeshivas . . . After that, we took a liking to the yeshivas and whether they needed payroll or to build a building, we'd do that on our own."

In early 1975 Prussin introduced Mordy to Marty Shulman, in data processing at American Express. Marty had dropped out of Hofstra in 1965, six credits short of getting his degree, to become a pro bridge player out on Long Island. Unfortunately, there was no money to be made playing pro bridge, only in teaching people to play at the clubs. Dissatisfied with the club circuit, Shulman went to work for Equitable Life as a systems trainee. He gained enough knowledge of data-processing systems there to become a systems analyst at American Express.

Marty Shulman: "As a systems analyst, you take something that is being done manually and try to figure out how to computerize it." Marty wasn't bad at that. He became a hardware evaluator, and a systems planner, joining Systems Planning, Corporate Division, in 1974. Systems Planning was theoretically supposed to oversee all data-processing activities throughout the company, but in practice each separate division was highly protective of its own autonomy. The divisions didn't want to hear from Systems Planning when trying to figure out whether to buy new computers, how best to get hold of them, or even how to use them.

Before 1973 American Express acquired computer hardware by buying or leasing straight from the manufacturer. By the time Marty Shulman went to work for the Systems Planning group, Corporate Division was putting heavy pressure on individual data-processing centers to cut costs and build profits. A suggested route was independent third-party leasing. Prussin introduced Weissman to Shulman at just the right time for all three of them. Marty Shulman had no compunction letting Mordy know at their first meeting that he happened to be in a very good position to "expedite" OPM's future at American Express.

Mordy arranged to pay Marty 1 percent of all equipment leased by American Express through OPM. That 1 percent amounted to a tidy sum over the years: Shulman says $100,000, Mordy says $300,000. Whatever the amount, the immediate results were that American Express leased two IBM 370 mainframe computers from OPM in March of 1975. From then on in, Mordy took control: he so successfully insinuated himself into the company's far-flung corporate structure he managed to lease them more than $130,000,000 worth of hardware over the next several years, even after Marty Shulman had long left American Express for the greener pastures of OPM.

Mordy sold OPM on service: getting the equipment in on time, getting the financing together on time, adjusting leases to meet the needs of the lessee. He aimed to please, and pleasing lessees was his major marketing tool, more major than money. Mordy took further control of American Express nine months after signing his first lease, when the company opened a big new data-processing center in December of 1975 in Florida. Amex was a nonunion company, and the building trade unions in the state started kicking up a fuss about computers being installed in its buildings without union labor. Mordy met with Marty. Marty, on behalf of Amex, authorized Mordy to spend up to one hundred thousand dollars to get that computer into the building.

Mordy flew down to Florida to personally take charge of the installation. In blue jeans, he helped move the computer from the loading dock into the building. To keep the unions off his back, he paid a contractor at the facility $25,000. It was Christmastime, and during the installation a few of the men refused to do any more scab work unless Mordy forked over a few hundred more to pay for a party. Mordy paid for the party; the computer was put in. Mordy returned triumphant to New York, dirty work done, having delivered on his promise to take care of it on only a quarter of his authorized budget. OPM did not call itself "The Custom Leasing People" for nothing.

In the summer of 1975, Fireman's Fund, a wholly owned subsidiary of American Express based in California, decided they needed a new IBM 370. They had already made arrangements to go out and buy one when Marty Shulman heard about it. As a member of Systems Planning he tactfully suggested Fireman's Fund could save themselves a good deal of money, and a lot of headaches, if they just went out and leased one from his good friends at OPM. Myron took Andy Reinhard out to California to meet with Fireman's Fund.

It was pure luck Myron took Andy along. Andy found a quirk in California state law by which OPM could evade state tax if

OPM formed an insurance company in another state that would lease the equipment to Fireman's Fund.

So OPM Life Insurance Fund was born. In Arizona, a state that would allow a corporation to be set up in about five minutes flat. By saving 6 percent sales tax on the lease, OPM was able to split the difference with Fireman's Fund, lowering its lease rate and effectively clinching the deal. OPM Life, as it became known to the few who ever heard of it, never gained permission from the state of Arizona to issue insurance, life or otherwise. Mordy confided to Joseph Verner, Marty Shulman's counterpart at Fireman's Fund, that OPM Life was "a total sham." It issued only one policy, either to Mordy or one of his kids.

Like Marty Shulman, Verner proved an efficient "expediter" of OPM leases, for commercial bribes totaling somewhere between $100,000 and $150,000. He expedited over $15 million worth of OPM leases at Fireman's Fund over a period of three years.

OPM Life might have been a sham from the word go, but Myron took it seriously. He might have been thinking about how Saul Steinberg diversified out of leasing into insurance, made himself a bundle, and got out of leasing for good. He might have just been suffering from another one of his evermore common grandiose delusions. Whatever it was, he asked John Clifton to look into ways of turning OPM Life into a real insurance company. Myron had great expectations for OPM Life: for a while, at least, it became the new way out. What Clifton's investigation into the matter turned up, however, was the fact that in order to sell insurance you needed a tremendous volume of business, on the order of one hundred million. OPM Life's leases with Fireman's Fund amounted to more like a tenth of that.

Clifton: "We're just not qualified."

Myron: "Don't worry, I've got Andy working on it."

Andy: "I'm not working on it. It just can't be done."

Myron: "It's a fait accompli."

Myron was always bullish about OPM. But John Clifton knew the numbers and they told a different story. Volume was growing dramatically, but the company was still sustaining constant losses. OPM could stay afloat only as long as business kept "pyramiding," bringing in new cash to pay off old debts. Volume had mushroomed from $3 million in 1972 to $12 million in 1973. Going into 1976 they were definitely up there in the $100 million category, but it was only such tremendous growth that allowed them to sustain such tremendous losses.

Myron's answer to Clifton's reality principle was to sprout more subsidiaries: AMG Leasing, which stood for *Anderre Menschens Gelt,* or "Other People's Money" in Yiddish. Dav-Na, a desk-drawer partnership, named after Mordy's eldest son, David, and Myron's oldest daughter, Natalia, a tax shelter operation deliberately designed to generate paper losses to give Myron and Mordy personal tax deductions. Myron's and Mordy's houses, which came to be known as "The Dav-Na Estates," were put into Dav-Na so the costs of purchase and upkeep could be chalked up as a loss to Dav-Na. Dav-Na became a convenient vehicle for making charitable contributions, and a container for certain losing lease transactions, which provided Myron and Mordy with additional tax breaks. OPM grew itself a holding company, Cali Trading, named after Mordy's wife, Carol, and Myron's wife, Lila, which presided over a tangled web of quasi-real subsidiaries: OPM Canada, Saratoga Leasing, OPM Life, OPM United Kingdom, Av-Jo Transport Services, Dutchess Data Processing, OPM France, Painted Post Computer Leasing, Rugby Leasing, OPM Airline Services, Madison Information Services, OPM Energy Resources, Nostrand Data Services, OPM Germany, Kings Data Processing . . .

Precisely what most of these paper companies did was a mystery to most at OPM. Some were set up to do certain somewhat unusual deals, others to do deals outside the country. OPM did eventually set up a European subsidiary with offices in London, headed by a man Myron referred to bitterly as "that arrogant Israeli," Moty Arielli, whom he had hired away from his largest competitor, Itel. OPM Europe was Myron's way of reminding his staff and customers that OPM was a heavy international hitter. He ordered thousands of plastic shopping bags printed up displaying OPM's elaborate corporate structure and widely distributed holdings, under the bold heading, "International

Presence." These went nicely with the Italian silk OPM ties, the briefcases embossed with the OPM company logo, the OPM hats, folders, memo pad cubes, and endless OPM paraphernalia distributed like party favors to anyone who happened to wander into the office. Myron dispensed sets of gold Cross pens like after-dinner mints, until finally John Clifton called him to task with a memo headed "Trinkets." Clifton politely inquired why Myron felt he had to give away the store in such a frivolous manner.

The inevitable reply memo was not long in coming: "Because I like to. Love, Myron."

6

Myron's halting "clean up" campaign was sailing ahead half steam. He used cash coming in from a very lucrative lease with Fireman's Fund in late 1975 to buy out most of the early bad deals. But at the same time they were cleaning up the double discounts, Myron and Mordy were embarking on new forms of lease fraud. Simple double and triple discounting had grown much too risky because with mainframe leases there were too many nosy lawyers snooping around closings. But cash-flow problems just wouldn't go away. Something bad just had to be done.

The first new form of fraud would later become known as "lease fission." In early 1975 Marty Shulman put through a fat lease at American Express for two IBM 370/158s at a total cost of four million dollars. Because the banks OPM relied on at the time did not want to finance multimillion-dollar deals, Mordy had a fresh idea: they could split up the two leases into fourteen leases and get the banks to go for a big fish cut into little pieces. For this they had to invent fictitious equipment, forging phoney IBM invoices to go with their phantom computers. They were able to finance one piece of equipment worth twenty thousand dollars for a million dollars and to get American Express to pay a total rent of nearly half a million for a fifty-dollar rack that held computer printouts. American Express, in the guise of Marty Shulman, happily signed for these separate, meaningless leases because the aggregate rent turned out the same anyway. According to Myron, Shulman would "sign anything we gave him for an appropriate fee." From "lease fission" to entirely fictitious leases was simply a leap of faith: from late 1974 to 1976 Myron and Mordy forged American Express signatures on four separate "phantom leases" covering equipment that didn't exist, for a grand total of three million in phoney financings over the period.

From there to "altered leases" was more like a hop, skip, and a jump. In October 1975, OPM leased some memory from EM&M through George Prussin and subleased it to American Express for $3,200 a month. But Myron needed extra cash, so Mordy magically came up with it. The duration of the lease was three months. Mordy blithely typed in a "6" before the "3," effortlessly producing a sixty-three-month lease. Financing that lease brought in millions instead of the thousands a three-month lease would have generated.

In November 1976, Mordy assumed that George Prussin could persuade The Bank of New York to lease an IBM 370 for seven years, but George could get them to spring for only three. Once again, OPM had been counting on that money to make its tattered ends meet. So Mordy sent The Bank of New York a "side letter" granting them the right to "walk away" from the lease after four years, but did not tell the bank putting up the money about it. OPM had to give the financing bank a Bank of New York "opinion of counsel" agreeing to the terms of the lease as stated. So Mordy got George Prussin to supply him with some Bank of New York stationery and got down to work. He forged the opinion of counsel, then realized he had to forge all the other Bank of New York documents to make the signatures match. This was really a Mordy solo masterpiece, and Mordy felt for some private reason he had to buy it out himself, without asking Myron for company money. He never came up with the money. That one was never bought out.

To produce all this fake IBM documentation, Mordy had to recruit a mole at IBM. He found one at last: Dick Monks, a product manager at IBM's Armonk headquarters. Mordy claims he gave Monks five thousand dollars for a package of blank IBM invoices and bills of sale. Monks claims he gave Mordy a few such invoices as a "courtesy," which did not explain the sizable stack of such documents found at OPM several years later. The blank IBM invoices proved invaluable for documenting the sale of computers that didn't exist.

Monks was also helpful on the marketing end. When Mordy was first trying to break into mainframe leasing he had a little talk with Monks. Monks agreed to give Mordy a highly confidential list of customers with IBM 360s on hand they might some day soon want to upgrade to the new 370s. Monks graciously updated that list with a new one of companies with IBM 370s on order, who might be persuaded to lease from OPM rather than buy or lease from IBM. Mordy cut a deal with Monks similar to the deals he cut with Verner and Shulman: 0.5 to 1 percent of the cost of equipment leased on leads from that list.

Mordy was willing to give Monks a check for his services but Monks tore it up, saying something about "a paper trail." Mordy's motto was We Aim to Please. He told Monks to wait for the cash in a Howard Johnson's parking lot on Long Island. Mordy switched the drop a couple of times, once telling Monks to wait for an OPM bagman at a Cadillac dealer; the man he was looking for would be driving the red Coupe de Ville.

By 1976 Mordy started getting suspicious of Monks. Mordy somehow got the idea into his head that Monks was selling the same secret list to other leasing companies, thereby reducing its value. Mordy casually mentioned something about lists for sale to a top IBM manager, who said confidently that no one outside of IBM ever saw those lists, they were absolutely top secret. To the manager's astonishment, Mordy just as casually tore off a corner of the list Monks had given him and gave it to the officer. This meant the end of Monks as far as Mordy was concerned, though he mercifully saved his job for him by only handing over the corner, thereby making the indiscretion difficult to trace back to Monks. In time, Mordy decided he didn't like paying Monks and his "control" inside the lessee; two commission payments on the same lease cut drastically into an already dangerously slim profit margin. He settled affairs with Monks for about $50,000. Mordy had an idea he had gotten off easy.

With OPM concentrating exclusively on mainframe leasing, they could no longer depend on Chase, Chemical, and Tilden

Commercial Alliance to supply the enormous loans they needed to buy mainframes at a few million a pop. Commercial banks wouldn't finance 100 percent of equipment cost, usually only about 80. When the total loan was in the hundreds of thousands, that difference didn't amount to much. But when you were talking about millions, the shortfall became significant. It was clearly time for OPM to get themselves an investment banker to go into the money markets and raise them money at a decent rate.

Someone at Mendy Weissman's told them about Goldman Sachs. Myron liked the sound of that: "Goldman Sachs: Investment Banker to OPM Leasing Services." He could easily see just such a phrase written boldly across the top of a fat tombstone ad in *The Wall Street Journal*. With Goldman Sachs hawking their deals, it would be hard for prospective customers to look at OPM as some sort of fly-by-night outfit. Goldman Sachs meant instant prestige in the financial community, prestige they really could use. And that means use.

At Goldman Sachs they were told to talk to Richard Santulli, who knew about computers and about lease financing. Santulli was a graduate of Brooklyn Polytechnic with a masters in applied mathematics. At Goldman Sachs he had specialized in working up computer models for predicting stock prices, calculating bond maturity, mergers and acquisitions programs, corporate finance analysis, even a little lease financing. Not so much equipment; more real estate, in the beginning. But the transactions were structured similarly, and by 1973 Santulli had moved to the Corporate Finance Department, having just put the finishing touches on a computer model of the structure of lease transactions. He was the only person in Corporate Finance who really knew anything about leasing. After all, he had written the programs. By then there was more and more equipment leasing and less and less real estate. Computer leasing was taking off and Goldman Sachs wouldn't mind getting a piece of that action.

Myron took Andy Reinhard with him to meet Santulli. Myron did most of the talking. Andy was just there to add class. Myron told Santulli they had been in minicomputer leasing and were now breaking into mainframes in a big way. They were used to doing half-a-million-dollar deals; now they were starting to do big deals for big machines and they needed help with the financing. They were just on the verge of signing some very big leases, worth $16 million, with Fireman's Fund. Myron pulled out a preliminary version of that lease. Santulli took a fast look.

He could tell right away that lease was "horrendous." Just not financeable. They were still using standardized forms used for minicomputer deals, which did not take into account any of the complexities used in leasing mainframes. With the minicomputers, they had been used to doing business with commercial banks, while the money market for the big deals was dominated by savings banks and insurance companies that operated by a whole new set of rules.

Santulli didn't say right away "Okay, Myron, we're going to be your banker." First they had to see whether they could do this deal, and before that they would have to do a reference check. But if they could do the one deal, assuming the references all checked out, they could proceed on a deal-by-deal basis: each deal on its own merits.

At that first meeting Myron struck Santulli as "just about the nicest guy . . . He listened to everything I said . . . very humble, very nice . . . Religion. At the time I thought he was the most religious person in the world." Myron was not only nice, he gave great references: American Express, AT&T, Western Electric. These were blue-chip companies, and from Goldman Sachs's point of view, excellent credits. Leasing deals were done on the credit of the lessees, not of the leasing company. It was the credit of the lessee that mattered because the notes given to the banks were "with recourse" to the lessee. Which meant it was the credit of the lessee the lease put on the line. If OPM went out of business tomorrow, the lessee would still be under an obligation to make lease payments to the bank. So the banks really didn't have to look so clearly at OPM's financial condition, which was a good thing, because Myron never gave out financial statements. As far as the banks and insurance companies were concerned, as long as the lessee was a good solid credit, an American Express or AT&T, and

Goldman Sachs was the investment banker, they really didn't care if OPM stood for "Other People's Money," "Other People's Monkeys," "opium," or anything else. For future reference, Myron let Goldman Sachs in on a little secret: OPM really stood for "Other People's Machines."

The financial services originally supplied by Goldman Sachs were relatively straightforward: (1) to get the leases into decent shape, and (2) to analyze the credits of the lessees. That was about it; the lessee was the crucial credit and Goldman Sachs was the banker. Who had heard of OPM out there in the money markets? Santulli told Myron right off the bat, "We are not your banker." He told Myron not to go running around acting as if Goldman Sachs was his banker. But Goldman Sachs did satisfy Myron's insatiable thirst for prestige and respectability by allowing prominent tombstone ads to be placed in *The Wall Street Journal* and other financial publications, announcing the latest debt financings it had arranged on OPM deals. OPM sent out brochures referring to Goldman Sachs as "our investment bankers" while Goldman Sachs did little to counter that impression. As Santulli would later admit, "Goldman Sachs has always been perceived as being an investment banker for very strong financial companies . . . We had done so much business for OPM that our name was certainly being used by OPM, and people very easily could perceive some strength of OPM from the name Goldman Sachs."

Going into the money markets to place debt for OPM depended entirely on the credit of the lessee. Myron would call up and say, "Hey, I've got Merck. How is Merck? A good credit? What kind of rate can you give me?" And Santulli would figure the rate based on the credit Myron would give him, and Myron would use the cost of the money to figure his lease rate to bid on the transaction. The better the credit, the lower the rate, the lower the lease rate, the better OPM's chance of winning the award of a lease. Occasionally Myron came up with a "no-brainer," a company so solid banks would lend their last dollar to it without asking any questions. AT&T was a "no-brainer." American Express was a "no-brainer." But occasionally Myron would come up with credits Santulli couldn't sell at all. Hospitals. No one in the financial community could analyze hospitals, where did they get their money? Who knew. Montefiore Hospital, Myron kept coming up with that one. Santulli couldn't sell Montefiore at all. OPM had to go out and finance those hospital leases on their own.

To satisfy its obligations of "due diligence," Santulli checked out OPM. OPM checked out. A man at American Express, Marty Shulman, spoke very highly of OPM. The same for Joseph Verner, at Fireman's Fund. And Myron gave another ringing reference: Rockwell International.

7

Sidney Hasin was director of Computer Planning and Controls (CP&C) at Rockwell International's Information Systems Center (ISC) in Downey, California. ISC was the central operating headquarters for the company's various regional data-processing centers at Seal Beach, California, Richardson, Texas, Cedar Rapids, Iowa, and Bridgeville, Pennsylvania. As one of the nation's major defense contractors, Rockwell was a prime user of state-of-the-art computer equipment. As director of CP&C, it was Sid Hasin's job to maintain sufficient computer capacity to support a wide range of government aerospace programs: the Apollo Project, the Minuteman Missile, the B-1 Bomber. Rockwell's privileged status as a premium defense contractor gave it access to all the latest data-processing hardware through the use of a high-priority "DX" rating, awarded by the Department of Defense. The "DX" meant that Rockwell received the latest equipment right off the assembly line, equipment so new IBM frequently used Rockwell as a testing ground for its most advanced products.

Sid Hasin had been put in charge of CP&C in 1971, when Rockwell decided to centralize its West Coast computer facilities into one, Western Computing Center (WCC) at Downey. All Rockwell computers were leased direct from IBM, at very high monthly rates for very short terms. By 1974 Sid Hasin had been promoted to Vice President of Information Systems. He did a study of various methods of hardware acquisition, concluding that by leasing computers from "third-party" leasing companies, Rockwell could save as much as 45 percent of total acquisition costs over IBM rates. Hasin proposed to start replacing the company's now outmoded 360 Series 155s and 165s with the new, more powerful 370 Series 168s by soliciting bids from leasing companies and awarding leases to the lowest bidder. This proposal was accepted by senior Rockwell management, and Rockwell's first leased computer was shipped out to the WCC in Downey in December of 1973.

Mordy called Sid Hasin up one day in 1976 to ask if OPM could be put on his bid list. Sid had never heard of OPM. He told Mordy his bid list was long enough. When Myron heard about the Rockwell rebuff he decided to try his hand at marketing again. Myron was on the Coast on other business when he called Sid Hasin. He used Mordy's basic opening gambit but pushed just a little harder: Would Mr. Hasin refuse to see Mr. Myron Goodman of OPM Leasing Services for just ten minutes? Mr. Goodman would be in the area anyway on other business.

Sid had been told by top Rockwell management to be polite to potential lessors so they couldn't complain to the Defense Department that they'd been turned away for no good reason. Yes, Mr. Hasin would be willing to meet with Myron Goodman for ten minutes, at Rockwell's offices at El Segundo, not far from LAX. Myron launched into a vivid description of his all-out master plan for the conquest of the leasing business. Itel might be Number One but he aimed to try harder. OPM didn't call itself The Custom Leasing People for nothing: to prove his point he proudly showed Sid a glossy four-color magazine ad depicting tailors cutting cloth, representing OPM's policy of tailoring its leases like a fine suit to fit its lessees' needs. Sid liked Myron's attitude. He was pleasantly savvy, very young, and charmingly aggressive. Myron threw around some rather impressive references for such a young man: American Express, AT&T, Fireman's Fund. His investment bankers were Goldman Sachs. He had good relationships with solid banks: Chase, Chemical, Philadelphia Savings Fund, Marine Midland. At the close of that first meeting Sid Hasin advised Myron that if those rosy references all checked out he'd be happy to put OPM on his list.

Hasin called Santulli at Goldman Sachs, who described Mordecai Weissman and Myron Goodman as "hard-working, aggressive, reliable people." Martin Shulman at American Express expressed much the same sentiments. Corroborated by Joseph Verner at Fireman's Fund.

OPM was put on the list, but their first bid was too high. Myron had developed the initial contact but Mordy was still in charge of marketing. Mordy worked the account until March of 1976, when Mordy told Myron he was getting "very flustered" with Sid, that if they were planning on dealing anymore with Rockwell, Myron was going to have to handle the account himself.

Myron: "Mordy and Sid are very similar types of people. Strong negotiators, connivers . . . putting them head to head led immediately to conflict."

Myron flew out to Rockwell with Andy Reinhard and Rich Santulli to see if they could rescue the talks and win back the lease.

Sid and Mordy had been haggling endlessly over the lease rate factor, which determined the cost of the deal to Rockwell, and the margin of profit to OPM. Sid was demanding a 1.08 percent, while Mordy was refusing to go a fraction below 1.11 percent. All of a sudden Myron found himself flying out to California to negotiate lease terms and he felt nervous because he didn't deal with many lessees. "Contract development talks," as they were called at Rockwell, were the very heart and soul of the business, and Myron knew Sid Hasin knew just what he was up to. According to Myron, Sid was extremely conceited about being known in the industry as someone who knew how to get the lowest lease rate in existence.

At ISC headquarters, Myron, Sid, Rockwell in-house counsel, Dan Byrnes, Rich Santulli, and Andy Reinhard sat up until all hours of the morning restructuring that deal. The transaction came together only, according to Myron, "through the good offices of Rich Santulli," who managed to get them money at a very low rate, and "the genius" of Andy Reinhard, who made the legal side go smoothly. And, of course, modest Myron, who took a very different marketing tack from Mordy's hard-ass approach. On the first go-round Myron did his best to stick to Mordy's guns: "I won't go below a 1.11 percent." But where

Mordy had been hard, Myron finally tried being soft: "Okay, Sid. You win. You've got the 1.08 percent." The long bargaining session was finally over, though the deal still fell apart a couple more times. The lease for the "E" machine was formally signed on June 14, 1976, financed by the Philadelphia Savings Bank. A certain bothersome clause in the contract caused Myron to pass out. This gave Sid Hasin his first real indication that Myron had serious health problems. Passing out got Myron exactly what he wanted: the offending clause was deleted, the lease was judged to be acceptable, and Rockwell and OPM threw a big party to celebrate the closing of the deal.

Sid Hasin let it be known early on he hadn't always been just a lowly procurement man. He had been president of a Rockwell subsidiary known as Narisco back in the sixties: North American Rockwell Information Systems. Narisco had been spun off from a division of Rockwell called Autotenics, which had been developed as a means of expanding Rockwell's data-processing activities beyond government, aerospace, and military contracts. Autotenics was supposed to win a share of the burgeoning software market by adapting programs developed by Rockwell for military projects to civilian purposes. Autotenics did indeed "capture" some lucrative contracts with HEW and the Department of Justice but the intended spin-off of Narisco as a software provider to the private sector was basically a flop. Hasin laid the blame for Narisco's poor performance not on any management failure on his part, but on the "great software depression of 1969." The division was "folded back" into Autotenics, Hasin was kicked back downstairs to general vice president, and another man was put in Sid's place as president of Narisco.

Sid's career at Rockwell never quite recovered from that debacle, in Sid's humble opinion. His present job as head of CP&C seemed to him a major comedown from such a promising past. Still, he took enormous pride in performing a less than ideal task with as much relish and ruthlessness as possible. Which consisted chiefly of browbeating lessors like OPM into deals practically guaranteed to break them.

In spite of these lovable traits, or perhaps because of them, Myron and Sid hit it off immediately. They prided themselves on similar things, being good wheeler-dealers, good connivers, while maintaining a rare capacity to sit back at a distance and enjoy the game of it all, taking a long broad view of a highly volatile business. Sid's fondest corporate memories, after being boss of Narisco, were of his halcyon days wheeling and dealing in the computer time-sharing market with a couple of guys known to the trade as "Bob & Bill." Sid had sold excess Rockwell computer time through Bob & Bill's time-sharing operation and turned a pretty penny for Rockwell on it.

He enjoyed the whole entrepreneurial exercise so much he drew up plans to start a full-time Rockwell time-sharing division he had high hopes of heading. But he never succeeded in selling the idea to senior Rockwell management in Pittsburgh. Sid cherished a fatal fondness for "real" businessmen, men with ideas and guts and ambition, men who really made money out there in the arena. To Sid, Myron had all this and more: vision and youth. Sid found in Myron a way to get a leg up at Rockwell. Myron found in Sid a final way out.

Myron: "Sid and I became very close from the inception . . . he was controlling OPM's various interests at Rockwell . . . he was the defendant of many things going on internally with Rockwell." As time went on, Myron would refer to Sid Hasin as "Mr. OPM," "my only true loyalist," and "the OPM man at Rockwell." Sid was Myron's control at Rockwell, just as Mordy had Marty Shulman at American Express, and Joseph Verner at Fireman's Fund. Myron: "To Sid, who never had a son . . . I was almost like a son . . . I maintained the father-son image to him." Sid had three daughters, and Myron became, according to Myron, the son he never had. As the Rockwell account started to heat up in 1977, Myron started heading out to the Coast once a week to "handle Hasin." Handling Hasin invariably meant taking Sid to lunch.

Lunch was important to Sid, more important than business. Whenever Myron spoke to Sid, it was always: "We must have lunch."

Myron: "No way in the world I would be in California and we wouldn't have lunch. If I was going out to SoCal Edison in the morning, no way could I have lunch with them. I would have to be at Rockwell at 12:30 sharp to have lunch with Sid. If God forbid I should have lunch with anyone else, it was always, 'Myron, why didn't we have lunch?' . . . of course I had lunch with Sid. Does the sun rise in the East?"

Over lunch, Sid liked to lecture Myron about why he should eat more than he did, which was rarely more than hearts of lettuce, maybe an order of French fries. To have lunch with Sid, Sid deemed a tremendous privilege. Sid was a true connoisseur of food. Myron: "God forbid it came not the way he liked it. That was even more important than the lease rate factor."

Myron paid for lunch. "The only time Sid ever paid for lunch he made sure he kept the receipt so he could be reimbursed by Rockwell . . . Sid is an extremely cheap individual." Myron soon found out that Sid put food before everything else in the world. "In the morning, Sid was only thinking about what he wanted for lunch. Half an hour after breakfast, he became deeply concerned about lunch. Whatever work could have been done in half an hour usually took two to three days . . . If we got there at eight or ten in the morning it didn't matter because by 11:30 the subject was lunch. After lunch, he was too full to discuss work. So we discussed dinner."

Sid grew accustomed to meeting Myron at his hotel. To Sid it was easier to do business outside the office where he wouldn't have to be always returning calls. Hotel suites had the added advantage of being closer to food. Sid constantly wanted room service so he could have his energy. As Myron and Sid grew closer, they enjoyed day-long sessions in the plush suites Myron favored, where lunch would gradually merge into dinner, and dinner would drag on into evening. Only very rarely would they discuss any actual business at hand. Sid could go on for hours about his problems at Rockwell, about his problems at home. His wife wanting to take too many courses and her passionate interest in China, Rockwell wanting him to move out to headquarters in Pittsburgh and his not wanting to go. As time went on Sid would indulge himself in endless soliloquies about Rockwell's not sufficiently appreciating his efforts to save them millions through third-party leasing.

Sid would always think of that early period, 1976 and 1977, as a sort of honeymoon; he called it Rockwell/OPM Phase I. It was a good time, a happy time, when the documentation was all in great shape, the deals moved smoothly, everyone got along, everything was in order.

Myron: "Sid is a very meticulous individual . . . very document oriented . . . extremely conservative, an excellent administrator." Sid felt in control of the situation. Myron played the neophyte, the slow learner; Sid played the fatherly authority figure.

Myron was forced to play the pussycat with Sid, because Sid was able to deal from a position of strength. Sid knew his computers, their inner workings; he grasped their capacity, their true worth. He had a fine technical background, which he bolstered with constant attendance at technical seminars and with night classes in accounting. He knew the formulas to calculate processing speeds, to forecast future values, to predict what a machine would be worth at the end of a lease, or in the middle. Which even Hasin admitted was "more of an art than a science," but an art Sid knew about as well as anyone. He could tell at any time whether a certain facility could use another mainframe, or more disk storage, and he knew just what that extra capacity should cost. To Myron, Sid was "a crackerjack technician, businessman, negotiator, financier." To Myron, Sid was maybe a little like Mordy: "What Sid had in his little finger about computing I didn't have in my entire head." And to Myron, "Sid wanted control. He always wanted control . . . and what Sid wanted, he usually got. Excuse me. What Sid wanted, he *always* got."

Myron soon realized that Sid's ego was much more fragile than he originally thought. He might have acted the big shot with him, but with his superiors at ISC he played the pussycat. Ego he saved for Myron, and for other hungry lessors he could push around. As for Sid's somewhat shadowy superiors, Myron hardly even knew Sid *had* superiors. To talk to Sid about leasing at Rockwell you would think he was the only boss, the emperor of acquisition. Only after many months of haggling did Myron meet Maury Dahn and Larry Manly, Sid's bosses at ISC. Sid kept them hidden, as if ashamed he even had them.

For all their haggling, occasional bickering, and interminable struggles for control, Myron and Sid grew close, rather quickly. Myron fell into the habit of calling Sid every Friday to wish him a good Sabbath. Sid would call Myron constantly to inquire, solicitously, about his health. They would talk for hours on the phone a few times a week, often as early as 5 A.M. California time. To Myron, "Sid felt he needed us more than we needed him . . . He didn't realize we needed him more than he needed us." Sid Hasin managed to virtually make OPM Rockwell's sole lessor, though he never succeeded in having that "sole source" relationship ratified by Pittsburgh. An interlocking relationship developed between OPM and Rockwell. Myron: "OPM controlling Rockwell, Rockwell controlling OPM." One of Sid and Myron's major problems was that neither one was ever quite sure who was controlling whom; both constantly connived behind each other's backs, like father and son and best of friends when dealing face-to-face.

Sid was not above using OPM's special relationship with Rockwell against OPM. OPM had developed an obvious dependency on the Rockwell account, for prestige, for cash flow, for volume, for ego. Sid used this as a weapon to beat Myron over the head: "If you don't sign this lease at this rate we are not going to look favorably on OPM." Sid would always say that Rockwell was willing to make special concessions to OPM because of "our relationship," but whenever that relationship was called on the line, Sid came up with the same set speech: "You want to do business with us, you do it the way we want to, or you'll never do business with us again."

Myron says Sid would "help out" OPM by calling up "his cronies" asking them to make bids higher than OPM, assuring them they would not be bound by the bid in the odd event that OPM ended up bidding higher. But he also screwed OPM by telling Myron that the others had submitted bids far higher than they actually had. In the beginning, Sid used to tell Myron the rate he needed. Sid would say, "You meet that number or else no deal." But after a while, Myron wised up to Sid's game and would force Sid to modify his number a bit, and Myron would modify his number a bit, and "we would finally come up to where Sid really wanted without him having to tell me." By the time Myron finally realized "what Sid wanted, he always got," it was too late to change things. By then Myron and Sid had become locked in a sort of frenzied minuet, in which Sid firmly held the lead.

Myron's fervent love fest with Sid Hasin and Rockwell troubled not just a few people. Mordy had long ago learned how to control lessees: you offered them money. Mordy gently suggested to Myron he should "feel Sid out" on the issue. As far as Mordy was concerned, you could never entirely trust anyone you weren't paying off. Mordy told Myron: "give it a try without coming right out and saying, 'Listen, Sid, here is a payoff.'" Myron decided to broach the subject one day in Sidney's office.

"You know, Sid, in this industry it is common for people who are called lessors to take care of people who are called lessees . . . And not just with rates or anything, we give gratuities, in effect, Sid."

Sid looked totally shocked. He did not accept; he did not want the subject brought up again. As far as he was concerned, the only thing Myron could do for him was to give Rockwell the best possible rates he could offer at a given time. Myron, apologizing profusely for any unintended insult, protested that all he wanted was "to ensure that Rockwell business kept coming to OPM." Sid said no problem, as long as he continued to have the best rates in the marketplace.

When Mordy heard that, it confirmed his worst suspicions about Sid. Mordy was more experienced than Myron in marketing. He knew honesty was not usually the best policy in the leasing business. The only way to get the business and keep the business in the face of cutthroat competition was to pay someone off and keep paying that person off, and the only way to make any real money was to take care of people inside the company so they would give you a rate that allowed you to make a decent profit.

Mordy was troubled about Sid Hasin, and as time went on Myron gave Mordy more and more to worry about. Myron became increasingly jealous of any attempt by anyone to interfere with that account. It was his own personal property at

OPM. His territory, his turf. To Alan Jacobs, the Singer Hutner partner who handled the Rockwell account from its inception, Myron was always going on about Sid, about how much Sid liked him, about how much Sid loved him. By late 1976, Myron was constantly crowing to Alan that he had Rockwell "in the bag." But the fact was, as Jacobs saw it, "Sid had Myron in the bag, and Myron just couldn't see it."

If Myron thought he had snowed Sid Hasin and hadn't, he certainly had snowed Rockwell's in-house lawyer Daniel Byrnes.

Myron: "After that very first deal was signed on the "E" machine in June of '76, Dan Byrnes never reviewed the lease documentation . . . his basic concern was to make it as small as possible. If there was more than two to three pages in a document Dan would get very upset . . . Kimi [his secretary] used to type up the opinions of counsel and he used to just sign them . . . he never even read them . . . Dan Byrnes was allowing OPM to do all his paperwork for him, prepare all the documents and take them over to be signed, and with . . . Kimi control the Rockwell account."

Sid and Myron would meet Dan Byrnes either in his office at Rockwell's building in El Segundo, right by LAX, or in a conference room in the same building overlooking the landing field. Dan Byrnes's favorite restaurant for lunch or dinner was the Host, in the airport tower.

Myron: "Dan Byrnes was more concerned with what types of airplanes were landing at LAX . . . than he was with the day-to-day flow of paper at Rockwell . . . My chief concern was to understand fully the distinction between a DC-8 and a 727. Because if Dan asked the question and I got it wrong, it would take at least a half an hour of explaining why I got it wrong . . . Sid used to act as referee because Dan would never speak to him again if after spending eighteen years at Rockwell he still didn't fully understand what all the airplanes were. He caught us once or twice on the Sabreliners, but we learned the large jets pretty well. Especially the 1:00 flight to Tokyo on the 747 SP."

So that was Rockwell/OPM Phase I. The Downey period.

When OPM was making money and Rockwell was saving money. When Sid was tough and Myron was tough but no one yet felt a loser. When Myron thought he had Sid in the bag and Sid thought he had Myron over a barrel. When the documentation was all in good shape and everyone was happy.

8

By late 1976, Myron was ready for another audit. It had been two years since his last. Goldman Sachs thought it a good idea, though they did not need financials to do OPM deals. Financials would come in handy if they ever took the company public, or took over another company. Financials were helpful when selling deals to tax shelter promoters, now becoming a major source of income. Mostly, Myron felt he owed it to OPM's evolving national image to show the world just how well he was doing.

Mendy was no longer the man for the job. Not because he couldn't do it, but because he wouldn't do it. Not unless the double discounts were all off the books. Something Myron had been promising for years, with distinctly uneven results.

A Big Eight firm wouldn't do. No more Touche Ross for Myron. OPM's books and records were in such terrible shape a firm like that would charge a fortune just to get started. Myron was looking for a firm large enough to do the job, small enough to have to play ball.

John Clifton: "Myron's preference at that point was that he wanted to be, as he put it, a big fish in a little pond as opposed to a little fish in a big pond . . . He wanted quite a bit of service and a lot of attention. So it had to be a medium-sized firm, maybe a little below the Big Eight."

Mendy knew of an outfit called Fox. Based in Denver, with a large New York office, the twelfth largest firm in the United States. Just the right size, maybe even the right temperament. Myron told Mendy to talk to Fox about a major engagement:

audit, tax management, extensive consulting. He also told Mendy to make some things clear to them. Five conditions he wanted satisfied before he'd even talk turkey:

1. Fox would have to treat as "immaterial" certain "problem" transactions, namely, double and triple discounts and phantom leases.
2. Fox would have to give at least 15 percent of equipment cost as "residual value" on all leased equipment.
3. Fox would have to classify OPM's leases in a way to produce the most favorable financial report.
4. Fox would have to let Myron "screen" any confirmations of leases to make sure confirmations were not sent out on any fraudulent transactions.
5. Fox would have to treat all "officer's loans" and "advances to shareholders" not as salaries payments or dividends, but as assets on the balance sheet.

Mendy, John Clifton, and Fox all deny that any such specific conditions were asked for by OPM or agreed to by Fox. Though Fox did end up accommodating Myron on most major issues. Mendy and Clifton do recall telling Fox about the double discounting.

Mendy Weissman: "I told them that OPM had engaged in improper lease financings . . . I also informed them that OPM was in the process of paying off the excess and we have a commitment from Myron Goodman that these would be cleaned up before the end of the year."

Marshall Zieses, who worked for Mendy, says Mendy told him to be "upfront" with Fox about the double discounts he was monitoring: "If . . . anybody . . . from Fox asks you about it, just tell them whatever you know. Don't hold back."

There was a meeting at Myron's November 2. With Myron, Mendy, John Clifton, and Andy Reinhard for OPM; Mort Berger, the partner in charge of the New York office, and Steve Kutz, a senior audit manager, for Fox.

Berger: "Goodman mentioned a problem that occurred during the year and wished to know whether it would require any type of disclosure. It seems that they had some defaults . . .

amounting to about $1 million . . . The Company was embarrassed by this and apparently used its own funds . . . to pay the rentals . . . Tentatively we responded it was probably not an item for disclosure but raised questions of credibility and internal control . . . we were assured this would not happen again."

Myron maintains this was simply a "cover" agreed upon in advance for the meeting. That Mendy told him he had talked things over with Fox and both sides had agreed not to mention the double discounts in the presence of "third parties." Mendy denies this. Berger denies being told the true reason for the so-called defaults, though he did later admit he viewed Myron's disclosure as some sort of "confession": "He used the word embarrassed. One can draw from the fact that he said 'I did it and won't do it again' that his state of mind was that he did something wrong."

Myron was "very impressed" with Fox's congenial attitude. It looked like they might have a few things in common. But he refused to hire them until he saw how they did on a little take-home test of his own ingenious devising: an evaluation of some hypothetical OPM leases to see whether their prospective treatment fit precisely what he had in mind.

One of the many reasons Mendy had been so willing, even eager, to pass the OPM ball to someone new was that lease accounting, already a tangle at best, had been recently rendered even more complex by a ruling issued in draft form by the Financial Accounting Standards Board (FASB). The FASB is a group of seven full-time members drawn from the ranks of accountants, professors, corporate officers, and financial analysts authorized by the SEC to establish standards of financial accounting and reporting. It writes the rules for writing financial statements, and those rules are considered binding. Accountants refer to FASB rules as "fasbee" rules, rhyming the name with "Frisbee."

Fasbee-13 was still so new few accountants could claim to understand it. Among other key revisions, it tried to take into account some essential differences between short-term and long-term leases. Before FASB-13, many companies indulged in a practice known as "off the books financing," which showed the computer as a monthly expense, not an asset, allowing the acquisition to be effectively hidden in a footnote under expenses. FASB-13 retained this form of accounting for short-term "operating" leases, where the leasing company is still the true owner, and the lessee is simply paying rent. But the new rule provided that with long-term leases, the lessee should be considered the true owner, with "effective control over the equipment over the majority of the useful life of the lease." With such a "finance" lease, the lessee's monthly rental is seen as an "investment" in the equipment, which turns the computer into an asset and permits the company to depreciate the cost of the equipment over its useful life.

OPM's financial health, as reported, depended on Fox's treatment of its $120 million in "lease-related" assets according to the new rule. Fox split OPM's leases into $65 million in long-term finance leases, $52 million in short-term operating leases, with the remainder of the cash coming in from equity sales of tax benefits. After taking a hasty survey of industry practices, Fox reported that estimates of residual values of mainframe computers ranged from 4 to 20 percent. Responding to Myron's complaint that he couldn't live with "an ironclad 10 percent figure," Fox was willing to give Myron an average of 15 percent. Guaranteed to boost OPM's forthcoming statement of income immensely, and Fox's chances of landing a lucrative engagement.

Fox sent the "superstar" of its New York office, Steve Kutz, down to 99 Wall Street to tackle the job. Kutz had been an auditor for fifteen years, with the title of Audit Coordinator. A quick look at OPM's books made it clear the postings were hopelessly out-of-date, entailing extensive "reconstruction" of the records before an audit could even begin. Kutz enlisted the aid of John Clifton and Mendy Weissman to do the necessary support work. Kutz also tried to get Myron to implement some long-overdue systems improvements. Though Myron "agreed to a lot of things . . . in practice he found it difficult to change his ways."

Fox started the confirmation process, which involved sending verification forms to lessees to confirm the existence of lease, and the location of the computer. Myron and Mordy had pulled off seven phantom or phoney leases in the previous year, none of which Fox uncovered in the course of its work. Myron claims he demanded and was given prior review of all confirmation requests; Fox denies giving any such thing. Myron and Mordy were able to buy back three of the bad leases by the end of the year, saving them from possible detection. A fourth was a real lease with The Bank of New York for which Mordy had forged a phoney "side letter" changing the lease terms without telling the financing bank. The Bank of New York, the lessee, confirmed the existence of the lease but did not disclose the secret "side agreement" to the financing bank.

Fox sent Myron a stack of confirmation requests for his signature, one of which was for the bogus Bank of New York lease. Myron took that one out of the pile, but Fox held on to its copy. When The Bank of New York did not respond to the first request, which would have been rather difficult as they never received it, a junior Fox accountant sent out another one, without telling Myron about it. The second version was sent out on a form bearing Myron's photocopied signature. Somehow, Myron found out about it. Alan Phillips, who worked for Fox, was a witness to the result.

"Mr. Goodman came downstairs . . . and he was rather indignant . . . And he came into the Fox room and started screaming that somebody forged a signature and sent a confirmation out. He was screaming . . . 'I didn't want this confirmation sent out' . . . why did we send it out." Myron's explanation, when Kutz asked him about it, was a little unclear: that The Bank of New York had "forgotten" it had ordered one mainframe computer and now he was trying to lease them another, and he didn't want them to "remember" they already had one. In spite of such shenanigans, Fox uncovered no evidence of fraudulent activity during its 1976 audit.

Which was just fine by Myron. Far worse, from Myron's point of view, was that Fox had an equally hard time uncovering any evidence of profit. By February of 1977, Rashba & Pokart had recently completed a "trial balance" for 1976 which showed not a gain, as Myron had led himself and everyone else to expect, but a rather substantial loss of over $2.2 million. Steve Kutz was delegated to break the bad news to Myron. Myron was understandably upset. It confirmed Myron's worst suspicions about accountants.

John Clifton: "Myron was always saying he was making a profit, it was just that the accountants didn't understand . . . Myron was convinced that with all the transactions he did, there just had to be a profit."

Myron's first futile stab at solving the problem was to simply slap another month onto his fiscal year, giving himself a thirteen-month financial period. Equity sales always picked up in December as tax shelter investors sought last-minute savings. Myron figured to pick up enough extra revenue to swing the statements well into the black. Mendy Weissman: "I remember a discussion that there were significant transactions in December . . . In substance Myron indicated that . . . he would have liked to see a profit." When Kutz went back and totted up all the figures, assets increased by more than $44 million, but the results came out the same: OPM's losses in fact increased, to almost $2.8 million. Rather than turning any major corners that year, OPM was going straight down the tubes.

Myron was outraged. This performance was even worse than Mendy's. Myron was particularly disappointed with "Steve Kutz, Superstar," whom he'd seen as a man after his own heart, someone who grasped his way of thinking. Myron met with Kutz, Clifton, and Mendy in early March to find some way to salvage a sinking situation.

Myron: "Get back to the grindstone and try to figure out some way to show a profit."

March 25, 1977, 1:33 P.M.: Myron was at OPM headquarters that Friday afternoon when a friend delivered a message ripped right off the stock ticker, "IBM Slashes Prices on 370 Series Mainframe Computers . . . New 3000 Series to Replace 370s." Myron took a look at the tape. One look was all he needed. He passed out. When he came around he sat down to try to assess the situation, which on the face of it didn't look good. He and

Mordy would just have to wait for the Sabbath to end before they could do anything.

Myron and Mordy worked around the clock starting at sundown that Saturday night. Mordy, typically, was more pessimistic than Myron. His initial reaction was that OPM should probably start filing for bankruptcy first thing Monday morning. But for all the bad deals on the books. Though Fox might not have uncovered them yet, a bankruptcy court would not be quite so indulgent. They would have to clean up the company first. Mordy had a fair idea of how such clean up campaigns had fared in the past.

The immediate effect of the IBM announcement on OPM's portfolio of 370 Series computers, which made up by far the bulk of its assets, was simple if a little extreme: an instant depreciation of 30 percent in the worth of those machines, the amount the price had been cut. If the company had gone into the market simply signing up lessees on long-term leases, the impact would not have been so immediate or so immense. OPM would have simply let all the long leases run out and write down the residual values, which might have hurt a little, maybe a lot. But in the long run OPM would have probably recovered by leasing out the new 3000 machines at higher rates, rolling slowly with the terrible punch.

Unfortunately, the situation was not quite so simple. OPM called itself "The Custom Leasing People," after all. They "custom-tailored" their cut-rate leases to meet discriminating lessees' needs. Lessees these days wanted their leases cut as short as possible, so they wouldn't have to keep outmoded equipment around if technology changed or their data-processing requirements shifted. The standard lease, ever since the industry's inception, had included what was known as a "hell or high water" clause, an unconditional commitment on the part of the lessee to pay rent for the duration of the lease. This was the real reason banks were so willing to lend money on leases in the first place, because as long as the credit of the lessee was good, they were sure to get their money back. Even if the leasing company went under, the lessee still had to pay.

Then Mordy had come up with one of his bright ideas. To lure large mainframe lessees into dealing with an unknown company, OPM started offering "early outs" on long-term leases, also called "early termination" clauses. Which lent the lessee the best of both worlds: the low rate of a long-term lease, the flexibility of a short-term lease. The banks didn't mind because the lease still had a "hell or high water" clause committing the lessee to pay up until the very end. But OPM agreed to reimburse the lessee if and when the company felt like walking away from the lease. Which effectively amounted to OPM's reshouldering the burden of ownership for the computer.

For a while, it all worked wonderfully. OPM volume grew exponentially, since the "early out" was not easy for customers to refuse. The banks were happy to keep lending money, because if OPM went under, the lessees would still have to pay them back. And the lessees were happy, because they could cancel their leases at will and still keep their cutthroat rates. The only danger was that they were all going to have to step up and pay out if OPM were ever to default on its obligations: a contingency they were led to believe was about as probable as the advent of the Messiah.

There wasn't much reason for lessees to cancel those leases early. As long as the machines they were leasing were the state-of-the-art, and the rates the lowest obtainable. But if the technology ever radically changed, as it seemed to about once every decade, the leasing market would radically change right along with it. Companies like Rockwell demanded the latest hardware available, and they were willing to pay top dollar for it. If a new generation of computer that was faster and better than the old one came on the market, they were going to have to have it; which was why they were so eager to sign up for those short-term leases in the first place.

Now IBM had gone and done it again. Cutting prices on the 370 to usher in the 3000 was really just a reprise of their move of ten years before, when they slashed prices on the 360 to make way for the 370. But this time around things were worse. Even OPM's major competitor, Itel, had been forced into matching OPM's softest terms by offering their customers flexible lease terms. They had at least taken steps to cover their flanks by obtaining insurance from Lloyds of London designed to guarantee the "back end" of the lease in the event of an early termination. OPM never could get Lloyds insurance, because of its poor financial record. And by the time OPM got around to asking for one, Lloyds had grown cautious about writing such policies.

As Myron and Mordy worked through that Saturday night after leasing's Black Friday, the first question was how soon would IBM be able to deliver the new machines? As long as the new hardware was still unavailable, the 370 should hold much of its value. If there was sufficient delay on the delivery, they might even be able to realize a little residual value on the old machines. All they could do was just guess; all they really knew was "1984 would have been just fine."

They talked about how to find the cash. They talked about investing in all sorts of get-rich-quick schemes, taking whatever cash they had on hand and getting something out of it, instead of investing in more suddenly-obsolete computers sure to drop right through the floor some time soon. In the end, speculation took them nowhere. They decided to brazen things out. On Monday morning Myron and Mordy emerged from seclusion with their own brave counter announcement: "The IBM announcement will not have any negative impact on OPM in the near future."

That is all. Stay tuned.

John Clifton knew how Myron was planning to manage accounts. By pushing for unsupportable residual values, 20 percent or even higher. It was the only way anyone at OPM could see to artificially brighten up an increasingly dismal picture. With the IBM announcement, nobody knew what residual values should be. All they knew was that they would be going down, not up. April turned into May with no sign of relief from Fox's dire financial forecasts. A big meeting with Fox was set for May 10. Clifton foresaw a very messy scene with Fox, a big fight over future values, followed no doubt by Fox's resignation. But the day before the big meeting, Steve Kutz burst into Clifton's office looking as if he'd just signed a long-term lease on the Holy Grail.

Kutz had put his nose to the grindstone all right. He had found Myron's profit. The solution had been there all along, staring him right in the face. But it wasn't until he stumbled across an annual report for another leasing company that it hit him: the equity income!

On a million-dollar lease that OPM had sold into equity, OPM would have actually invested $150,000, which represents the difference between what the bank put up and the equipment cost to OPM. From the equity sale, OPM might have taken in $200,000, which left OPM with $50,000 left over. That was money that OPM should not ever have to pay back out, if the lessee lived up to the full terms of the lease, and the residual value was what the company thought it would be a few years down the road. So, Steve Kutz said, why not take that full $50,000 in as income from the first day of the lease? And consider it not "realization of residual value," which would have to be accounted for over the full life of the lease, but as income garnered from the sale of the tax breaks? In other words, current income.

Now the famous FASB-13, on the face of it, did not exactly bolster Kutz's clearly controversial position. It flatly stated that on a "sale-leaseback" transaction, "any profit or loss on the sale shall be deferred and amortized" over the life of the lease. In order for "the Kutz method" to work, Kutz had to claim these sale-leasebacks were not really sale-leasebacks, because a further line in FASB-13 defined most of these deals as "entered into as a means of financing, for tax reasons, or both." FASB-13 went on to describe such transactions, quite accurately, as "transactions that are infrequent, incidental, or extraneous in nature." Kutz took this to mean that OPM's sale-leasebacks were not sale-leasebacks at all, because they "represented a fundamental part of its business activity and generated significant cash flow."

Kutz was ecstatic. He just knew Myron would go for it. He had been depressed, apparently, by the dismal prospect of displeasing Myron and sorely disappointed when OPM had turned out to be a losing proposition. According to Alan Phillips, who worked under Kutz, "When [Steve] realized they weren't going to show an income . . . that's when he came up with the new treatment of how he was going to handle the money from the equity sources." Kutz was eager to unveil his new method at the big meeting the next morning. With his eleventh-hour inspiration, Steve Kutz was bound to become a company hero: a veritable knight of OPM.

Kutz was clearly excited about telling Myron. Right away, if not sooner. But Clifton suggested he wait until morning and put it all on the table at the meeting, so everyone there could take a fresh look at the bold new idea together. Kutz agreed. But something strange happened the next morning, in the conference room at Singer Hutner. Instead of Myron going in all aggressive and take-charge and chairing the meeting, as he usually did, he took a seat in the back and kept his mouth shut. And when Steve Kutz bustled in with his papers, Myron waved him graciously into the chairman's seat.

Myron stood up to make an announcement: after a good deal of thought and consideration he had come to the inescapable conclusion that he was prepared to adopt a more conservative position on the question of residual values. Clifton would have been astonished at Myron's meekness, if he hadn't guessed that Kutz must not have been able to wait until morning. He and Myron clearly had this whole little charade well rehearsed.

Kutz unveiled "the method," with the help of a few charts and graphs. He broke the application down to two modest proposals: (1) to take the equity income up front, resulting in additional income of about $4.5 million; and (2) to extend the estimated useful life of the equipment on lease, resulting in an increase of another $0.5 million. More magic: an extra $5 million where there had not been one red cent before. Myron himself couldn't have done any better.

May 27, 1977: Fox & Co. issued an unqualified opinion on OPM's 1976 financial statements, reflecting a net income of $1.7 million, a positive net worth of $750,000. The first real report of income in OPM history; the first dim sign of net worth.

9

Rockwell had finally outgrown its Western Computing Center in Downey, California. The original WCC had started out in a single building housing one IBM 360. Now it was scattered across three buildings at three separate locations in the Los Angeles area, housing five IBM 370/168s and one CDC-175 scientific computer, with three more 370s on the way. The machine room in WCC Building Four was dangerously overcrowded, with no room left to reconfigure equipment, add equipment, or perform routine maintenance. Rapid expansions were being projected in the ISC data-processing load due to the increased use of computers in the design of advanced aerospace vehicles: the Space Shuttle and the B-1 Bomber, both expected to be approved by Congress shortly. Something had to be done about the computer housing shortage.

As director of Computer Planning and Controls Sid Hasin reported to Larry Manly, general manager of Information Systems Center, who reported to Maury Dahn, vice president for Information Systems, who reported to Robert DePalma, corporate vice president of Finance and chief financial officer in Pittsburgh, who reported directly to Mr. Rockwell. Neither Manly, Dahn, or DePalma had any expertise or training in computer technology. So the highly technical job of making sure Rockwell had enough computers, the right computers, at the right cost, fell to the underpaid, unappreciated director of Computer Planning and Control, Sidney Hasin.

Sid Hasin, Maury Dahn, and Larry Manly came up with a proposal to consolidate all Western's regional data-processing activities at a new WCC at Seal Beach. Rockwell already owned a fine new eight-story building there, part of an elaborate three-building complex which was underutilized. Dahn, Manly, and Hasin proposed the building be taken out of the hands of Corporate Real Estate and handed over to them.

Myron: "Maury wanted his own building and to be emperor of it."

Maury's job was said to be on the line with this proposal. Sid's job was on the line because Maury had asked him to spearhead the project. Sid told Myron that if the move came off without a hitch, ISC was going to be sitting pretty. But if the move caused Pittsburgh problems, heads were going to roll.

Sid was obsessed with keeping Maury happy. Maury was obsessed with keeping Bob DePalma happy. Sid would call Maury a tough son of a gun and a bastard and a dry-as-toast accountant who never could understand people. But then Sid would sit there shaking his head and say, "But Maury's my ticket to the future, however long that might be." And then he would go off on one of his endless soliloquies on the subject of his never being appreciated, and how he'd show them someday when he was gone how much he had done for them. Myron used to have to calm him down, like a psychiatrist.

Myron: "Anything I can do for you Sid, you know that."

The move was set for the "Christmas interval" at the end of December. Most everyone would be on vacation that week and computer usage would slump to its annual low. Sid could have simply shut down the old center at Downey, sent his forty van loads of equipment down to Seal Beach, thrown the power switch, and hoped for the best. But a much safer solution, less likely to cause Pittsburgh undue anxiety, would be for ISC to set up a parallel operation at Seal Beach, while keeping Downey on-line as a backup until the new WCC was up and running.

Sid decided to install three IBM 370s at Seal Beach to get it going while he was closing down Downey. He proudly referred to these as his "swing machines." Sid dangled the award in front of Myron while insisting on bread-and-water terms: eighty-eight-month leases with rock-bottom rates, with an option to walk away without penalty after five months.

On the face of it, the deal was nuts. OPM was locking itself into an obligation to reimburse Rockwell for the full amount of the three leases if and when Rockwell terminated. The only way Myron could at all break even on the deal was if he managed to re-lease the machines for what he was paying Rockwell.

Myron agreed to Sid's insane terms on one condition: that Sid sign a sublease agreement permitting OPM to make monthly payments in the event of a termination, not the lump sum equal to the remainder of the lease, which was OPM's standard suicide clause. Myron claims Sid told him that would be fine by him. But less than a week before the closing, Sid reneged.

Sid: "It has to be a clean deal. You buy out Rockwell. No sublease."

Myron: "Sid, I can't do it."

Sid: "Either you do it or you'll never do business with Rockwell again."

Myron: "Sid, it's a wonderful award . . . but I'd prefer to conceive of the termination as a 'guaranteed sub-lease' . . . not a lump-sum buy-out."

Sid reminded Myron for about the hundredth time that "I did not have the power, the authority, to grant his request . . . but any reasonable proposition I promised to bring to management's attention."

Myron had been counting on his sacred relationship with Rockwell to save him when the time came. He would fall on bended knee before Dahn and beg him to let him make the payments. The three "swing machines" were terminated after five months. OPM now owed Rockwell $13 million. At which point the sacred relationship was quickly forgotten.

Sid: "Buy it out."

Myron: "But, Sid, you told me I could make the payments."

Sid: "Buy it out."

Maury: "We're terminating. We want the thirteen million. Now."

Sid just sat there coolly while Maury went on "like a real bastard" demanding his pound of flesh from OPM. Myron waited until they were back in Sid's office before letting him have it.

Myron: "What in hell is going on here? You told me it was going to be okay to make the payments."

Sid: "Don't worry about Maury. He's having his period."

Sid must have also had his.

Sid: "You have to buy out the deal, Myron, you must buy out the deal. You renege on your contractual obligations to Rockwell and you will no longer be looked upon favorably here. You won't do any more business with us, I can tell you that right now."

Myron had only agreed to the deal in the first place for two reasons:

1. To save Sid's ass
2. Because Sid told him they'd make it up to him in the future

That was the start of the Black Book. An unwritten, informal, under-the-table agreement by which Rockwell was supposed to make up for all the harm done to OPM.

Myron: "It was all being done on the basis that Rockwell would in effect give us back the $13 million by taking future transactions and making it up on the monthly rental . . . and in effect charging it to the government, because the government gave them 85 percent of it back, so Rockwell wouldn't even have to have been out of pocket."

Myron maintains there was a real Black Book: "It was nothing but one of Sid's ledger books, he had lots of them. But he had a special one for OPM and it was black."

Sid's Black Book was not a book at all. It was more of a "situation."

Sid: "We discussed internally . . . the difficulties caused to OPM by this termination . . . and it was suggested that we not make it up to OPM [so much as] take it 'easier' on OPM . . . that we not negotiate them down to the bottom that we could . . . but we would still keep it at a competitive level."

To Sid this never was such a cut-and-dry deal. It was always "a very subjective type of agreement." Any entries in such a book, according to Sid, "would have to be somewhat fictitious."

Myron was finally forced to admit to himself that the Black

Book was just another one of Sid's less palpable shams. Myron finally found a better word for it: "It was blackmail by Sid Hasin, if you really want to know."

Haggling over the Black Book went on for years.

Sid: "I need this rate."

Myron: "I can't give you that rate. I will give you this rate."

Sid: "Myron, I really need this rate. I can't go below it."

Myron: "But what about the Black Book?"

Sid: "I can't do anything until the next deal. The next deal will be in the Black Book."

Myron: "But, Sid, it's fifteen deals already and every time you say the next deal will be in the Black Book."

Sid: "Don't worry, Myron, I told you, I'll take care of it. The next deal, I promise, will be in the Black Book."

There always was a next deal. But it never was in the Black Book.

10

By the end of 1977, business was certifiably booming. Fox's financials for the year showed net income up 40 percent, to $2.5 million. Lease-related assets had shot up 100 percent, to over $250 million. "Income from equity participants" had climbed to nearly $14 million, without which the company would probably have been forced to report a net loss of more than $10 million. Still, net worth had more than quadrupled, to over $3 million.

Some signs of trouble had turned up even on the balance sheet: debt incurred in the purchase and lease of equipment from vendors now exceeded the minimum income due the company from lessees by more than $150 million. All those "early outs" reduced by a large margin the money OPM could actually count on if and when lessees terminated leases in force early.

Fox did disclose a $6-million receivable due from Dav-Na, Myron and Mordy's not very tidy desk-drawer partnership. Without bothering to mention that Dav-Na was merely a paper shell, and an insolvent one at that. Dav-Na had generated a convenient tax loss for the year of $440,000. The statements did note in passing that the deliberate transfer of losing leases into the partnership "which generate a variety of tax benefits . . . could be attacked as lacking economic substance." The IRS had been good to OPM up until now. Fox clearly saw no reason that this pleasant state of affairs shouldn't continue indefinitely.

Myron and Mordy had withdrawn an additional $500,000 in shareholder advances, listed as an asset on the balance sheet.

Fox neglected to mention that the personal estates of Myron and Mordy did not possess the cash to repay such a debt. This could have been charged against income, in the form of a dividend, but was not. It could have been shown as an expense for salary payments, but was not. It could have even been shown as an asset, with a reserve held against the risk it would not be collected, but it was not. Fox called the loan an "advance" and left it at that.

OPM: solvent by the grace of God and Fox & Co.

Myron and Mordy knew better. They might be pulling in enough cash now to meet obligations, but as soon as those early outs started coming down full force, they were going to be in big trouble.

Richard Santulli of Goldman Sachs gave Myron and Mordy a piece of advice when the IBM price cut went through: "See what equipment you own free and clear, what your obligations are, what your early terminations are." And, it hardly needed to be said, do what you have to do to keep the business going. Goldman Sachs advised that OPM "put its house in order." But Myron and Mordy were not by nature good housekeepers.

They preferred to play games. Make up stories. Keep up appearances. They assiduously avoided doing what Santulli told them to do, a hardheaded analysis of their long-term obligations. Hardheaded analyses had never been their strong suit.

There must be an easier way out. There was: buy a company.

Their first serious takeover target was Century Factors. Henry Singer of Singer Hutner, a mergers and acquisitions specialist, apprised Myron and Mordy of its vulnerability to a sneak attack. OPM promptly retained Skadden Arps, the leading legal experts on hostile takeovers, and bought a large block of Century stock from the estate of a major shareholder. They hoped to use Century's extensive line of credit to finance more acquisitions and underwrite current operations. But they ran into stiff resistance from another major shareholder, who also happened to run the company. Century's banks threatened to cancel its lines of credit unless Myron and Mordy put up personal guarantees for the full purchase price. OPM was forced to back off. According to Myron because the price was too high. According to Mordy because the lawsuit threatened by the hostile owner would have forced OPM's double hocking into the open.

In December of 1977, Singer thought he might have found just what the client ordered. Three brokers he met were on the lookout for a buyer for a small bank in Louisiana. The First National Bank of Jefferson Parish (FNJ) in Gretna, a suburb of New Orleans. Henry Singer liked its looks. Myron liked the first thing Henry asked him about it, "How would you like to be Chairman of the Board of the 468th largest bank in the United States?"

Myron had always fancied himself a bit of a banker, ever since leaving Chase. Mordy's own gloomy assessment, which amounted to a yes vote in the end, was that buying a bank "might add a degree of respectability to OPM."

Everyone was pleased with the deal except Goldman Sachs. Rich Santulli:

1. They had a leasing business to run. If they had excess cash, it would be better off going back into their business.
2. They knew zero about the banking business. Going from the way they ran a business, like a candy store, into the most regulated industry you could possibly be in . . . It was insane.
3. We didn't feel that the New Orleans area was the right area for two Jewish boys from New York to be operating in.
4. They had obligations to pay off, like the big Rockwell buy out, and they shouldn't be defaulted on so Myron could go down south and play "American Banker."

In two and a half years Goldman Sachs had placed debt on over $200,000,000 worth of OPM deals, earning well over $2 million in the process. But things had been going badly between them for some time.

Santulli: "It was a growing thing . . . we felt it wasn't fair for us to keep telling them they can't do things . . . they didn't need our advice . . . the relationship had gotten worse and worse." Santulli chalked the "new coldness" largely up to the experience factor: in the beginning, OPM had relied heavily on the advice of Goldman Sachs as to how to structure leases. Now they knew how to write leases, they didn't need Goldman Sachs anymore.

Myron's decision to go ahead with the bank purchase was the last straw. The two senior partners on the account, David George and Pete Sacerdote, had devoted a great deal of their time trying to persuade Myron & Company not to buy the bank.

The conflict finally came to a head at a five-hour meeting at Goldman Sachs, attended by Myron, Mordy, Joe Hutner, and five Goldman Sachs bankers. After what Joe Hutner later characterized as "a long, boring, very confusing, and very directionless meeting," Hutner finally tried to press them for their final view of the bank acquisition. According to Hutner, Sacerdote declined to express any definite opinion.

Sacerdote: "We are in the business of aiding companies in closing transactions . . . If OPM has a certain transaction to discuss we will be happy to participate . . . We are not going to express a view on this particular matter . . . We do not regard that as part of our role."

Hutner figured he must be dreaming.

"Mr. Sacerdote, you just drew up a whole report on this subject. Who else should have an opinion? What is your role here except as financial advisers to OPM?"

Hutner insists Sacerdote refused to take sides on the issue, which Myron ascribed to pure timidity: fear of losing the lucrative OPM account. The meeting was on a Friday afternoon and running late. Myron had to head home to observe the Sabbath. He walked out without saying a word to anyone, grabbing Hutner on the way. In the hallway he finally exploded.

"Those miserable pricks! Find me another banker, right away. Call that friend of yours at Lehman Monday morning."

Goldman Sachs sent OPM a rather reserved letter of resignation.

> OPM's leasing business has experienced rapid growth and we believe we have been helpful to you in this regard. While we appreciate your desire to grow rapidly, we believe OPM must not out-

strip its financial or managerial resources . . . Goldman Sachs has found that our views on these matters are more conservative than OPM's. We find it awkward to be continuing in a posture of advising restraint when it is evident that this is not one of your desires.

When Myron received this letter, he called Rich Santulli. "We could hear him clearly on the phone . . . he was very loudly crying . . . He may have turned into a tremendous actor along with the other tremendous talents he had, but he was very upset, and cried."

Myron hated to see anyone go. Even when he forced them into it.

11

Joe Hutner's friend at Lehman Brothers was David Sacks. A former head of the Tax Department at Simpson, Thacher & Bartlett. Sacks had joined Lehman in April of 1976 as chief legal and administrative officer, a member of the board of directors and of the executive committee. Hutner had known Sacks less than a year, ever since Sacks had bought a house from a friend of Hutner's in Larchmont. Hutner had handled that sale "as an accommodation" and they had gotten to know one another. Hutner called Sacks in early March 1978. A client of his, one of the two largest computer-leasing companies in the country, was now represented by a major investment bank but was looking to make a change.

Sacks: "Is it Itel?"

Hutner: "No, OPM."

Sacks had heard of OPM. Mostly from those impressive tombstone ads placed by Goldman Sachs in *The Wall Street Journal*. A meeting was set for later that week. Sacks called Alan Batkin, a thirty-two-year-old Lehman partner with an M.B.A. from NYU, with a four-year stint as a C.P.A. with Coopers & Lybrand behind him. He had an idea Batkin might know something about the leasing business. Batkin did know something about leasing: he had even written a chapter in an accounting text called *Retail Accounting and Financial Control* on "Leasing Versus Owning." His primary experience at Lehman Brothers had been in the airline, timber, and retailing industries.

Joe Hutner and Mendy Weissman turned up at Lehman Brothers a few days later. Myron, as usual, was late. They talked in Sacks's office for an hour or so before retiring to the dining room for lunch. Sacks asked the OPM delegation "the sort of questions an investment banker asks a prospective client." What could a new banker do for you? What was your source of unhappiness with Goldman Sachs? Who are your customers? What sort of track record do you have? How do you make your money?

Myron complained bitterly about his lack of contact with senior people at Goldman. He hadn't minded when they were a small potatoes outfit, but now they were generating fees of $2.5 million a year, it was just a little insulting to be "stuck talking to a couple of associates." He hadn't been getting along well lately with the senior partners on the account, who had been strongly opposed to his buying the bank. Myron said he had paid Goldman over two million in fees in 1977. It was actually just a touch over one.

Before taking on OPM, Sacks paid a visit to OPM with Harvey Kreuger, head of Lehman's banking division and the former CEO of Kuhn Loeb before it was taken over by Lehman. Sacks was quite taken with Mordy, whom he found "perfectly charming . . . he regaled us with a number of reasonably pleasant stories." Mordy conducted himself modestly, describing himself as just a humble salesman; Myron was the financial whiz. They called themselves "The Custom Leasing People" and they seemed to take their responsibilities very seriously. Myron and Mordy had the arresting look of brash young men who meant to make their mark in the world.

Lehman's cursory reference check certainly reinforced that impression. Batkin called references supplied by Myron at Rockwell, American Express, National Bank of North America, Manufacturers Hanover, Singer Hutner, and Fox. "Sidney Hasin said . . . Rockwell thinks these guys are terrific . . . they always live up to their word, if they ever shake hands on a deal and there is change in rates or pricing between the time they shook hands and the closing . . . they will always live up to the deal they had shaken hands on."

Batkin was about Myron and Mordy's age. He found it "quite impressive that these two young men had developed a large business with such major corporations as those on their client list . . . these were very blue-chip corporations these two young people had established ongoing business relationships with . . . everyone referred to them as people you can trust, people of the highest integrity, people who could be relied on to live up to their word."

Batkin's final analysis concluded with the crucial question: Who could get hurt on an OPM deal? The answer seemed simple: the lessee. Financing was extended on the credit of the lessee. If OPM were to default on its obligation to "buy out" a lease when a lessee decided to walk away early, it would be the lessee who got stuck paying the rent on the machine, not Lehman Brothers, not the bank.

To confirm Myron's bullish projections that OPM was "a fast-growing, profitable company," Batkin went over Fox's certified financials for 1976. The financials showed a positive net worth, and a large amount of debt in relation to equity, not all that unusual in a young, highly leveraged company like OPM. Batkin spoke to Kutz and Mendy about OPM's financial prospects. Kutz was tremendously positive, upbeat; Weissman provided no cause for concern. Batkin was even shown a "highly confidential" internal projection of future cash flow and buildup of equity, which showed "a rather marked and rapid increase." He did not question the Kutz method. To Batkin, OPM's substantial equity income seemed to provide a considerable margin for profit. He described the equity concept in a memo to Lehman Brothers' commitments committee.

> OPM makes a large profit up-front . . . if the present value of the rent equals 100% of cost, and then they raise 20% in equity, OPM has an initial profit of 20% of equipment cost.

It was this equity cushion, Steve Kutz and Mendy Weissman explained, that allowed "the residual values on the balance sheet of OPM [to be] very conservatively stated." Batkin took "considerable comfort" from this, and from the fact that OPM had recently plunked down three million in cash to buy the FNJ bank and apparently had been able to raise an additional six million in loans without any problems. A company on the brink of bankruptcy could hardly claim to have done that. Myron confided to Batkin that "his goal was to have the entire purchase price [nearly ten million] available by July . . . in cash."

Lehman Brothers' banking planning committee met twice in mid-March to consider OPM. Based on Batkin's positive analysis, Lehman elected to become investment banker to OPM. The Lehman Brothers/OPM relationship began like so many other OPM relationships, as a love fest. Myron would later describe their attitude as "the pampering of Myron Goodman." This Myron considered little more than his due, as he had been led to believe by Batkin that "OPM was in the top 5% of Lehman clients . . . OPM was pure profit . . . two maybe three guys working on it at any one time . . . expenses versus revenue was minimal."

As with Goldman Sachs, Myron insisted on frequent and prominent placement of tombstone ads in all the right periodical places, attesting to the prestige of OPM and its exclusive connection with Lehman Brothers. Though David Sacks, who had to approve the placement of all such advertising, considered such ads largely a matter of "pandering to client ego." Myron Goodman knew better: "The tombstone ads were to enhance OPM credibility . . . the entire OPM sales force was supplied with photocopies of these ads . . . OPM had thirty, forty plaques made up with an ad on each to give out to all OPM offices . . . Bob DePalma [Rockwell's chief financial officer] said the only reason Rockwell continued to do business with OPM was because of our association with Lehman . . . same with Polaroid, TRW, Lockheed . . . and others. Mordy had Batkin call Polaroid and Lockheed." In a pinch, tombstone ads could even take the place of certified financial statements to satisfy overly curious lessees or banks in need of reassurance as to OPM's financial health. For many OPM customers, the Lehman connection alone was enough to make them rest easy.

An article, "Leasing's New IBM Jitters," appeared in the February 27, 1978, *Business Week*. It questioned nearly every supposition made by Batkin in his analysis of OPM. The accompanying photograph was a closeup of Mordy standing before a bank of IBM 370 mainframe computers, holding an open-reel data tape in both hands. Beneath the photo ran a caption: "Weissman of OPM: Competitors are calling his computer-leasing deals 'crazy' ".

The lead quote, from an anonymous industry "insider," set the basic tone of the piece: "In the computer leasing business . . . everything can be explained in the balance between greed and fear—greed for making money, and fear of I.B.M." The equally anonymous author went on to state the do-or-die question then facing the industry: "Will the imminent delivery of IBM's new 303X series of large computers continue the downward slide in value of its older models . . . Some observers expect many leasing companies to take another drubbing [some] go so far as to say that there will be a 'bloodbath' ".

With the price of a new 370/168 having already dropped from $5 million a year before to $1.8 million at the time of the article, *Business Week* challenged the industry to justify the high residual values underlying most leasing deals. A prime doer of such dubious dealing was none other than OPM:

> Last November, Itel offered to lease two computers to The State of Iowa for $17,000 a month for five years. OPM Leasing Services offered the same machines for only $300 a month for the first year, and $28,000 annually for the remaining four years. And a clause in the OPM lease allowed the state to terminate after one year with no penalty. "It's insanity the way deals are structured," says one OPM customer.
>
> Itel and others complain bitterly that OPM often steals customers with terms and residual values that are far better than they feel they can prudently offer. Admits Mordecai Weissman, who with his brother-in-law Myron S. Goodman runs OPM: "We are the most hated leasing company in the industry. Most of the other leasing companies were sitting around like fat cats until we came on the scene . . ." OPM (which does not stand for "Other People's Money," Weissman insists) did $300 million worth of computer leasing business in 1977, 75% of it in IBM 370's.
>
> Many in the industry are skeptical of OPM deals. One investment banker with a large Wall Street firm . . . refuses to handle them. In a lease structured a year ago, OPM counts on a $4.8 million computer being worth more than 50% of its original price after

seven years, and 20% of its cost after nine years. Such terms, competitors say, are "crazy."

Lehman Brothers could hardly help but see that article. Few people concerned with computer leasing managed to miss it. A Lehman partner by the name of Joel Peck, who worked with Batkin on the account, contacted Sid Hasin at Rockwell to ask him "the real story" behind the allegations. Hasin vehemently denied the story as mere rumor mongering by jealous rivals, saying "OPM's competitors are the ones that do that, not OPM." Singer Hutner sent Lehman Brothers a letter purporting to find numerous inaccuracies in the article, adding that OPM was considering taking legal action against *Business Week*. Lehman Brothers did little else to investigate the charges. They asked for and received oral assurances that OPM leases were economically sound. Myron never provided even a wisp of documentation to back up his shrill assertion that the article was baseless, scurrilous, and utterly libelous.

Myron's personal solution to this outrageous assault on his corporate image was to throw a series of lavish parties in celebration of OPM. These "seminars" were held in the dining rooms of some of the better downtown hotels in most of the major cities in the country. Alan Batkin, Joel Peck, or another Lehman banker attended most if not all of these bashes. A high point of the presentation was the Lehman partner's standardized five-minute oration describing the role of Lehman Brothers in arranging OPM's debt financings. All of which served admirably to counter the negative impression generated by the *Business Week* article.

OPM seminars were held in New York, Boston, Atlanta, Los Angeles, San Francisco, St. Louis, Detroit, Minneapolis, Pittsburgh, Houston, and Dallas. The grand finale was the New York seminar, where five hundred serious students of leasing attended a lavish luncheon at the Waldorf-Astoria. Guests included lessees, vendors, prospective lessees, banks, and other potential financing sources. Myron insisted on elaborate security precautions to ensure that "competitors" would not act as gate-crashers bent on stealing his precious trade secrets.

12

When Rockwell terminated the "swing machines" after just five months, it was the start of an ominous trend. For the buy out of those leases, OPM needed to get its hands on $13 million. Myron might even have had it, except that he had gone and bought himself a bank.

Sid Hasin was not helping any. He was dangling yet another major award before Myron's hungry eyes: a long-term lease on a Control Data Corporation (CDC) 176 scientific computer, which Rockwell needed to help design the Space Shuttle. But when you dealt with Sid Hasin, there always was some sort of catch: in order to win the award for the 176, Myron would have to buy out a lease on a certain elderly CDC-175 Rockwell was hoping to unload. Since the 175's lease still had seven years to go, that buy out would require another three million.

Then there was the recent expansion of OPM into the "international marketplace." Which involved opening a London office. Very prestigious. But very costly. The endless flights on the Concorde alone, for OPM diplomats bent on pursuing better relations with foreign countries, were driving the overhead over there through the roof.

Myron summed up the basic problem: "A general overall need to keep the company afloat."

Myron had his own ideas on how to keep afloat. Which did not involve putting his ship in order, straightening out OPM, or cutting costs. He hatched a bail-out plan, which even he was willing to admit was not exactly foolproof. Its major charm lay more in the realm of originality. He was going to buy the Boston

Red Sox. And that wasn't all. There was a secret part: he planned to trade Carl Yastrzemski, Carlton Fisk, and Bob Linn to the Yankees. For cash on the barrel, of course. Trading ballplayers shouldn't be all that different from trading computers.

There was an additional noncommercial beauty to the concept. Myron was a fanatical Yankee fan. The infusion of talent Myron had in mind would surely give his favorite club a new lease on life. Myron told people at OPM his desire to own the team had spiritual roots as well: he planned to forbid them from playing on Saturday. At the same time, he was conducting exploratory talks on the acquisition of Madison Square Garden. Not out of any particular lust for the building itself, but more out of a spirited devotion to the art of self-love. The building bore his favorite initials: his own. He confided to a few sympathetic souls that once he was King of the Garden, there would be no more Friday night games.

July 7, 1978: two weeks before buying the bank Myron stayed up all night furiously dictating missile memoranda to Sullivan of the Red Sox, Auerbach of the Boston Celtics, Grant of the Mets, Steinbrenner of the Yankees, expressing an interest in taking any one of these franchises off their current owners' hands. Alan Batkin could not just dismiss this as one of Myron's pipe dreams. Sullivan and partners had recently acquired the Red Sox for a bit over $20 million. Myron and Mordy were about to buy a bank worth ten.

Myron grew close to Batkin from the beginning. Myron: "He was extremely bright, friendly, and status-conscious . . . I used to go into his office and he'd say, 'You see what I've got? what Peck and Wolitzer haven't got? My own office . . .' He wasn't obnoxious or anything about it, it was all done in good humor." Like everyone else Myron respected, Batkin was no pushover: "When I did something wrong he said so in the decibels he knew . . . he wouldn't take any guff." And like Sid Hasin, Batkin's main concerns seemed to be to "make Lew [Glucksman] and David [Sacks] and Harvey [Kreuger] happy." Things were the same all over.

Alan Batkin was Myron's friend and contemporary, but Myron liked to take out extra insurance when cultivating a new company. Someone to whom he could play the beguiling part of fair-haired boy, one of his favorite corporate roles.

Lewis Glucksman was then chairman of Lehman Brothers' operating committee, and president of Lehman Commercial Paper.

Myron: "I first met Lew Glucksman running around the bond trading room . . . in his shirtsleeves, with his collar open and tie down, yelling and screaming and keeping everybody in line."

He admits, unabashedly, that he "saw a little bit of myself in Glucksman." He describes their incipient relationship in all-too predictable terms: "Father/son, in the beginning . . . he used to praise me when he liked the things that I did, and he used to put me down severely, like a father with a son, on things that he didn't like."

Glucksman did not like some things about OPM.

Myron: "Glucksman was not pleased by reports he heard from Batkin about OPM . . . day to day operations, chaotic closings, everything always urgent." But Myron was confident that Glucksman looked fondly on OPM because "he thought OPM was a hard-working company with a constant flow of business for him. We kept a constant flow of transactions going, a constant flow of fees." But from his very first meeting with Glucksman, Myron recognized an essential distinction between them: "He was organized."

Lew Glucksman saw his role in managing the OPM account as more avuncular than paternal: "conceptualizing and understanding the strategic needs of a company and trying to supply for that company the best advice." But that summer of 1978, Alan Batkin and his colleagues on the OPM account asked him for more than that: help in arranging short-term financings for OPM.

OPM frequently needed "bridge loans" to tide it over the awkward period between the closing of a financing and the commencement of a lease. OPM frequently purchased a piece of equipment some months before the lease began, which meant that the lessee would not begin its flow of payments until the machine was installed. Closings frequently were delayed, financing institutions occasionally bowed out of a deal. Bridge loans were the only way OPM could avoid forking over its scarce cash until the permanent loan came through.

As president of Lehman Commercial Paper, Glucksman was widely acknowledged to be an expert in arranging these sorts of financings: "I knew a large number of banks and bankers throughout the U.S. and that was a field in which I had specific areas of expertise." When Batkin first asked him to look into finding OPM a reliable short-term lender, Glucksman thought immediately of the First National Bank of St. Paul: "They were very aggressive in the business of trying to find paper . . . with very rapid growth as a result of that . . . It is not possible to grow a bank in the city of St. Paul alone . . . they had to go far beyond Minnesota." St. Paul's aggressive commercial instincts had drawn them frequently to Lehman Brothers on more than fifteen previous occasions.

Glucksman called Clarence Frame, president of the First National Bank of St. Paul. He had known Frame for nearly fifteen years, though Glucksman refused to call the relationship a "friendship": "It was a business relationship. I have almost no outside relationships, none that I can think of." Friends or no, Frame was happy to help. Glucksman: "That's the only call I ever made . . . Because I have more and more withdrawn the scope of my working involvement as I became more and more involved with the broader things in the business." Once was quite enough: the first St. Paul/OPM bridge loan was closed on August 31, 1978.

St. Paul was forced to rely on Lehman Brothers' reputation for representing only solid companies on such transactions. Unlike a permanent lender, a bridge lender had no committed lessee to ensure repayment of the loan in the event of default by the leasing company. As protection against its exposure to OPM, St. Paul insisted on (1) an assignment of the lease itself, (2) first security interest in the equipment, and (3) a firm commitment from a permanent lender to "take out" the transaction as soon as the bridge financing ran out. Bridge loans were gravy for the bank as long as the loans were promptly repaid, because interest rates ran several points above prime. But bridge loans created a problem for Myron: bridge lenders insisted on seeing financials.

An even more rigorous test of Lehman's unbounded affection for OPM was passed with flying colors in December. OPM was going crazy with year-end closings, when a major deal ran into trouble and OPM had to pay IBM for the equipment or the whole deal was going to go sour. Lehman Brothers promptly arranged an emergency $10 million loan from St. Paul, guaranteed personally by Myron and Mordy. To be paid back within just a matter of days. Alan Batkin told Myron that it was only because of Lehman Brothers that the bank would ever have considered making such a loan. This time around, St. Paul was not to be disappointed. Myron: "The loan was paid back a day before it came due, and everyone was happy."

October 30, 1978: Myron's thirty-second birthday. Joe Hutner of Singer Hutner joined with Lehman Brothers in organizing a little tribute to the young financial genius. As Myron was such a Yankee fan, Yankee Stadium was rented out that night for a cozy birthday party. Two to three hundred people: Lehman people, OPM people, Singer Hutner, Fox, Rashba & Pokart people. The guest selection was handled by Hutner, whose criteria were simple: "An appetite for hot-dogs, a tolerance for cold damp air, a modicum of affection for Myron Goodman, a business relationship with OPM."

Myron was suitably touched. Lehman Brothers presented him with a trophy, four feet tall, a slender silver statuette with at the top what might seem to represent, with considerable squinting, Myron at bat.

Myron: "When I broke my leg playing softball . . . they [Lehman Brothers] gave me a trophy . . . at Yankee Stadium . . . they also donated [$50,000] for a library in my name at Hebrew University . . . It was all part of not just servicing a client, but the pampering of Myron Goodman . . . They even koshered their kitchens for thirty-forty people for a big dinner at the 1979 OPM corporate anniversary . . . It was a very nice affair."

13

New Year's Day 1979: Myron and Mordy took the plane to L.A. Mordy was acting nervous. Myron was acting scared. Myron was scared OPM was about to go under. Myron was scared of dying. Mordy wanted two million to go away and leave OPM alone. The question was, as always, simple: how to obtain more money. Mordy, always so sharp and cool and full of ideas, was fresh out of ideas.

Myron: "Mordy wanted to live with a million or two million off on some island, and not to get involved with all this anymore . . . but he wouldn't leave unless the bad deals were taken off the books because he didn't want me to have them as a headache without him being there." Mordy wanted to file for Chapter Eleven under the bankruptcy laws. But Myron was dead set against it: "At that point my ego was very high, and I saw me becoming President of OPM, and I agreed he should leave only when he felt he should . . . He always wanted to go off on his own safaris or his desert trips or whatever and just be free to do what he wanted to do . . . And the only way to do that was to have his $2 million in the bank and not have to worry about anything."

They sat in anxious luxury at the Beverly Wilshire, trying to figure things out. To Myron, it was worth trying something daring. Mordy was sick of the risk. Myron wanted to go for broke. Mordy just wanted to go.

This one was Myron's idea. Myron's last-ditch salvage scheme. They were either going to make it big, or go bust in a very bad way. Mordy was not going to have anything to do with it. Not much, anyway. It was going to have to be Myron's baby, on Myron's personal turf: the Rockwell account. Just a few quick easy ones to tide things over, to keep the wolf from the door, until something better could be worked out. Something clever with the bank.

Myron: "There was no intent for it to continue up to the dollar amount that it did . . . It was to be a transaction that would be done and removed from the books within six, eight, twelve weeks, a short period of time . . . not until well into the major fraud did I think we would have a major fraud."

There were reasons it had to be Rockwell.

Myron: "Sid Hasin wanted to communicate with me two and three times a day . . . If there was going to be a problem with Rockwell . . . in all likelihood it would come to him. He, in turn, would not do anything other than call me for an explanation, and I, in turn, would be able to buy out the deal relatively fast, and wipe it out . . . Dan Byrnes was allowing OPM to do his paperwork for him, prepare all documents and take them around to be signed, and with his secretary, Kimi, control the Rockwell account."

Rockwell's credit was good, which made banks sit easy. Rockwell was such a busy account that if a bad deal happened to be discovered "it would be easier to explain because there were so many good deals." Because Myron was sure he could "handle Hasin" he was sure he would always be in a position if something went wrong to "discuss the matter with Sid and end it right there." Dan Byrnes, Rockwell in-house counsel and chief policeman on the beat, was apparently too busy identifying the profiles of airliners landing at LAX to look for shady details in dubious documentation.

As always, the immediate need was for short-term cash. Myron's first ploy was to build a "bridge to nowhere." This was the latest form of double discounting, dispensing with the computer. All Myron needed was a reasonable-looking IBM bill of sale and an IBM invoice marked "paid" to show to the financing bank. And a signed and executed Rockwell lease. Myron had a stock of such leases on hand from Rockwell, which he had procured by persuading Hasin that they should be considered cancelable purchase orders to "reserve" hard-to-find equipment and "lock in" interest rates. Once Rockwell signed a lease, Myron could safely "bridge finance" it. If Rockwell really wanted the equipment, he could buy the machine and have it put in. If Rockwell decided against it, he could buy out the bridge loan and forget all about it. Except that he had freely enjoyed the pleasant use of all that short-term cash.

Mordy was at the office for once the night Myron called: January 11. A major bridge loan with the First National Bank of St. Paul was due to close the next day. They had to get their hands on the cash, but the paid invoice from IBM had been inexplicably "delayed." Whether Mordy bought this or not, there was in fact no invoice due, there being no such equipment. Myron told Mordy to talk to Allen Ganz, their twenty-five-year-old brother-in-law, in charge of Contracts/Finance. Allen had a list of equipment descriptions Mordy could use as inspiration for the task. Weissman typed up a new IBM invoice using the blank forms Ganz gave him. He signed it with the name of the appropriate IBM rep, stamped it "paid," and blithely dashed off the date.

This one might be Myron's baby, but Myron needed constant advice, and occasional physical aid. On February 1, Myron and Mordy were together again on a transcontinental flight. Myron admitted he needed to do another lousy Rockwell deal, that the lease was a fiction and the equipment a fantasy. This time around, Myron came down heavily on the desperate situation they faced, that if they didn't do another one they'd have to close the doors for sure. Myron said that they'd never get the money in to buy out the bad Bank of New York deal Mordy had done, without getting it from a bad Rockwell.

Mordy didn't mind helping, but he minded being caught at it. In the first of many artful maneuvers designed to distance himself from the fraud, Mordy begged to be allowed to do the job at home, away from the prying eyes of OPM personnel. He waited until the Sabbath was over to get down to work.

Sunday morning, February 4: Mordy had an OPM chauffeur load an IBM typewriter into an OPM limo for the trip out to Long Island. Mordy painstakingly worked up the fake IBM invoices in his den. Myron forged the signatures this time around, marked them "paid," and five days later closed the deal without a hitch for $4.5 million. At which point, Mordy retired as OPM's IBM writer-in-residence. From that day forward, Mordy stood back and watched, or closed his eyes, but never touched a false document again.

Myron was reluctant to ask Mordy for help, if he could possibly avoid it. But Myron couldn't possibly handle the complex administration of an ambitious fraud all by himself. Myron at heart was a team player. He set about recruiting a team. Fortunately for the success of the scheme, he had a ready pool of candidates to draft from his own staff. Myron's distinctive executive style had always been to surround himself with men his own age or even younger, all strictly bound to him personally by ties of family, fear, or financial dependence. OPM was like one big raucous family in a constant state of crisis. A few family members might be willing to help, a few might even be eager, the rest he could probably intimidate.

Steve Lichtman was Myron's assistant. A tall, curly-haired, affable type. He had been a high school classmate of Mordy's, recruited by OPM in March of 1977 after four years with Chase. His exacting duties included accompanying Myron to service the Rockwell account, handling messages, luggage, and travel arrangements, a job that gave him the imposing title of vice president and a salary to go with it.

Sunday evening, February 4: Myron called Lichtman at home. He asked him to ride with him into work Monday morning. Lichtman knew this meant one of Myron's mornings, which began at 4 A.M. Reluctantly, he agreed. Myron's car pulled up at four-thirty sharp and Lichtman got inside. Myron didn't say anything; he just kept looking out the window, looking bored, sick, or something else; Lichtman couldn't quite place it. Not a word out of him the whole ride in. Not a word more, and Lichtman was ushered into Myron's office. Myron sat down behind the huge, imposing, trapezoidal desk on which all his papers were soon to be piled. He stood up and started pacing around. He looked out the big windows at Trinity Place. Finally he came out with a word. He started talking about "it."

The whole future of OPM depended upon "it." On the willingness of Steve Lichtman to do "it." If "it" couldn't be done, OPM was dead. If "it" could be done, there might still be a chance. The future of OPM was now resting in the hands of Steve Lichtman. Could Steve Lichtman handle the strain?

Lichtman had no idea what "it" was. Gradually he began to gather that whatever "it" was, "it" was not strictly kosher. In time, Myron let slip a few key details: he needed cash to buy out a Fireman's Fund deal. He needed the cash from a Rockwell financing. The Rockwell lease could not be put together in time to meet the closing date of the Fireman's Fund deal. What they had to do was bridge finance a fake lease to tide them over until the real Rockwell lease was put through. Now it was Lichtman's turn to pace up and down. Myron swore the bad deal would be bought out right away, it was coming right off the books. No big deal.

Friday, February 9, 1979: Steve Lichtman's first full day of crime. Myron had lied. He was not pulling off a bridge to nowhere, but a full-fledged phantom lease. The equipment did not exist, never had existed, and never would exist, not if Myron could possibly prevent it. The permanent lender would be fooled into thinking this deal was a long-term, real-life, major rental, covering three separate, high-ticket pieces of computer equipment: OPM/Rockwell E.S. 80-1, E.S. 80-2, and E.S. 80-3. Lichtman spent the entire day trying to learn how to forge. Myron had signed most of the Rockwell signatures, but he asked Lichtman to try his hand at the signature of Rockwell's purchasing officer, Robert C. Peterson. Myron showed him how to forge without knowing how to forge, by tracing the real signature from a legitimate Rockwell lease. Lichtman was eager and willing, if not exactly proficient; tracing one signature took him all day. He also misidentified the procurement officer's title: Vice President, Aerospace Personnel. There was no such job at Rockwell.

Steve Lichtman needed help to help Myron. Myron told Lichtman to talk to Allen Ganz. Allen had known Myron and Mordy ever since they both started going out with his sisters in 1968. Allen had been living with his parents in Rockaway then, and Mordy had a bungalow at the same Catskills colony where the Ganz's spent their summers. Allen was still in high school, at the Hebrew Institute of Long Island in Far Rockaway, known for short as "HELI." HELI merged with another Hebrew school called Hillel and was renamed "HAFTR," for Hebrew Academy Of The Five Towns and Rockaway. Allen graduated in 1971 and went to Baruch College, where he earned his B.B.A.: bachelor of business administration. Concentration: marketing. Summers, he worked part-time at OPM.

After college, he went to work as Myron's full-time assistant. His chief duties that summer consisted of "making sure the pool people were at Myron's house . . . and the basketball court was up, important things like that." After a few months of minding Myron's house, Allen was put to work on transactions. He would attend closings, get documentation in place, check lease calculations. In two years, he was put in charge of Contracts/Finance. By June 1977, Allen was a full-fledged "overseer," working with Goldman Sachs and the banks, obtaining financings, sending documentation to attorneys, checking numbers, reporting directly to Myron. As the volume of transactions grew, Contracts/Finance grew. Allen was given Toni Pierre, who had been Myron's personal executive secretary, as his first assistant. Before long he had five full-time people under him. When OPM moved into its palatial new headquarters at 71 Broadway in February of 1978, "things just sort of ballooned."

While still in college and working part-time as an OPM messenger, Mordy had asked him to take a $15,000 check to a rabbi in Brooklyn. Mordy said he should give the rabbi the check; the rabbi would give him cash. Allen could tell something funny was going on, just from the way Mordy was acting: "Just go, don't worry about it, forget about it, just bring it back." As if nothing was going on, which meant something was going on.

Later on after college, Allen would be asked to deliver "special packages" to Marty Shulman at American Express, to Harold Farkas at Jerry Silverman, a dressmaker in the garment district, to Richard Monks at IBM in White Plains, always in envelopes that bulged and crackled: Ganz assumed it was cash. In May of 1977, Allen was called into the "executive suite" at 99

Wall, two drab adjoining offices, nothing fancy, not yet. Allen had been knocking himself out working up the documentation on a deal with American Express, with four or five separate leases all involved in one closing. The deal was supposed to be for a mainframe computer and a whole cluster of peripherals, but as he went along Allen got to wondering about it: whether the deal was for real.

Mordy gave him the papers and told him to take them to Marty Shulman to be signed and brought back. From the way Mordy said it, Allen knew his suspicions were absolutely founded. He kept saying, "Don't worry, we'll take care of it, get it out of your mind." Then he launched into the whole family thing: "We trust you as a brother-in-law, you're family, you'd never betray us." This gave Allen a few things to think about: he knew about Harold Farkas at Jerry Silverman, who got first eight hundred and then twelve hundred a month for favors. You were supposed to feel sorry for Farkas because he had a retarded son and a lot of medical bills, and Mordy used to get him tickets to take his son to the circus. He knew about Richard Monks at IBM because he had personally handed Danny Ascher, the OPM chauffeur, a special envelope to take up to Monks in White Plains with explicit instructions to deliver it directly into Monks's hands. Then Allen had to send Danny out again, this time to Denver, with fifteen thousand dollars in cash to give to Joe Verner at Fireman's Fund. They were supposed to meet at the airport and since they might have a problem recognizing each other, Allen gave them a password: "Merry Christmas." It was nowhere near Christmas.

All of this came down from Mordy. Allen had always gotten along better with Mordy. Myron was weird; that was all there was to it. Myron was weird when he first started going out with Lila Ganz in 1968. Myron was basically a bully. He knew how to yell and scream and intimidate the hell out of you, and make you shake in your pants and say, "Okay, Myron," no matter what it was. He knew how to make you fly to the moon and back if he wanted. Sometimes by being nice, usually by being mean. Allen was scared of Myron. There was no getting around it. And he was not the only one. Most people at OPM learned to be scared of Myron.

Now Allen was twenty-five and an OPM vice president. Now it was 1979 and business had gone crazy: volume growing out of sight but money also getting tight, so the pressure was on all the time to close that next deal yesterday if not sooner, to get that cash in, to stay ahead and afloat. And everything that came down, came down direct from Myron. Mordy was hardly there anymore.

You were given just enough information to get the deal done and nothing more. Which slowed things up, created bottlenecks, because everything had to wait until Myron could personally attend to it. If something did not make sense, you were not about to question it. If Allen suggested maybe once or twice that the company could save itself a few dollars by going to a bank where the rate was a little lower, Myron would just snap, "Don't you tell me how to run my business, I do what I want." And when he was always putting on the pressure, half of it was created by Myron himself. If a law firm was taking too much time on a closing, he'd get all excited and start to make threats. He'd make Allen get on the phone to move mountains: "I don't care what they say, it's got to get done, it's got to get done . . . It's got to get done!"

The first weeks of 1979 were total hell. Allen was supposed to be closing about twenty transactions in about two weeks. He'd been killing himself and killing his staff trying to get everything moving smoothly, but there were endless snags and drags and he had made plans to go on vacation the twenty-fifth. In the middle of everything, he took off. For seventeen days of bliss, away from it all. He came back in February, the tenth or eleventh. He stepped into Steve Lichtman's office to say he was back.

Steve was looking tired, and troubled. He kept alluding to something that was obviously bothering him, but he wouldn't say what it was. Allen finally had to say, "Listen, what's going on?"

Steve had been up all night with Myron working on a Rockwell deal. And the important thing about the Rockwell deal was, the deal wasn't real. Myron had put the screws in him until he'd finally gotten sick. Not just tired, but physically sick. Now they were going to have to do another one. And the worst part was that he'd only been willing to go along with Myron once because Myron had promised him it would be only once. Now Myron was making him do another one and telling him to ask for help. Allen's help.

"It was like a mountain falling on my head." It was one thing to be a kid and be given certain things to do. You were told to do certain things, maybe you even saw certain things, or thought certain things. But the point was you didn't have to know, you didn't have to find out. You could follow orders and listen to Mordy. "Forget about it, don't worry, we'll take care of it." Now he was twenty-five and a vice president. Now he was no longer a messenger boy running around with peculiar packages.

"Frankly," Allen said, "I think this is a pretty sick, pretty sad, scary situation."

Steve Lichtman agreed.

Allen thought, "What do I do? Do I walk away from a family-type situation where family is involved? And by me walking away it would cause the whole downfall of everything, and everything to crumble?" It was either getting out of there and running away or "succumbing to all the pressures that were happening, and everything which soon followed." Later on that same day, Myron came to see him. And he went through this whole long song and dance: how OPM was in dire straits financially, how even with all these transactions being closed and all this money and all this volume there just wasn't enough money coming in, how they were in terrible, terrible shape. Myron said, not a word to anyone about this, except to him or Steve. Not to Mordy, not to Andy Reinhard. "If you ever have any questions, go through Steve or me."

So he and Lichtman were given a job: creating false documentation. Steve Lichtman knew Rockwell, so he would work up Rockwell. Allen Ganz knew Contracts/Finance, so he would work up IBM title documentation and any versions of a lease to be financed. They started work early before anyone but Myron was in, in OPM's fancy, wood-paneled, windowless library on the "executive" floor, a small, cozy, round room with a heavy marble octagonal table and soft, deep leather-covered chairs, bookshelves lined with leather-bound tomes, and silk yarmulkes, waiting to be donned for the daily mincha service, on the shelves beneath the elaborate and heavy brass Moorish chandelier.

Allen would start with copies of legitimate IBM bills of sale. He'd make a good copy and white out the date, equipment description, and serial numbers, then type in new numbers based on descriptions Lichtman gave him from his phoney Rockwell leases. Then he'd copy it again, and he had a presentable IBM bill of sale. The copy looked close enough so that even when Singer Hutner started to demand originals, no one ever detected a difference.

Lichtman was in charge of working up fake leases. All leases were fabricated on a word processor at Singer Hutner. With a real lease, the lease was worked up and sent out to Rockwell to be executed. With a fake lease, Rockwell obviously couldn't see it or the whole scheme would be blown. Myron had an idea: departing from normal procedure, Myron told Singer Hutner that all Rockwell leases should be sent first to OPM, which would then "forward" them to Rockwell. Real leases could go on to Rockwell, fake leases stayed at OPM. Locked away in Myron's myriad briefcases, and in special file cabinets kept by Lichtman and Ganz on the eighth floor. On phantom leases, Lichtman would take genuine signature pages from "surplus" Rockwell leases Sid Hasin had been persuaded to sign on the grounds that they wouldn't have to be binding. He would then insert the signature pages into the fake lease, so the Rockwell signatures would not have to be forged. Lichtman kept an accordion folder of genuine Rockwell signature pages on hand for use whenever needed.

Lease terms were known to shift right up to the closing. Changes usually linked to the cost of money. On real leases all changes would be confirmed by a letter of authorization from Sid Hasin, which would be telecopied from Rockwell to OPM and presented at the closing. When lease terms were adjusted at the closing of fake leases, Ganz would have to forge the appropriate Rockwell signature on a letter he would type on Rockwell stationery. He would then simply telecopy the letter from the ninth floor of OPM headquarters down to the eighth floor, where Lichtman would be waiting patiently to present it at the closing.

14

On those very first phantom leases, Myron was nervous about the closing. On closings of leases involving IBM equipment, an IBM rep always came. Since no IBM equipment was being leased on the bogus deals, IBM's absence might look strange. Myron claims he went to Andy Reinhard to ask him for help and advice.

Myron recalls staying at the Mark Hopkins in San Francisco the night of January 31. Andy was supposed to show up that evening for dinner to go over closing documents for a package of impending Rockwell transactions: Rockwell/OPM 80–1, 80–2, and 80–3. Andy had no idea the deals were bogus. Myron was planning to tell him at dinner. But Andy was late coming in from New York and didn't even bother to call. Myron was furious, but kept his cool; he couldn't afford to have Andy get any madder at him than he was going to get anyway. Myron held off until they boarded the plane back to New York. He recalls the flight clearly: TWA First-Class, "day going into night . . ."

Myron sailed into the same pitch he gave Lichtman and Ganz. OPM was in a severe cash bind, and they just had to do one questionable transaction. The problem was purely temporary. He would be taking the deal off the books within three or four weeks. No one would ever know.

Andy: "You can't do that."

Myron: "We've got to do it. If we don't I'm going to have to close the doors . . . We're going to buy out the transaction, don't worry. You've got to go along with me . . . You've got to do me this personal favor."

Myron says he needed Andy's help because he "wasn't too involved with the closings . . . it was the first time I was doing leases like this." He was worried about the appearance of the fake IBM invoices. Neither he nor Mordy, and certainly not Steve Lichtman, was a polished forger. If questions came up at the closing about why no one from IBM had bothered to show up, Myron was planning to say, "Don't worry about it. It's all taken care of. We paid them already so they don't have to be here."

According to Myron, Andy had serious reservations about the scheme. But Myron kept pushing him to it: "You have to do it, you've got to do it. For me. For all our years together, for our families, our friends. For OPM. For Singer Hutner. We can't go down the tubes now." He says he persuaded Andy that if they didn't do it, OPM was bound to go under. And in the end, Myron says, Andy agreed to help out.

Closings between OPM and the First National Bank of St. Paul were handled by two sets of attorneys: St. Paul counsel Briggs & Morgan in St. Paul, and Singer Hutner in New York. No one from the bank attended closings. When Singer Hutner received the final papers they would call Briggs & Morgan to say the deal was ready. After the closing was consummated Singer Hutner would simply send the papers to Briggs & Morgan.

Myron says Andy refused to have documentation on any bad deals sent out by Singer Hutner. Myron would have to send it out from OPM. But when Singer Hutner called Briggs & Morgan after the closing to say the deal was on its way, Myron wanted to make sure that Andy made that call. Not Alan Jacobs, who ordinarily handled lease transactions. Myron was worried "Jacobs would bring up questions to make sure he understood what was going on." Myron didn't want questions. He wanted those papers sent out without any fuss. Jacobs was a careful attorney, and he might have even picked up the phone to call Sid Hasin to ask him about the deal.

Fortunately for Myron, Jacobs hated Sid Hasin's guts. He had been furious at Hasin ever since Rockwell had terminated the "swing machines" after promising not to. Myron's main worry was to make sure Andy handled that deal himself. This was a little unusual, because Andy handled the equity deals, and Alan Jacobs the leases.

Reinhard does not recall any such discussion with Myron on any sort of airplane. His diary reflects no entry for a flight on February 1 from San Francisco to New York. Myron's diary shows a dinner date with Reinhard in San Francisco for the night of the thirty-first, canceled, and a flight back to New York with Reinhard on the first, and a second meeting with Reinhard on the second. But Mordy recalls flying with Myron back to New York on that day, when Myron first broached his daring plan to do a series of fraudulent financings in order to buy out the bad Bank of New York deal Mordy had done.

Myron claims Andy looked closely enough at the Rockwell documentation to spot Steve Lichtman's clumsy forgery.

Andy: "This is ridiculous."

Myron: "Leave me alone. It's good enough."

In any case, Reinhard did end up handling that first dangerous deal himself, contrary to normal Singer Hutner procedure. Reinhard says he took over because Alan Jacobs was busy working on other OPM matters. Jacobs does not recall the transaction at all, or asking Reinhard to take care of it. Reinhard transmitted the bogus lease documents to Steve Lichtman in California on February 6, including a message to a Rockwell lawyer concerning a provision in one of the leases. Which was either a clever attempt at disguising his knowledge that the leases were bogus, or a sign that he really had no idea what was going on.

The closing took place on the ninth. It went off without a hitch, with or without the help of Reinhard. On the thirteenth, a paralegal at Singer Hutner sent Sid Hasin and Dan Byrnes copies of a letter referring to the bogus financing "on behalf of Andrew B. Reinhard." If Reinhard was deliberately "papering" Rockwell's files to distance himself from the fraud, Myron never knew about it. But if Myron had wanted Andy to keep all details of the bogus deals out of Rockwell's hands, this sort of thing was not exactly what he had in mind.

Steve Lichtman told Singer Hutner, on Myron's instructions,

that all Rockwell documents were to be sent to OPM, not to Rockwell, from now on. This "new policy" was supposed to make things easy on a favored client, by graciously cutting down on paperwork for Dan Byrnes and Sid Hasin. Lichtman told Reinhard's paralegal about this. She even asked Reinhard about it. Reinhard reportedly responded, "No problem."

Either she forgot about it, or just didn't get it; she sent the false transmittal letter to both Hasin and Byrnes. When she told Lichtman what she had done, Lichtman became slightly unstrung. He called Kimi, Dan Byrnes's secretary right away. The transmittal letter that had just come from Singer Hutner was to be disregarded. Kimi seemed perfectly willing to follow instructions, but Myron was not comfortable having her cover his tracks all by herself. He sent Lichtman out to Rockwell that night to make sure the letter was found and ignored.

Lichtman's cover story was carefully prepared: the letter was connected to a Lockheed lease, it had nothing whatsoever to do with Rockwell. Kimi gave the letter back, unopened, and obligingly sent for Hasin's copy straight from his office. On her own copy of the letter, Reinhard's paralegal noted, "Steve Lichtman retrieved." Mission accomplished.

Allen Ganz assumed Andy knew about Rockwell. Myron and Andy talked OPM all day, every day, for hours. There couldn't have been much going on at OPM Andy didn't know about. They had known each other from sleepaway camp. Allen decided Myron's virulent insistence that Andy didn't know was just a way of protecting his friend.

After the first few bogus deals closed without incident, Allen asked Steve Lichtman right out, "Who else knows?"

"Andy Reinhard."

"But how are we getting away with it? I mean, at the closings?"

Steve said Andy was "aware" but not involved.

"What about Rockwell?"

"No one knows."

"Not even Sid Hasin?"

Allen was flabbergasted Hasin didn't know. Myron solemnly confirmed it: "No one at Rockwell will ever know."

For all of their sakes, Allen hoped he was right.

Lichtman says he talked to Reinhard about the first bogus leases. He avoided mentioning Rockwell by name, but he tried to get Reinhard to get Myron to stop doing deals he would "just have to buy out." Reinhard promised Lichtman he'd talk to Myron, but when the day of the closing came, it went ahead without a peep out of Reinhard. Lichtman assumed Myron must have talked Reinhard into cooperating.

Myron puts it more bluntly. "The fact of the matter is I told Andy, unfortunately." He says he told Reinhard to make sure any problems that came up at Singer Hutner would be dealt with from the inside. When problems did crop up, Myron would tell Allen or Steve, "Call Andy, he'll take care of it."

Jacobs was always a problem. He had a way of asking questions: "Why is OPM paying the bank on certain Rockwell deals, and not on others?"

Myron: "Alan, what can I tell you? It's a fact of life. What it says, it says. What we do, we do. What difference does it make? They're getting paid, aren't they?"

Jacobs would stare at one of Myron's bogus IBM invoices, purporting to indicate that OPM had just paid IBM four million dollars for some piece of equipment.

Alan: "Myron, how could you possibly have paid for this? You're always crying you don't have any money, so how could you have already paid them on this one?"

Myron: "We have enough money. Look, I'll show you."

Just to keep Jacobs happy, Myron would flash an OPM check, or sometimes a letter "with an address to some fictitious IBM box number." Such a check could even be ledgered and sent out if that would keep Jacobs happy. To wend its way back to OPM in the end.

If Jacobs was in one of "his particularly obnoxious moods," Myron would just have to call Andy in "to put the fire out."

Andy was always there to "make sure the deal got closed." And if Alan Jacobs asked too many questions, Andy was always able to "keep Alan quiet." Myron controlled Rockwell. Andy was his enforcer. According to Myron.

The worst problem was any time Singer Hutner wanted to call Rockwell.

Myron: "Don't do it. It bothers them. They don't want to hear from you. Dan Byrnes doesn't want to hear from you. He's busy. He doesn't like to deal with things. We'll take care of it."

They didn't always get the message.

"But I get along very well with Dan Byrnes."

Myron: "Don't call. Okay?"

15

The Rockwell fraud was not the real way out. Even Myron knew that. The real way out had to be legit, and Myron still believed there must be some straight way for OPM to generate clean cash. The bank looked like the answer. Myron: "The intent was to make Cali Trading [OPM's parent company] a bank holding company, put OPM under FNJ, and funnel . . . leases through the bank and have the tax shelters and all the money in the bank out to OPM." Simple enough, and on the face of it, totally legitimate. But they needed approval from the Federal Reserve Board of Governors for the transaction to go through.

In the meantime, Myron and Mordy bought the bank in their own names. They had themselves elected directors and set about searching for a new president who would not be too hard to handle.

They retained George Moran, a retired senior vice president of Manufacturers Hanover Trust, as a consultant to the bank. Moran and Joe Hutner conducted a nationwide search for the new CEO. They saw somewhere between twelve and twenty people before picking William Weathersby, a native Southerner, a former senior financial officer at several Southern banks, and a former chief executive officer of a bank in Baton Rouge.

Myron and Mordy were directors, but only Myron took an active interest in the bank. Myron showed up at every board meeting and took charge. Mordy made it to one and was visibly bored. Myron finally had his hands on a bank of his own. Bank relations had been a particular trouble spot at OPM over the years, and Myron was thrilled by the prospect of being able to tell a bank what to do, instead of the other way around.

Myron's problems with banks stemmed from one unshakable habit: writing checks on uncollected funds. In 1974, OPM banked at Chase. Myron grew accustomed to writing checks in anticipation of proceeds from closings. The OPM check would sometimes clear before the bank's did, and Chase would bounce Myron's check, and Myron would start climbing a wall. By 1975 Myron and Chase had had quite enough of each other. Mendy Weissman took him over to Irving Trust. That relationship began to show signs of strain over Myron's refusal to let Irving see his financial statements. But his biggest problem remained writing checks on money he hoped to have, but didn't have yet.

Within a month after taking over FNJ, Myron was overdrawing his accounts at the bank. Weathersby had been handpicked by OPM to be sympathetic to OPM. Myron had hoped to keep Weathersby in line by extending him a substantial personal loan at the time he became FNJ president. Instead, Weathersby started calling Myron on the carpet for his cavalier attitude toward his own bank.

Myron: "Be quiet and leave me alone."

Myron promised to stop. But by the end of 1978, Marvin Mayer, FNJ's executive vice president, complained to Weathersby that OPM had overdrawn its account at the bank 354 times between October and the end of that December.

In December 1978, Myron had John Clifton write out a series of checks in the amount of $100,000 on OPM accounts at Irving Trust and Chemical Bank. Those checks were deposited at OPM's account at FNJ. He then had Clifton draw up a corresponding series of checks on the FNJ account, to be deposited at Irving and Chemical. In the matter of days it took the checks to clear between New York and New Orleans, OPM had upward of five million extra dollars with which to "play the float."

Myron says this one was Mordy's idea. John Clifton didn't think it was so hot. He even went as far as to warn Myron, as tactfully as possible, that "it wasn't such a good idea." But "in the beginning, and to the extent that no one was hurt by it . . . and the amounts were relatively insignificant," Clifton was willing to go along with it. Unfortunately, what to some might be known as "playing the float" is more commonly known as "check kiting."

During a routine review of OPM's account for December, Weathersby was struck by multiple checks written out to large, neat, round amounts deposited at FNJ from Chemical and Irving Trust, while corresponding checks were being written by OPM on FNJ accounts for deposit at Chemical and Irving. Weathersby asked his internal auditor, Anthony Leone, known affectionately as "Chopper" ever since his days piloting a helicopter in Vietnam, to conduct a full-scale audit of OPM's activities.

By March of 1979, the auditor's report was complete. Weathersby was all set to confront Myron with clear evidence of his wrongdoing, when Myron pushed things just a little too far. OPM had to pay cash for a mainframe after a closing had been delayed. Myron was back to his old tricks. He wrote an FNJ check to IBM and forced Weathersby to certify it. They both knew there was not enough in the account to cover it. Weathersby knew if he didn't do what he was told, his job was going to be on the line. But this was the last straw. Instead of calling Myron and begging him one last time to stop, he decided it was time to play hard ball.

March 17, 1979: Weathersby called Joe Hutner to say that FNJ's internal auditor had detected a check-kiting scheme at the bank involving OPM. He insisted that Hutner and Mendy Weissman come down to Louisiana to see a presentation on the problem put together by Chopper.

Hutner called Mendy that afternoon.

Hutner: "What are you up to this evening?"

Mendy: "Oh, I don't know . . . I guess dinner at home."

Hutner: "You're coming with me to New Orleans."

Mendy: "What for?"

Hutner: "I can't explain now. We'll have time to talk on the plane."

Joe asked Mendy to tell him all about check kiting. Mendy told him. Joe told Mendy what Bill Weathersby had told him. There wasn't much left to do but look at the facts.

Chopper made a dismally effective presentation, complete with flip charts and enlarged views of featured checks. Hutner: "I was very depressed . . . it wasn't one of the brighter moments of my life." Weathersby and Hutner and Weissman took a look at the guidelines on check kiting put out by the Comptroller of the Currency. The course was clear: inform the Comptroller of the Currency. And the FBI.

Hutner found appropriate advice for the moment. He told Weathersby: "Just do what you have to do." He went back to his hotel to try to reach Myron in London.

He tried calling Mordy first. Mordy was, after all, a director.

Mordy: "I really don't want to hear about it. Discuss it with Myron."

Click. Mordy hung up. Hutner finally reached Myron and told him the jig was up. Myron had Lichtman call Clifton to see if he was going to resign as OPM treasurer.

When FNJ first detected the scheme, they called Clifton. Clifton went to see Mordy. Myron was in London. Mordy was a big help.

"Use the float."

"We can't use the float. That's the whole point. Myron was using the float."

"Oh I see, well in that case, I guess you can't use the float."

Mordy shrugged, fresh out of ideas. It was sad. Mordy, once so bright and full of initiative, just didn't seem to care anymore.

FNJ called again to ask that all OPM accounts be closed: "We have examined what has been transpiring over the last few months, and we are going to have to inform the Comptroller of the Currency."

Clifton didn't wait to hear from Myron. He went to see his lawyer. He ended up resigning as treasurer, on advice of counsel, but agreed to stay on at OPM while a campaign was vigorously mounted by Myron to downplay the scandal and emphasize "the various things OPM was going to do for the bank." The furor seemed to die down soon enough. An investigation was being conducted by the Comptroller of the Currency, but until that was over and done with there didn't seem to be much to say about what had transpired. The bank holding company merger was put off indefinitely until OPM was either cleared or convicted.

Myron returned from London on Wednesday, March 21. He waited until Friday to call Alan Batkin. Myron knew the hardest part of all would be facing Lehman Brothers. He had to talk to Batkin right now, "face-to-face."

Batkin: "Myron acted very solemn . . . He was quite concerned . . . he took this as a very serious matter." Myron confided that between December of 1978 and March of 1979 there had been a number of "instances of overdrawing the account at FNJ . . . issuing checks against uncollected funds." This was apparently in violation of federal banking laws, which prohibited a bank covering an overdraft of a principle, officer, or director of the bank as "an unauthorized extension of credit." The Bert Lance problem, basically.

In view of all this, OPM was closing all accounts at FNJ. He and Mordy would not be standing for reelection to the board.

Myron: "No one lost any money on those overdrafts . . . We even paid interest on the money . . . But it was a mistake and we never should have done it."

Batkin: "Why did you do it?"

Myron: "It was all part of our efforts to live up to all our commitments on a very timely basis."

Batkin: "You know, I'm going to have to tell David [Sacks] about this, and he will have to tell Lew [Glucksman]."

Myron hung his head. "I know. You do what you have to do."

Batkin told David Sacks, who told Lew Glucksman. Batkin called Myron right back.

"Be at Lehman Brothers at eight sharp Monday morning. Don't be late."

Myron: "That whole weekend I was petrified Lehman was going to resign." Lew Glucksman took charge of disciplining Myron: "I am the senior partner in our firm . . . the disciplinarian or bad guy or whatever . . . Somebody has to play that role . . . some sort of authority figure."

Glucksman tried to be straight with this brash young man: "On those accounts at this firm I have any involvement with, I expect to never have any surprises . . . If there is any repetition of any action of this kind, we at Lehman Brothers will have to look upon it as having very serious consequences for our relationship . . . Are there going to be any more surprises?"

Goodman: "No, there are no more surprises."

Glucksman asked everyone to step out except Myron. He wanted to be alone with him, so if he had to "read the riot act to him," which might prove humiliating, it would be far better "not to humiliate a client in front of the people he is going to have to work with." If he was going to have to "scorn, ridicule, or abuse" Goodman, "it would have been embarrassing for Myron for Alan to be there . . . He had more than a certain amount of pride, I'm sure."

Goodman might have had his pride, but not at that meeting.

Myron: "I was extremely upset . . . I was crying at that meeting . . . I told him I didn't understand how it happened, and I promised him no surprises, ever again."

Glucksman: "He was very contrite . . . he got very emotional. In fact, he broke down and cried. He said he would never do anything like this again."

Glucksman felt it was his job to "get a feeling as to what had happened . . . whether this was a regrettable action by a young man who was running a big business, and who may have made a mistake . . . or an action by someone whose pattern was such that I should be careful or worried about."

The crime allegedly committed by Myron was a rather ambiguous act to Glucksman, who tended to hear "quotes around the word 'kite' " when he heard the phrase "check kiting": "Writing checks on uncollected funds is a practice that is followed more frequently than it should be by both large and small companies . . . check kiting is one of the great debates in banking. It depends on who you are whether the check kiting is going to float or becomes illegal activity."

Glucksman, in his Solomon role, had to decide for himself whether Myron had done something "intentionally wrong," or whether he was "just another young man who had made a mistake." Through tears, promises, abject contrition, apologies, and charm, Myron was able to persuade Glucksman that he was not a criminal by nature, that his action did not constitute "a pattern of illegal activity," that he was just an honest young man gone astray, bitterly ashamed of what he had done. In forming his opinion of Myron's conduct, Glucksman was admittedly swayed by Myron's conspicuously pious demeanor.

Glucksman: "You couldn't come into contact with Myron Goodman without knowing he was a deeply religious man . . . I think he wore a yarmulke . . . he observed dietary laws, all that sort of thing . . . The precepts of a deeply religious man would tend to suggest a certain [something] in which promises not to do something or statements to that effect would tend to give you a feeling of comfort."

Armed with that feeling of comfort and a marked conviction that Myron was not a dishonest man, Glucksman and Batkin and Sacks brought the matter formally before the Lehman Brothers' operating committee, which reached the collective conclusion that this regrettable incident was "not indicative of the nature of the individual . . . it was aberrant behavior limited to this event."

Alan Batkin: "All indications seemed to point to an image of Goodman and Weissman [as] people of very high integrity . . . very zealous about living up to their obligations . . . deeply religious people, with great moral conviction . . . that in their overzealousness to serve a client . . . had exercised very poor judgment and had acted wrongly." It was not clear which client Myron might have been trying to serve by playing the float.

Myron, for one, was thrilled and a bit surprised that his unrehearsed command performance had gone over so well with the likes of Lew Glucksman. "They said because of me they were going to stick with OPM."

16

While Lehman Brothers was sticking by Myron, Myron was minding his fraud. Controlling Rockwell meant controlling Lehman Brothers, making sure financing banks did not call lessees. Myron claims he "laid down an edict" at Lehman that under no circumstances was a lessee to be contacted, period. He persuaded Alan Batkin and Joel Peck to "put that down in the terms of the offering." Myron: "If they wanted to place Rockwell debt, that was the condition under which they would place it. Or I would place it myself."

More than anything else, Myron was scared of attorneys who might want to contact lessees at closings. He tried to "blacklist" certain firms he considered "white-shoed, ultrafascist," an epithet he freely applied to just about any firm "obnoxious" enough to do anything more than what they were told. The firm most frequently retained by Lehman Brothers for OPM closings was Cleary Gottlieb. Myron: "They were very lax about their closings . . . very easy to get along with." The sort of firm Myron liked: dark-shoed, liberal.

Other firms were not so nice.
Sullivan & Cromwell: "I don't like them."
Davis Polk: "They were obnoxious."
Milbank Tweed: "We never got very far with them."
Stroock & Stroock & Lavan: "Just like Davis Polk."

Myron could influence the selection of closing counsel because OPM paid the legal bills for closing its deals. Criteria for the yes list: "Speed of closing, ease of closing, meeting our needs in terms of timing . . . no formal changes in standard lease documentation . . . accepted our documentation . . . and if they had to work Christmas night, they worked on Christmas night."

Keeping "white-shoed, ultrafascist attorneys" from snooping around Rockwell closings remained just as important as the fraud moved into a new phase: altered leases. Forging phantom leases had been particularly dangerous because if anything went wrong, the lease number did not even correspond with anything Rockwell had in its files. Altered leases provided something of a safeguard because at least there was a legitimate lease at Rockwell for every lease falsely financed by OPM. The difference was in the lease terms: the rent, the duration, the equipment values, and the equipment itself. Starting with a real Rockwell lease, Allen Ganz would remove the pages showing the actual lease terms and substitute new figures, allowing OPM to finance the lease for enormously inflated sums. From a purely technical point of view, altered leases were something of a refinement over phantom leases, because the Rockwell signatures at least were genuine and the actual leases existed, if in a very different form.

No documents showing Rockwell's version of an altered lease could ever fall into the hands of Singer Hutner, Lehman Brothers, or the bank. They all had to see the inflated version, and that version only. OPM would call Singer Hutner to provide them with lease terms, which would then be sent to closing counsel for the bank. No Rockwell rep ever attended an OPM closing after the first, so Rockwell and Singer Hutner never had a chance to compare lease terms. All Rockwell leases were sent by Singer Hutner to OPM to be "sent on" to Rockwell, so Allen Ganz could switch the signature pages back and restore the original figures.

New recruits were added to the fraud team: Mannes Friedman and Marty Shulman. Mannes met Myron in 1975 when he was a salesman for a New York textiles concern. When Myron offered him a job as his assistant, Friedman was understandably concerned about his ignorance of the leasing business. Myron told him not to worry, no one at OPM knew anything about the leasing business, not when they started out. Friedman's inexperience was a plus; in fact, Myron could train Friedman his "own way."

Mannes Friedman became an integral part of Myron's traveling road show, staying with Myron and Lichtman and the others at the Beverly Wilshire, running messages, carrying luggage, ferrying documents back and forth between Rockwell and OPM. One night in the late spring of 1979, Mannes confronted Myron in a hallway of the Beverly Wilshire.

Mannes: "Why are you going into a different room in the hotel with Steve and talking to Allen Ganz on the phone? Don't you think I know what's going on?"

Myron: "I don't know what you're talking about."

Mannes: "You know, doing deals with Rockwell Sid Hasin doesn't know about."

Myron: "What's your point?"

Mannes: "Just that rather than me being an outsider I think you should know I know all about it. And if I can do anything to help, just let me know."

Myron: "Okay, if you keep your mouth shut."

Steve Lichtman seemed to be having trouble keeping his mouth shut. Myron was not exactly thrilled to hear Steve had taken Marty Shulman into his confidence.

> Steve told me [Shulman] was involved in a few deals so you might as well talk to him about it. To make sure he keeps his mouth shut. I used to ignore Shulman in total. I got angry at Steve and asked him why he did it. He said because Shulman had ins with equipment suppliers other than IBM.
>
> So I spoke to Marty and he said any time I needed him he'd be more than glad to help. He volunteered right in my office, sitting opposite my desk. So I said okay, and I also raised his salary. I even kept him on board when Mordy wanted to fire him.

OPM's former "mole" at American Express had been hired by Mordy in July of 1978 as head of "Operations." Whatever that was. He was supposed to work with refurbishing houses in maintaining and restoring equipment that came off lease, so that it could be eventually re-leased. As OPM suffered more and more from "returns" on old 370 Series equipment, Shulman was asked by Mordy to "look over the portfolio for dangers, exposures, to make projections as to the future of the portfolio over time."

It didn't take a genius to see the portfolio jumping right back at them. Shulman: "OPM was not geared to handling used equipment, and they knew they were going to have a lot of stuff coming back." He was hired initially as a consultant and paid fifty thousand dollars for four months' work. His conclusions, submitted in a formal report, were not complex: (1) expand the Operations Department, and (2) hire people experienced in dealing with used equipment. Who was more experienced than Shulman? Shulman was hired.

Shulman was a mystery man at OPM. No one could quite figure out what he did. All they knew was it wasn't much. Myron: "Marty Shulman was a total waste as an employee. I think he would admit that . . . He didn't do anything except get other people involved in fights he shouldn't have gotten involved in." At first Myron tried to encourage Shulman in his efforts at putting together an inventory of OPM equipment, one of those minor things OPM had always meant to do but had never gotten around to.

Myron to Marty, June 15, 1979:

> I am pleased that you are pleased that I am pleased to see you think I feel you are making progress with respect to the inventory.

John Clifton was baffled by Shulman's presence at the company. When Marty first hired him, he told Clifton he could do anything that did not involve contact with American Express, because American Express was not supposed to know he was there. But then he told Clifton, even more conspiratorially, that "Myron and Mordy were playing some sort of game with him because American Express knows all about me anyway." Myron told Clifton that Marty had "a definite problem fitting into organizations, a problem being a team player."

Shulman never really found his niche anywhere until he became a key player on the fraud team. There he came into his own: this was a team he knew how to play on. Allen Ganz says that Shulman, more than any other participant, "got off" on the fraud: "It was always like a challenge to him . . . he was excited if a deal went through and nobody caught it . . . And when he had to pose as a bank officer he could not only handle it, it turned him on. He didn't mind at all."

To account for the fact that no one from IBM ever turned up at bogus closings, Shulman suggested they simulate the leasing of used equipment, his own particular speciality. IBM had only recently come out with a product known as a mass storage unit (MSU), which was nearly as expensive as a mainframe but not as easily identifiable. The best thing about MSUs was that nobody knew what they were, certainly no one at Singer Hutner, Lehman Brothers, or any of the financing banks. When in doubt, Shulman always listed an IBM 3851 mass storage unit on a fraudulent lease. In a single year, Shulman created title documentation attesting to the presence of sixty-one MSUs at Rockwell. In fact, only one such unit was at Rockwell. Sixty MSUs would have constituted more than 30 percent of the entire planetary supply.

Shulman referred to MSUs in his equipment descriptions as "slightly used memory." Which in itself should have been somewhat suspect, considering the unit had been on the market less than a year. No one at Singer Hutner, Lehman Brothers, or the banks ever bothered to check. Only Alan Jacobs, at Singer Hutner, ever raised even the issue.

Jacobs: "Boy, they must be turning over a lot of numbers at Rockwell they have to remember."

Myron: "Of course, that's the whole idea. You don't have to get more CPUs, you just add MSUs."

Myron had no idea what he was talking about, but it shut Jacobs up.

Another potential problem spot was keeping up payments to the banks. On all bogus leases, OPM had to meet the payments promptly or the banks would start asking questions. Allen Ganz's father, Sam, was in charge of Billing/Receiving. Allen Ganz kept a list of all the bad deals, which would be given to Mannes, who would pass it on to Sam. Sam was known around the office simply as "Pop."

When Allen gave his father payment instructions on the bad

deals, he always tried to make sure the old man didn't get ideas: "Myron wants it this way," or better yet, "Here it is. Don't ask questions." If Sam dared to question Myron about a questionable payment, he didn't do it more than once. Myron: "Sam did not bother me ever again . . . If I told him to stop asking . . ."

The fraud team did not always pull together. Coach Goodman would have to whip them into shape. Allen Ganz at twenty-five was the junior member of the team and always the most nervous and frightened. By mid-1979 he had developed a full-fledged ulcer. Everyone figured it must be Myron hounding him all the time. Occasionally he would balk.

"Myron, please, this has got to end somehow."

Myron would fly into one of his rages.

"There is no point to live anymore! Do you want me to jump out of the window right now?"

Sometimes he would go further.

"You want me to get rid of your sister? I'll kill your sister and both your nieces!"

All Allen could do was tell himself, "Oh my God, this is getting really out of hand now. It's going to have to end some day, somehow."

It was the loneliness that drove Allen crazy. No one could talk to anyone but the other conspirators. They were all in this horrible thing together: "We all cried to each other. It was terrible, his word was so powerful." At OPM, Myron was standing in for God.

Allen Ganz started searching for someone who might be able to discipline Myron, someone strong enough to stop him. Sitting in that dark, windowless library whiting out numbers, photocopying fake forms, Ganz would find himself becoming obsessed with finding ways to put them all out of their misery.

"Why don't we just talk to Mordy about this?" he'd whine desperately to Lichtman. Lichtman would nod sympathetically but say nothing.

Then it was Andy Reinhard who might be able to put a stop to Myron. Allen would plead with Lichtman, "Please talk to Andy. He's got a sensible head. He can talk to Myron, Myron trusts him." But Allen knew it was grasping at straws. Steve would say he'd talk to Reinhard, then he'd say he had talked to Reinhard: "Andy's going to talk to Myron. Don't worry. He's going to try to talk sense to him. But it's hard." Then it became: "Andy's talking to him, don't worry, he says this is the last one." But there never was a last one. Only a next one.

> Memo from Myron to Allen Ganz:
> If [a certain transaction] fails to close on time, someone's head will be very smoothly severed from the remaining parts of their body. That person being the last person to lastly have another part of his anatomy removed—I.E. Mr. Allen Ganz.

Myron never once dropped the charade that Mordy didn't know anything. Allen started to wonder if Myron could have somehow forgotten Mordy's seminal work, at the beginning, forging IBM invoices. Myron would be forcing Allen to swear up and down he'd never breathe a word to Mordy, when Allen would stop and think, "What's he trying to pull here? Why can't I speak to him?" Because it was getting so Allen was desperate to speak to someone, even Mordy. Ganz: "It was weird, we actually followed his instructions . . . God forbid you should talk to Mordy."

The year when everything just started to go was 1979. As OPM's financial position continued to deteriorate, Myron stepped up his lavish giving to charity. John Clifton began to see his job as simply "getting Myron to acknowledge that there was a problem." By mid-1979 it was all too clear "no way were we going to show a profit." The only question was the size of the loss. Clifton kept urging Myron to "take a bath" for the year, take maximum write-offs on the old equipment, clear all the old debts out at once. But Myron just kept giving more and more to charity, at a time when the company was teetering on the brink of insolvency, if not falling right over the cliff. Clifton talked to Andy Reinhard about it to see if he could get Myron to stop. Andy said Myron felt "it was a good deed he'd be blessed for by giving."

John Clifton: "Myron should know he can't bribe God."

By May, Steve Kutz, always the booster, was projecting a loss for the year of at least $6 million.

Steve Kutz to Myron Goodman, May 4, 1979:

> It should be noted, Myron, that the attached statement is not overly conservative . . . Specifically, toward the end of 1978 certain equipment came off lease . . . and was re-leased at rentals significantly below the original rentals . . . If this represents the beginning of a trend . . . the situation calls for bold and decisive action.

Mendy Weissman saw Kutz's letter to Myron and wrote himself a note in the margin, "OPM experiencing a shortfall of $800,000 a month on early terminations."

Alan Phillips, a former Fox accountant who was to become OPM's next comptroller, saw the writing on the wall. "By the summer of that year [1979] I realized the equipment kept coming back and they were re-leasing it all at a lot lower rental . . . And it seemed to me that between their normal overhead for the offices and for all the offices they opened up around the country they needed at least a million dollars a month just to stay alive . . . So each month there was a big nut to cover . . . Whenever John Clifton would ask Myron 'How are you going to cover it this time?' he would open up his blackboard and show him all the good deals he had coming up."

And by that summer John Clifton had finally come to see through Myron's pathological optimism. "Myron was always expressing confidence that we would overcome . . . that the company would be able to make it through, that it would be tough but we would survive . . . around the second half of 1979 it became clear to me that that was just not the case . . . That in fact we were losing money on every 158 and 168 [370 Series] that we had to place somewhere else . . . Two things became clear during that period: 1) there is a big difference between cash flow and profit 2) there were a lot of problem transactions."

The problem, as Clifton saw it, was that OPM had created an image for itself as a well-off company: you had to travel first-class, stay in hotel suites, run up huge expenses, because that was the way Myron acted. Clifton kept trying to get across to Myron that the company was going to have to run as leanly as possible in order to survive. He made specific recommendations: stop opening more branch offices, stop writing "negative" deals, cut down on staff and expenses. When Clifton criticized Myron for spending $36,000 on Cross pens, "just one of the gifts Myron would dole out to various persons in favor at the time," Myron asked Clifton if an extra $36,000 here and there "really made any difference."

Clifton felt as if he was talking to a little boy who still believed in Santa Claus: "Yes, Myron, it does make a difference."

Clifton just could not understand where Myron got his confidence, or his cash. Allen Ganz had a better idea. During that long hard summer, whenever Myron would get depressed about business, he'd boast to the fraud team that "Rockwell is the fifth largest user of IBM equipment in the world . . . particularly if you include all that fictitious equipment they've got out there."

The collapse of OPM's lease portfolio stimulated new attempts to diversify out of the leasing business, taking whatever cash was on hand and investing it in something other than computers. Henry Singer of Singer Hutner, who had brought in the bank, brought in someone named Eli Houseman in July of 1979. Eli Houseman had a company called 34th Street Development Corporation, though its precise connection to the street itself was somewhat obscure. Houseman knew a man named Dewey Smith, who was in the barge business.

Dewey Smith was supposed to be "an old barge hand." Smith was convinced, and had managed to persuade Houseman, that with oil prices going through the roof the coal transport business should start booming any day now. Smith wanted to sell OPM four coal barges, for use on the inland waterways. John Clifton strongly opposed the venture, but Myron was captivated: a new OPM subsidiary, Bargeco, was formed, with the intrepid Dewey Smith at the helm.

Gary Trock, a former gofer for Myron who had been taken off the West Coast entourage as part of a halfhearted cost-cutting campaign, became OPM's "liaison man" with Bargeco. Trock's major contribution to the barge business was the naming of the barges after Myron: *MSG 101, 102, 103, 104.* Problems arose with the barges: no one seemed sure where they were, or whose they were. At one point, a question arose as to whether Dewey Smith had ever owned the barges in the first place: certain liens someone else had on the barges surfaced after a while. Dewey Smith turned a neat trick on the deal, buying the barges for $65,000 apiece and selling them to OPM for $100,000 each. The end of Bargeco was hastened by a disaster at sea: the sinking of *MSG 102,* apparently on its maiden voyage to no one was quite sure where. By the end of August, Clifton thought he had persuaded Myron to bag the barges, cutting their losses at around $120,000. Myron seemed perfectly willing to forget the whole thing.

After the mystery of the sunken barge, came the saga of the lost airplane. In the halcyon days of 1977, Myron and Mordy had bought themselves a corporate jet.

John Clifton: "Myron wanted an airplane . . . He had been reading a book called *Winning Through Intimidation* and the guy in that had an airplane . . . So they bought a Convair prop jet which they outfitted with beds and everything, like a real executive aircraft. He had asked me to do a feasibility study on buying a plane, but I never got around to it. One day we were in the elevator and he asked me about it. I said, 'Myron, you know it's not feasible and I know it's not feasible.' And he laughed and said, 'Yeah I know. You're right, it's not.' We got the plane anyway."

Myron himself eventually admitted, "The plane was very expensive, even for OPM." As an image builder, it was a smashing success. As a means of travel, it was a headache. OPM kept a pilot on duty twenty-four hours a day, but the plane was never there when they needed it. Myron and Mordy conducted a series of "in-flight orientation sessions" for newly hired executives, and it allowed them to spend their nights gambling in Las Vegas while commuting daily to L.A. for business. But Clifton was right, it really wasn't feasible, even for OPM. Myron and Mordy came to their senses at last.

Steve Kutz: "It was very expensive to operate and the company attempted to charter it out, and then sell it . . . and then somebody who was involved in the management or attempted sale of the plane . . . somehow misappropriated the plane . . . at the time we had details, we had at least sketchy details . . . somebody sold the plane who wasn't entitled to do so."

Only one survival mechanism still seemed to be working: the Rockwell connection.

17

On August 1, Rockwell treasurer William Neely was due to pay a special visit to OPM. Neely had recently figured his total exposure to OPM at just under thirty million, the amount OPM would have to come up with if Rockwell decided to walk away from all its leases at the earliest possible moment. Rockwell had no objection to OPM's standard early-out clause, which Neely considered "a nice fringe to a lease, a very handsome provision." But if OPM were to go under trying to bear the weight of all its obligations, all the nice fringes and handsome provisions in the world would not be worth much. Neely: "If everybody started pushing early outs at them . . . they were going to have a problem. People were assuring me, saying, well, you know, that really isn't going to happen." Sid Hasin and Maury Dahn provided the reassuring chorus from California. Neely's boss, Robert DePalma, Rockwell's chief financial officer, was OPM's most vocal critic at headquarters in Pittsburgh. Neely decided to take a trip to New York to find out for himself how OPM was doing, and report back to DePalma.

Sid Hasin was moving to increase Rockwell's dependence on OPM by proposing a sublease extension agreement, by which OPM would sublease a number of obsolete 370/168 computers and related peripherals that Rockwell no longer wanted. The advantage to Rockwell was perfectly clear: they could relieve themselves of a lot of useless equipment at rates exceeding market levels by at least 50 percent. Why Myron had been willing to make such a deal was less clear: Myron told Hasin he planned to use the old machines to "gain entrée" to new customers. The only catch for Rockwell was a reliance on OPM to meet $12 million worth of rental payments. If OPM went under, Rockwell would be stuck without the machines, and without the cash from OPM to offset rent Rockwell would still have to pay out on its original leases. Rockwell's total exposure to an OPM default would be raised to more than $40 million.

To meet the challenge of reviewing his financial statements before the treasurer of a Fortune 500 company, Myron spent several hours going over his latest Fox financials with John Clifton. The meeting was scheduled to last five hours, but Myron was hoping that Neely's financial review would take no more than a few minutes.

Myron took the Rockwell delegation on a red-carpet tour of OPM headquarters. They met Mordy, who was bashful, friendly, and charming, and Marty Shulman, who was bald, fat, unfriendly, and not charming. Myron kept the upbeat patter flowing smoothly: Lehman Brothers was doing a fine job; OPM Europe was taking off beyond their wildest dreams; OPM didn't need insurance from Lloyds of London to back up their "early outs" because they were writing equipment values down so rapidly they could realize a profit on re-lease much faster than Itel. The new 3000 Series? No problem. OPM was getting into the 303Xs very cautiously, conservatively, because didn't Mr. Neely know about the rumored new 4000 Series, which would do to the 3000 what the 303X had done to the 370? OPM was reacting to changes in the industry in a sober, serious, conservative way.

It finally came time to get down to business. Myron turned coyly conspiratorial: he didn't show his numbers to just anyone, they were strictly confidential. But seeing as Rockwell was his biggest and by far his favorite customer, he was willing to break corporate policy and let Mr. Neely sneak a peek. No copies, of course, nothing to be taken away. But his honored guest should feel free to take notes, and take as much time as he liked.

Neely spent about half an hour going over the statements. He focused first on total net worth: $44.9 million. He was "reasonably impressed" with that figure. He was more impressed and a bit surprised by the net profit figure: $10.2 million: "It was higher that I thought it might have been." Though he duly noted the many millions in "stockholders advances" made in the past year, Neely did not become unduly alarmed: "It was a company owned by two individuals who don't disclose their statements to anyone. If they wanted to have an advance from their corporation it was up to them to do it."

He did come across one somewhat disturbing item: a shortfall. Footnote Two, Lease Receivables: $400 million. Footnote Four, Equipment Purchase Obligations: $500 million. He wrote: "Oblig 500; payments 400. 100 short." Neely decided to not let a mere $100-million-dollar gap bother him unduly. "Looking at everything I was seeing, it seemed to me that over a period of time it was reasonable to assume that they would meet this obligation." Myron's suave explanation of the discrepancy was that comparing the two numbers was "really like comparing apples and oranges . . . because there was more in that obligation than just the stream of lease payments . . . if you just compared the two you weren't looking at the whole business." Neely: "I think that was part of the explanation given to me."

Myron concluded his presentation with a ringing, patriotic send-off: he was proud to be doing business with Rockwell, playing an "important role in the nation's space and military efforts." And in all humility, he felt he was helping, in the only way he knew how, to keep America strong, its national defenses healthy. Bill Neely left before lunch, prepared to write Bob DePalma a glowing report of goings-on at OPM. Sid Hasin and Maury Dahn stuck around for lunch; Myron was buying.

Sid had a question about the financial statements.

Sid: "You're always telling me you've got cash flow problems. It says here you've got $5.7 million in cash on hand."

Myron: "Sid, that's just one day. That's just one minute. Dec. 31, 1978 we had all that, but Jan. 1 we had a lot of problems."

In fact, Bill Neely had been neatly taken in. The financial statements Myron had shown him were fake. Spending hours going over the certified Fox financials with John Clifton had been merely a means of doing his homework before writing his own illicit take-home test. He inflated total assets by over $200 million, from $400 to $600. He increased retained earnings from just over $2 million to $35 million. He expanded his net worth from $4 million to $45 million. And he finished off the fabrication by removing the date from a genuine Fox auditor's report and stapling it to the altered statements.

Bill Neely: "I obviously wasn't there conducting an audit. I had a limited amount of time. And I was, you know, attempting to pursue the thing in a fashion that would give me an answer of reasonable assurance or reasonable doubt . . . They were being held out as one of the largest leasing firms around. Their financials seemed to be reasonable. As far as I knew, they were audited . . . It didn't say, you know, the people were ready to go bankrupt or anything like that."

Before the meeting even began, Sid Hasin said what he could to reassure a nervous Myron. "He doesn't understand financial statements anyway. So you can double-talk your way around it. And you should have no problem."

The First National Bank of St. Paul had at least as much reason to worry about OPM as Rockwell. As the major bridge lender to OPM, St. Paul had no lessee on the hook if OPM ever ran into real trouble. They had only the closely linked names of OPM and Lehman Brothers on which to rely. Their confidence in the good name of OPM was sorely shaken on March 22, when the Comptroller of the Currency called St. Paul's parent company to advise that OPM was under investigation on criminal charges of check kiting. On March 26, Lew Glucksman called St. Paul president Clarence Frame. Glucksman: "It was not a bitter exchange . . . He didn't seem to get very excited about it . . . They were clearly not shocked or outraged." But St. Paul did suspend all loan activities on OPM transactions pending the results of an "internal review" of the entire OPM/St. Paul relationship.

In May, Myron flew out to St. Paul with Alan Batkin to try to persuade the bank to come back into the OPM fold. Myron assured them: "Nobody lost any money. It was a terrible thing to do. We realize now it was a terrible thing to do, and we're never going to do it again. It was just one of those lapses, having the bank gave us the temptation because we were in charge . . . we're going to turn over a new leaf entirely." Myron referred to a "technical violation" of federal banking regulations, to "the uncollected funds situation," but never once to the "check kiting." He had "cut a deal" with the Comptroller of the Currency to close all his accounts at FNJ, and as far as he was concerned all that unpleasantness was now well behind him.

St. Paul was perfectly willing to accept Lehman Brothers' conclusion that the check kiting was a matter of poor business judgment, not outright dishonesty. St. Paul was apparently less concerned with the personal integrity of the principals than with their financial fortunes. To Jeff Werner, "It was apparent as they discussed the way they operated and the nature of the market that the company was a one-man operation . . . Everything revolved around Myron. He made all the decisions, he ran the company himself . . . I don't think we were quite certain as to where Mr. Weissman fit into the picture." That was fine as far as it went. But as long as everything depended upon Myron, St. Paul needed to be satisfied that Myron knew what he was doing.

Werner was a 1973 graduate of the Harvard Business School. Myron cannily used every bit of business school jargon he could summon up in his campaign to win back St. Paul. They had "identified a shift in strategic objectives" and were "currently in the process of implementing that shift." They were concentrating on the leasing business; forgetting about diversification; "actively seeking" a buyer for the bank; seeking to "maximize value of the current portfolio with aggressive remarketing of equipment coming off lease"; not buying many new machines; "laying off" on new lease buildup: they were going to do their very best with what they had. OPM was going conservative. Or at least talking that way.

Werner wasn't terribly impressed by Myron's B-school palaver. He wrote himself a note: "Myron is not a businessman. Not good at setting goals and objectives and making sure he has adequate control of the administrative systems in his corporation." His comments were "totally volume-oriented," he seemed to feel that "if he were just left alone he could show a profit. He could make money." Myron was basically an entrepreneur, a deal doer, not a corporate manager: "He didn't think he needed an accounting staff or administrative staff to tell him he was doing his job correctly. He didn't think there were any limits on growth he should have to observe."

From the last available financial statements, Werner could readily see Myron was failing to cope with a real problem: equipment in inventory, machinery sitting in a warehouse somewhere waiting to be leased out, had shot up from under $2 million in 1977 to $20 million in 1978. Werner: "He was reacting to a situation he had let build up. If he had been on top of his business he never would have let his inventory of leases build up. He had begun to address it only when it threatened to become a real problem." Now it was probably too late, given the sorry state of the market. In business school Werner had studied the "classic abuse" committed by the computer-leasing industry in the previous decade, when technology had outstripped the projections of future value, slashed residual values, and driven dozens of paper-rich companies into bankruptcy. His own assessment of OPM's future prospects was not nearly as bullish as Myron's: "OPM must have a steady stream of new business to offset the losses and negative cash flow generated by existing leases . . . At least until residual values can be generated in material amounts; this point will not be reached for several more years . . . They must have new business to survive. Therefore, incentive is probably to get the business out, using just about any residual value assumption."

Myron did not exactly win Werner over by confiding that he, for one, drew a definite distinction between "business principles" and "accounting principles." Werner: "If everyone would just pay attention to what he said in terms of business principles instead of in terms of accounting principles, everybody would be a lot happier . . . he entered into profitable deals . . . although the transactions might not appear to be as profitable as he said they were." Myron: "I'm in the business of making money, not producing profit statements."

Werner: "I would say I was not persuaded by his logic." Werner wrote himself another note: "The company is run as a Myron S. Goodman personal vehicle."

Division Head Diane Arnold to Jeffrey Werner:

> Every abuse in a privately-held company has been committed here . . . transactions of the company mingled with transactions of the owners . . . advances to shareholders exceeding the total net worth of the company . . . donations by the company for owner's private purposes . . . with no discernable business purpose behind them."

St. Paul had not lent any money on OPM transactions since March. On June 15, Alan Batkin called Jeffrey Werner with a few thoughts that might help St. Paul assess its relationship with OPM: "OPM's business practices were . . . a bit unorthodox . . . But Myron and Mordy are solid individuals . . . probably willing to personally guarantee OPM debt on an ongoing basis." Lehman Brothers was "doing all it could to control Myron, and to get him to pay more attention to administration, and the day-to-day conduct of his business."

The bottom line for the First National Bank of St. Paul was that doing bridge loans on OPM deals was just too lucrative. On June 21, Werner met with Clarence Frame. Werner was proposing to work up some sort of "loan agreement" so that "we could continue to lend money on OPM transactions for the benefit of ourselves and OPM." Frame gave Werner some sage advice: "OPM principles are not 'crooks' but have very sloppy practices . . . Their conduct has forced us to be very careful and formal . . . to define very carefully the framework of our relationship with OPM. The loan agreement should contain very onerous conditions . . . Be very careful what you do, define it well, and have it understood by everyone involved."

Despite all of Werner's and Arnold's and Frame's obvious misgivings, the First National Bank of St. Paul elected to continue lending bridge money on OPM deals, as long as a lessee was firmly committed to the lease, OPM was willing to grant St. Paul a "first security interest" in the equipment, and St. Paul limited its exposure to $10 million outstanding. But St. Paul never did get its formal loan agreement. Werner: "We went ahead with simply a general understanding . . . between Myron and Diane, myself and Lehman Brothers, for a general framework within which we could operate." To Werner, the point of a loan agreement was "to establish guidelines, not to have a piece of paper signed. As long as the guidelines were being followed, we saw no urgency about ratifying the agreement . . . I felt the objectives of the loan agreement had been substantially accomplished without having it signed."

While Werner was looking for guidelines, he might have done well to consult a "check list for loans" distributed by St. Paul to its loan officers, designed to "cover the major points on which the loan officer should be informed." The final item on the checklist:

> Beware of any customer who:
> 1. overemphasizes his honesty
> 2. overemphasizes his ability
> 3. is "too important" to bother with or is annoyed by legitimate requests for information
> 4. can now afford to be honest

American Express was OPM's biggest customer until 1979. Mordy had so successfully insinuated himself into the good graces of the data-processing managers at the various divisions that in the heyday of OPM/Amex relations a typical lease would be worked up like this:

"Hey, Mordy, I need a———but I can't pay more than X per month."

"How many you need?"

"Three, and I'll need them a couple of years at least."

"Okay, I can have them there by Friday. How does X sound?"

"Great, that's about 30 percent off IBM's price. I can handle that in my budget. Send them over."

"The deal," such as it was, was usually just a few notes scrawled on Mordy's memo paper, to be "fleshed out" after the equipment was already installed. A central office known as Contracts Administration had the responsibility of overseeing and executing all leases. It was headed by an American Express lawyer named Frank Aiello. Aiello more than once caught Mordy playing games with Amexco leases.

Amexco had leased an IBM 370 from OPM. Myron financed the lease at Chemical Bank. Chemical thought the lease was a "hell or high water" contract binding Amexco to a full six years, but in a secret "side letter" Chemical never saw, Mordy gave Amex the right to "walk away" from the lease after two years. Two years went by, and Amexco sent the machine back to OPM. As usual, OPM did not feel like parting with the cash. OPM kept up the lease payments to Chemical Bank, which thought the computer was still at American Express.

Early in 1979, Chemical hired a company called Equifax to verify the location of the computer. They contacted the data-processing center in question to arrange for an inspection. American Express had no record of that machine being still at that location, so they called Mordy to see if he knew anything about it. Mordy said he'd check into it.

He checked into it all right. He called Equifax. He said he was with American Express. He was terribly sorry to inconvenience the people at Equifax, but they happened to be going through their year-end audit right now at American Express and could not possibly handle an on-site equipment inspection at this particular time. He managed to have the inspection put off, which gave Myron time to buy out the lease. A few weeks later, Frank Aiello called Mordy into his office to ask about a notification Amexco had just received from Chemical Bank, advising them of their delinquency in meeting payments on three more IBM 370s that American Express had long since terminated.

Mordy looked a bit sheepish. He mumbled something about how they had meant to buy out those financings, but had forgotten to, somehow, by mistake.

Aiello: "We've had a problem with Equifax. Now a problem with this addendum. What else is there?"

Mordy promised there would be no more surprises.

At a company retreat in May 1979, Aiello warned a gathering of American Express data-processing managers against "getting hooked" on OPM, "Technological developments threaten OPM's ability to remarket its own equipment at levels sufficient to pay back its obligations on 'early outs.'" The marvelous "walk away" leases they so loved to sign could easily become "crawl away" leases if OPM went under, or were unable to come up with the cash to pay on its commitments. He urged them to stop giving OPM business without competitive bidding, to start steering business away from OPM, and to "develop a strategy of exercising our early termination rights before other OPM customers start doing it." He calculated their total exposure to OPM at over $115 million.

American Express signed only six more mainframe leases with OPM after that. The loss of American Express was the worst blow ever to hit the company. According to John Clifton, Amex had frequently allowed OPM to "finance transactions and get cash out of them in excess of the value of the equipment." About all Myron had left was that enormous backlog of rich transactions he claimed to see every time he opened up his magic blackboard.

Myron responded to the loss as best he could. He got mad. On one of the very last Amex deals, he wrote a memo to Steve Lichtman:

> Unfortunately, as usual, there could be a change in the American Express deal. However, what's the surprise? We are dealing with idiots, we will always be dealing with idiots, and they will never change. They happen to be the biggest jerks walking the face of the earth. Unfortunately, we have to lower ourselves to their level. Why? Simply because some of their transactions happen to be lucrative . . . However, have some self-respect. Don't lower yourself too much. Even though they are basically putzes and idiots and jackasses who basically have no brains . . . As things progress, I will instruct you in what to do. Thank You. Best Personal Regards, Myron.

Toward the end of that terrible year, Myron started to lose his grip. His health was deteriorating rapidly; his tunnel vision was getting worse; his hearing was gone in one ear. His intake of pills and painkillers was on the rise; his moods were getting harder to control. He was under constant pressure from Lehman Brothers to produce financial statements, without which they didn't feel they could continue to do his deals. And the deals were coming in slower and slower, for smaller and smaller amounts, which put additional pressure on each deal to produce desperately needed results: hard cash. In November, Myron heard rumors of discontent in Accounting, which was falling behind in its lease records, largely because Myron was keeping his Rockwell records to himself. Myron had a habit of blowing off steam by dictating furious memos to his secretary, usually quite late at night.

> To All Accounting: From Myron Goodman
>
> Any member of the Accounting Department who feels he is not recognized by anyone in the Company, I have nothing to say to them. That is, let him get up and get his ass out of here. I am sick and tired of having to cow-tail and watch every GD move I make. I am not walking on a pile of horse manure. I am not wasting my time thinking about other people's feelings. Not with all I have to do."

He got mad at Singer Hutner too. Even relatively haphazard scrutiny of some of his more dubious lease documentation was capable of driving him crazy.

> Nov. 14, 1979: Myron Goodman to Andrew B. Reinhard
> RE: Games Playing By Singer Hutner with OPM Personnel
> If for any reason any partner or associate has any problem with regard to documentation . . . I want to be informed. If the problem persists, management at OPM (i.e. Myron S. Goodman) will determine whether or not we want to continue our relationship with Singer Hutner, or pursue a more accommodating law firm . . . I would hate to see a relationship between you, myself, Joe, and Alan and any of my other dear friends at Singer Hutner end because of some stupid, obnoxious, egotistical, aggressive, associate."

"The changing of Singer Hutner," Myron wrote, "is the only solution . . . I don't want to be associated with a white-shoed, conservative, neo-Nazi fascist law firm."

Myron also lashed out at his closest associates.

Memo to Mannes Friedman (regarding the closing of an impending transaction):

> I am trying to make believe that you won't screw [this one] up . . . Because if you do, you'll be hanging upside down like Mussolini (sp?) was when he was hung. However, there will be one big difference: you will be castrated before I hang you.

Fortune did an article on OPM for its December 3, 1979, issue, complete with a picture of whiz kids Myron and Mordy sitting on top of the leasing world. The day the photographers from *Fortune* showed up to take pictures, Myron was putting a lot of pressure on Allen Ganz to close a Rockwell transaction. Lichtman was talking to him on the speakerphone, "Myron wants you to know this, Myron wants you to do that."

Allen: "You can tell Myron to go fuck himself."

The phone clicked shut. No sound came from the other end. Allen got this terrible feeling Myron might have been listening in. Only seconds went by before Myron burst into Allen's office, looking like death on wheels. He took his brother-in-law and hurled him across the room. Then he started rearranging Ganz's office, starting out with his desk.

Ganz: "I back up and he comes by me. I am on all fours, so to speak. I had these plaques for the tombstone ads sitting on my desk and he took them and hurled them at me . . . and they all went on the floor."

Myron started screaming about everything under the sun. He said terrible things about two black men who worked under Allen, one of whom sat in the next office. The man's name was Harold, and Allen happened to know Harold had a license to own a gun. Harold couldn't help hearing every racist, ethnic slur Myron was shouting, at the top of his lungs. Harold stood behind his office door holding one of those heavy metal bars you use to secure lateral files. If Myron stepped just an inch through that doorway, Harold was going to let him have it over the head. Which might have at least brought Myron to his senses.

Fortunately for Myron, Harold, and Allen, Steve Lichtman came down and managed to subdue Myron. Allen: "Hey, Steve, thanks a lot for letting me know this was going to happen." Steve didn't say anything.

None of them was in his right mind at that point. Myron was just going out of his head, putting everyone and everything down all the time, ranting and raving about just about anything. Allen was starting to lose it too: "They took great pains in keeping things from me when it came to distress calls because they knew I would open the window and go right down to the street."

He definitely should have just quit. Walked away from it all. But he had no more perspective. Ganz: "I was programmed to believe that . . . if I left that would be it . . . Eventually it would crumble and they could not have continued my work . . . and my mother and father would die and my sisters would be all out on the street . . . He was a deranged person, and it was a very sick situation . . . Myron got me to cry . . . No one else ever got me to cry . . . I was a sandwich between my two brothers-in-law and my only job . . . I was living two lives, one at home, one at OPM . . . which was a nightmare every day I went to work . . . I wasn't aware of the real world out there . . . It was a fantasy world."

Steve Lichtman was having his own problems keeping quiet under the strain. At the urgent request of the Bank of St. Paul, John Clifton was working up an "interim audit" to give them all some idea of just how badly things were going. Hoby Shapiro was helping Clifton with the internal audit, though Hoby had decided to resign from OPM in the wake of the check-kiting scandal. Hoby had been OPM's acting comptroller since August, but had resigned as of October 3. He let Myron persuade him to stay on until the end of the year to help Clifton over the hump. John and Hoby had been trying to get some information on Rockwell leases from Steve Lichtman, but Lichtman kept putting them off: "It isn't ready yet. Myron doesn't want you to have it. Myron hasn't had a chance to go over it yet." Lichtman kept saying, "Myron wants everything to be perfect with Rockwell before it goes to Accounting, because it's Myron's account." That made Clifton suspicious. He told Lichtman that if there were any "problems" with the Rockwell leases, they would be bound to come up in the audit.

Late one afternoon in early December, Lichtman walked into John Clifton's corner office on the eighth floor. He looked upset, and sick, and frightened. Hoby Shapiro was there. Lichtman looked at them both like total strangers. "I'm dead," he said. "I'm dead."

"I've done something wrong," he went on. "I might have to go to jail."

John Clifton: "He said he had spoken to someone at Singer Hutner and they told him he could go to jail and he would be the only one to go to jail and not anyone else . . . Myron had asked him to do him a favor, and he had helped Myron out . . . Myron was supposed to do some bridge financings . . . which would enable him to get over a cash flow crunch for a short period of time, and the transactions would be bought out relatively shortly from cash flow he was anticipating from his backlog of transactions . . . It was Steve's belief that once these transactions took place, that the bridges would be bought out and that would be the end of the matter."

It had not been the end of the matter. Just the beginning. A few days later Lichtman told Hoby Shapiro, "I'm getting pressure from Myron to do another one."

Shapiro told Lichtman he'd be "a schmuck" to go along. He should get himself a lawyer and follow his advice. Shapiro left OPM for good after that, ignoring all Myron's entreaties to stay.

Shapiro: "I really wanted nothing to do with it . . . John was staying, and I felt he would have to do what he had to do, knowing he was staying, knowing what he knew . . . I didn't want to know anything. I just wanted to get out. I felt the facts would come to light soon enough."

On December 18, Clifton had a meeting with Myron about the interim audit. Clifton told Myron he needed certain information related to the Rockwell account. Steve Lichtman had been holding out on him, and that was just going to have to stop. Myron agreed, profusely.

John Clifton: "You know, Myron, if there are any problems with those transactions, they're going to come out in the audit."

Myron kept acting cagey. Clifton decided to call him on it, "Are there problems with Rockwell?"

Myron: "We'll be able to document all the transactions. Don't worry about it."

Lichtman told Clifton he'd "cut a deal" with Myron. He would help Myron do a few more transactions, until Myron had all the cash he needed. Then Myron was going to stop for good, and they all would be off the hook. Lichtman said Myron had said he could ask Clifton "for help, to work on the documentation."

Clifton: "I'm not doing any such thing."

Lichtman relayed this to Myron. Lichtman came back to report, "Myron says that's right, we can go to you for certain things, but not that kind of thing."

18

DUE DILIGENCE.

That was all Myron ever heard out of Alan Batkin these days.

Lehman Brothers had to see financial statements. They had to make sure OPM was run in a proper manner. With proper capital structure. With conservative plans for the future. If Lehman Brothers was going to keep working with OPM, it was going to have to start being run like a business, not a candy store. "You don't know what's going on," Batkin would tell Myron until Myron wanted to scream. "You don't know if you've got profits or losses. You don't know where you are. The only thing you know is that you own the First National Bank of Jefferson Parish, and since that is audited, at least you know you've got an asset there." It always came back to that: audits, assets, numbers. Batkin used to make the situation obnoxiously clear: "We cannot and will not allow Lehman Brothers Kuhn Loeb to be a banker to a company without financial information."

After New Year's, Myron was summoned for a little heart-to-heart with Lew Glucksman. Myron knew this was it. Before they pushed for an audit Myron would always put them off, "It takes time, it takes time." Now the time was up.

They had their meeting in Glucksman's office right off the bond-trading room. The whole thing took ten minutes.

Lew Glucksman: "We are going to have to take the ball in the management end of the business . . . We are not getting anywhere in terms of the organization of OPM. I am telling you you have to get the toughest, meanest accountant I know, and that is Lou Moscarello . . . You need him because you need to be put into shape."

Myron: "Yes, Lew, whatever you say."

Myron listened to Lew Glucksman because Lew Glucksman was a tough guy. If Myron didn't listen, he was going to start yelling. Myron: "It was not a question of do I agree. I agreed before I walked into the room. They wouldn't have waited more than five minutes literally to say good-bye."

Glucksman turned to Alan Batkin: "You will supervise this for us."

Myron was petrified. He'd never heard of Lou Moscarello, but he was beginning to get the idea. "You're not going to like him," Glucksman said. Myron nodded meekly; he didn't like him already. "He's going to be tough and obnoxious," Glucksman added. Myron was starting to feel bad. "But that's what you need," Glucksman went on. "Discipline." Myron decided he'd better sit down. Discipline?

Glucksman assured him Moscarello would be just going in to do a "management survey," not an audit. Just some new systems design to whip OPM into shape. But Myron knew this "management survey stuff . . . was really just a sneak move on Lehman's part . . . to prepare us for an audit . . . which would have been a total disaster." What Lew wanted in the end was financial statements. Myron: "At a minimum, any financial statement. Utopia would have been an audited statement." Myron was sure all this would end with Lew calling him back in to say, "Moscarello is doing a good job. Now it's time to do an audit." That would mean the Rockwell files. And that would be the end.

Lou Moscarello had been with the Big Eight accounting firm of Coopers & Lybrand for thirty-five years, and a full partner since 1959. When Alan Batkin first called him on January 3 about a client "experiencing difficulties getting out financial statements," that one phrase alone told him much of what he needed to know.

Moscarello: "They wanted me to ride herd and achieve a measure of success. I am willing to delegate responsibility. I am not willing to abdicate it."

Moscarello knew perfectly well Lehman Brothers was calling him because of "my reputation, my competency, and my ability to get things done in difficult circumstances." Alan Batkin's description of OPM made circumstances look pretty difficult. Moscarello trusted Alan Batkin not to exaggerate. Batkin had worked at Coopers & Lybrand under Lou Moscarello up until the late seventies. He had been "an outstanding young man" there. Batkin added that he was making the request on behalf of Lew Glucksman. Moscarello's personal contact with Glucksman had been sporadic over the years, no more than a few lunches. But he agreed to take on OPM because "the initial request came from Lehman Brothers, and a man like Lewis Glucksman."

Moscarello sent two men from Coopers' Management Consulting Services Division down to "scope out" OPM: Robert Lage, a senior manager, and Marty Zelbow, an M.B.A. from Amos Tuck, a former consultant with Ernst & Whinney, and corporate planner with Gulf & Western, who had been with Coopers only two weeks before being put on the OPM case full-time.

Zelbow was struck by "an incredible sense of confusion" as soon as he walked through OPM's front doors: "a purely entrepreneurial environment . . . no discipline at all." He talked to John Clifton, head of Accounting, Marty Shulman, head of Operations, Allen Ganz, head of Contracts/Finance, and Sam Ganz, head of Billing/Receiving. He found Dave Hanlon, audit manager for Fox, trying to load lease data into a small computer on the eighth floor, using a computerized account system that just wasn't working. Nothing seemed to be working at OPM, particularly the people.

On January 17, Lou Moscarello "pitched" for the OPM engagement in the big conference room at 71 Broadway with the electronic movie screen that lowered from the ceiling, and the immense burled-oak swiveling Magic-Marker boards clearly custom-made for the splashiest of presentations. Moscarello, in keeping with his reputation as the meanest, toughest accountant in the business, did not pull any punches: "OPM is a chaotic, undisciplined, poorly controlled environment . . . with accounting records not updated for months on end . . . with some areas of posting four to six months behind . . . lease data deficient . . . This situation is at least as bad as any I have ever seen."

As Lew Glucksman sat there taking in Moscarello's award-winning performance, he thought this should supply the ingredient that would impress Myron with the importance of the work being done. And Myron did seem impressed: "He seemed to be reaching out for the kind of help that was in his own interest . . . [he was] very receptive." To Glucksman, Moscarello's blunt criticisms were all just part of his job: "Lou outlined what they were going to do and where they were going to come out. And he outlined how they were going to get there and the rough regular discipline of reporting, reporting, reporting, that would be just what OPM needed to get itself straightened out." Myron looked perfectly willing to be disciplined; he was good at being contrite. Moscarello's harsh view of OPM's management problems hardly made Glucksman alarmed for the future: "All consultants try to make the world look like Armageddon has arrived."

Early in February, Marty Zelbow and Steve Kutz had lunch at The World Trade Center. Kutz was visibly worried about OPM. As he explained to Zelbow, the whole leasing industry was in terrible shape because of early outs handed out like party favors during the good years. Now the market could not possibly absorb all the obsolete 370s flooding back to the leasing companies. OPM's entire portfolio was dangerously overvalued; Kutz expected to have to report "substantial losses" for 1979. As they walked back to OPM, Kutz shrugged. "I just don't know how Myron keeps going." A question that kept nagging at Zelbow as time went on.

Coopers instituted a strict weekly regimen of "progress meetings" to review OPM's flagging performance. Myron would sit at the head of the conference table flanked by John Clifton and Mendy Weissman; Lehman Brothers took up the other end, represented by Alan Batkin or Joel Peck, sometimes Harvey Kreuger. Andy Reinhard usually came; occasionally Steve Kutz.

Coopers initially proposed a six-to-eight-week interval to complete the missing lease files. By February 1, they counted 116 missing lease files for 1979. Two weeks later, the count had risen to 206 and still climbing. Moscarello: "We knew we had a mess when we started, but we didn't know how big a mess it was until we started digging and going about trying to do the assignment."

There were endless obstacles to progress, with Myron proving by far the most formidable. From the start, Zelbow couldn't help noticing that Myron didn't seem to want financial statements prepared, "that it would have been to his benefit to delay rather than to have them prepared and . . . for us to find some potentially bad news that there was for all the world to see." Precisely what that "bad news" was was not immediately clear. But Zelbow's lunch with Kutz clearly implied that staggering losses would very likely turn out the least of it.

There were a number of other human obstacles Zelbow might just have dismissed as "deadweight," but he preferred a more polite term: "bottlenecks." Allen Ganz, jumpy and nervous, operated under some terrible emotional strain: "Ganz was a very young man . . . overburdened . . . unable to respond effectively to a very difficult environment." Zelbow gathered that Myron liked to browbeat his brother-in-law, but this hardly explained why Ganz was "totally unresponsive" to Zelbow's requests for information about the missing lease files. Marty Shulman was even worse; he was "totally arrogant, uncooperative, no follow-through at all." Shulman compounded his definite attitude problem by hardly ever being around. Zelbow was hardly surprised to hear he was supposed to be running some sort of consulting operation on the side. Zelbow considered Shulman "a real sleaze bag . . . the kind of guy you'd expect to smoke cigars and hang out at the racetrack all day." For all Zelbow ever knew, that was all he did.

Sam Ganz was a nice enough man, but clearly incapable of handling his responsibilities as head of Billing/Receiving. Myron's father, Leon, was practically the only employee who functioned smoothly, though his only visible regular tasks were handing out pencils and paper from a cage on the eighth floor and keeping the Coke machine full in the kitchen. Howie Walfish, a highly paid employee in the Contracts Department and a high school pal of Mordy's, was basically "a bandleader . . . he plays all the company bar mitzvahs." Mrs. "Boom Boom" Washington, in charge of the innumerable company messengers, drivers, and chauffeurs, was a colorful enough character and very impressively built. But as an addition to OPM's management team, she seemingly lacked a certain sense of direction.

As for a sense of direction, Myron's conduct in business meetings did not provide much of a model. From the day Coopers first pitched for the OPM engagement, Zelbow had been shocked by the sight of these tip-top corporate executives like Lew Glucksman and Harvey Kreuger treating Myron Goodman as if he were the chairman of General Motors. At the first few weekly progress meetings, Myron was incoherent half the time; he kept nodding out like some sort of junkie. Zelbow started to feel like the kid in "The Emperor's New Clothes."

Late on a Friday afternoon early in February, Zelbow was working in a spare office on the eighth floor when he got a call from one of Myron's secretaries: Mr. Goodman would like to see Mr. Zelbow immediately. Zelbow dashed up to the poshly decorated "executive area" on the ninth floor and was kept cooling his heels on the reception area couch for at least an hour. Finally he was summoned into Myron's vast chamber, where the big boss was slumped behind his long trapezoidal desk, too exhausted to speak. He couldn't remember what he had wanted to see Marty about. He scratched his head, swiveled around in his chair, and finally mumbled a slurred word or two before drifting off in midsentence. Soon after that, he passed out.

Zelbow ran down the hall to the library. Steve Lichtman and John Clifton were closeted in conference.

"I think someone had better go down and take a look at Myron."

Lichtman jumped up and ran. Zelbow called Bob Lage, the Coopers engagement manager. "I want to come over right now. I've got to talk to you."

He described to Lage, as best he could, Myron's behavior:

"He's a very tired man, almost irrational, hardly able to carry on a coherent conversation." As Zelbow saw it, Myron was a very sick man trying to run a very sick company. He had a serious heart condition and was being kept alive with the aid of a pacemaker. He was under all sorts of powerful medications which were clearly affecting his state of mind. For someone Lehman Brothers was looking to as the man to turn around a troubled company, Myron looked like the worst possible candidate.

Lage called Alan Batkin. Zelbow had heard good things about Batkin. But when Lage relayed Zelbow's story to Batkin over the speakerphone, Batkin sounded so nonchalant Zelbow could hardly believe his ears. Batkin: "The company is going through a difficult period . . . he does have a serious heart condition, but he's under very close medical supervision." He said something about Myron's personal physician having been recommended by Lehman Brothers. He said the man was "operating under tremendous pressure" due to constant cash-flow problems. Zelbow gathered they were being told in a roundabout way to stop worrying about nothing.

Zelbow had been at Coopers only a few weeks before being sent to OPM. Lou Moscarello hardly knew him. Lehman Brothers was Coopers' prime account, and the OPM engagement had come directly from them at the very highest level. Zelbow knew Bob Lage was not exactly eager to offend Harvey Kreuger, or Lewis Glucksman. If Zelbow was going to persuade his superiors to drop OPM, he was going to have to find something a little more substantial.

Myron didn't like Zelbow, but he had a certain grudging respect for him: "He was obnoxious and arrogant and a difficult-to-get-along-with individual . . . But at the bottom line he did his job and did it well." But the last thing Myron wanted Zelbow to do was his job. Once the missing lease files were located and up-to-date, an audit would be ready to start. So the only way to keep Rockwell going was to stop Zelbow: "I wanted Zelbow out, or controlled in some way." Even Myron suffered certain regrets: "If not for Rockwell, Marty Zelbow might have been the best thing to ever hit OPM."

Myron's opening tactic was to undercut Zelbow with his superiors. He fired off a series of angry letters to Moscarello and Batkin complaining of mistreatment by "junior accountants," demanding more attention from "senior people" at Coopers to justify the expense of the engagement. When that brought only mixed results, he did his best on the home front to exploit a growing antagonism between Zelbow and the various OPM "family members," who deeply resented this arrogant outsider questioning their competence and openly criticizing their performance. Myron: "I couldn't afford to have upset people in general."

Myron always believed the best defense was a good offense. Under direct attack from Zelbow, he had to strike back from behind, or if at all possible outflank him. He did his best to intimidate him, bully him or get him fired. Anything but let him keep snooping around the Rockwell files. At the weekly progress meeting of March 24, Zelbow openly protested Myron's "reduced commitment" and "procrastination." He accused him of deliberately delaying the implementation of a number of suggestions made by Coopers.

Zelbow prepared a memorandum to be circulated at that meeting:

> Due to the chaos and confusion in the company it is quite impossible to prepare any sort of reliable analysis of cash flow. However, after more than nine weeks on-site we are concerned that the company's cash management situation is dangerously out of control."

This opening broadside had the advantage, at least, of bringing a cold war into the open. On March 28, Myron struck back. He sent a memoranda to fifteen key OPM executives, ordering them to ignore all documents created by a new system of reporting instituted by Zelbow:

> It is my opinion that the current system (however chaotic it might be) is better than the new one. That is, until I determine that the new one is better than the present one, I have to be under the impression that the old one is better."

Zelbow: "He had directly countermanded a directive I made . . . it was open warfare from then on." The conflict blew up the first week in April. During a progress meeting at which Myron was not present, Zelbow remarked to Dave Lesnick, an OPM vice president on temporary assignment tracking down missing lease files, that OPM's books were "in such lousy shape they could cause a bankruptcy that would be very embarrassing for the entire Jewish community." Lesnick just happened to be an Orthodox rabbi, who generally took charge of the afternoon mincha services held in the OPM library. Lesnick didn't mind Zelbow and had even recruited him a few times to make up the minyan of ten men needed for the afternoon prayers. But Lesnick was married to Myron's sister. He was a family member. His loyalties were clear in this case.

He gravely wrote Zelbow's offhanded comment on a piece of paper and had it passed out to Myron. Myron burst into the meeting and went "totally beserk." Zelbow: "He went off for two hours of just an unbelievable tirade." John Clifton remembers Myron screaming about "something someone had done behind his back," refusing to even speak the unmentionable Zelbow's name. Myron happened to have a cold at the time, so he kept sneezing and blowing his nose and throwing crumpled-up tissues into the basket while ranting and raving at Zelbow.

Myron went straight to Alan Batkin. He showed him Lesnick's hand-written note, evidence that Zelbow was waging an insidious internal campaign of innuendo against him. Zelbow met with Batkin later on that same day. He told Batkin that OPM's 1979 financials "might be a real source of concern." Zelbow's concern about OPM's financial condition resulted in a decision by his superiors to collect from OPM every two weeks. One week in May, OPM fell behind on its Coopers bill. Zelbow planted himself outside Myron's office waiting for the check to be signed. He waited out the entire afternoon, telling Myron's secretary that all work was going to stop until Coopers got its money. When Myron found out about this final insult, he retaliated by banning Zelbow permanently from the executive area: exile to the lowly eighth floor. But Zelbow didn't mind the ban; it was starting to feel like a badge of honor.

19

By June, Marty Zelbow was convinced Myron was up to no-good. He heard from an OPM employee that the company had to keep moving its checking accounts around because Myron could not stop bouncing checks. Weekly charts prepared under C&L supervision projected cash-flow deficiencies of up to $13 million. Both John Clifton and Steve Kutz told Zelbow that new business had fallen off dramatically, and early terminations were flooding in fast. After spending a few days looking over OPM's financial statements, a C&L manager named Al Brink decided the only way OPM could stay in business was if volume kept increasing to bring in cash to make up for losses on current leases. Zelbow: "He may even have used the words 'Ponzi scheme.'"

Martin Zelbow to Bob Lage, May 28, 1980:

> Our client is experiencing severe adverse business conditions and could, during the course of the engagement, become insolvent or be petitioned into bankruptcy."

All Zelbow's instincts forced him to wonder "how Myron was getting enough in through the front doors to stay afloat, unless it was coming in through the back." He believed it was "not uncommon" for businessmen in the desperate straits Myron was in to "generate cash by borrowing from tomorrow" to pay off the debts of today. He knew Myron was "committed to his business almost irrationally" and that he was entirely capable of shady dealing to stay afloat.

Zelbow was more than "curious" about the Rockwell transactions. More than half of the missing lease files were Rockwell; most of the others were American Express. But American Express business had fallen off sharply, while Rockwell seemed to be booming. Those "absent" Rockwell leases were generating unusually large amounts of cash at closings, $5 million here, $10 million there, which seemed a bit peculiar considering the leases were supposed to cover used equipment. OPM's business was heavily weighted toward new equipment, and Rockwell was a state-of-the-art equipment user. The sheer bulk of used high-ticket equipment going out to Rockwell struck Zelbow as highly suspicious. When Steve Kutz said he planned to personally review the Rockwell transactions, Zelbow couldn't help wondering why.

Zelbow: "By June, I was becoming more and more convinced that something highly questionable was going on, and I did not want to see Coopers & Lybrand get any closer to it, to put the firm in a position where they could conceivably be accused of negligence, or some sort of failure to detect a fraudulent scheme." He decided to go to Lou Moscarello and lay his suspicions on the line. He didn't mention Rockwell by name because he felt that would be "pure conjecture." But he warned Moscarello and Lage:

> We are in a situation where we have a client who is in a desperate situation. I cannot prove the man is committing fraud, but we are in a situation where we have an unusually high risk that our client is committing fraud."

Zelbow strongly advised that C&L withdraw from the OPM engagement.

Moscarello took Zelbow's suspicions as just that, "pure conjecture." To question a businessman's personal integrity simply because he might be going broke struck him as just plain irresponsible. He told Zelbow to stop worrying about OPM's financial condition; his job was to design new systems, not to perform an audit. Snooping around looking for fraud was not what OPM was paying C&L for; for that they could hire a private eye at half C&L's rates. Moscarello bluntly told Zelbow to get back to work and mind his own business.

Zelbow desperately wanted to understand Moscarello's position: to withdraw from an engagement referred by Lehman Brothers on the unfounded suspicions of a junior consultant would have been bound to offend Lehman Brothers. You couldn't make hard decisions in business based on soft speculation. Not when you were dealing with people vouched for by the likes of Lew Glucksman. Still, it burned Zelbow up that "if these people were not going to see what I saw, they might just as well have been prepared to use me as cannon fodder."

Zelbow placed a great degree of confidence in the personal integrity of John Clifton. When Clifton started coming and going at odd hours during the day, not exhibiting much of an interest in goings-on at the company, Zelbow's worries jumped to a new plane of suspicion. From the distracted way Clifton was acting, Zelbow could only assume he was planning to leave; all those unexplained absences could only have been for job interviews. When Zelbow tried to ask him about it, he played his cards "very close to the vest."

John Clifton was much more than suspicious. He had a pretty fair idea of what was going on. Steve Lichtman's mumbled references to "doing bridges" amounted to a virtual confession of some form of Rockwell fraud; Rockwell was Myron's only account and Steve Lichtman was Myron's assistant. But Clifton didn't know the nature of the fraud, or the amount. Clifton simply assumed it must be less than the worth of the bank: in the range of $10 million. Which, if true, meant that Myron should be capable of paying it back by putting the bank on the block.

What bothered Clifton most about all this was the callous way Myron had put Steve Lichtman "in the jackpot." With the double hocking, and to a lesser extent with the check kiting, Myron and Mordy had done what they had to do, and they would have been the ones to catch the heat if everything blew up in their faces. Now they were using underlings to carry out these outlandish escape schemes to keep themselves out of bankruptcy court. Using underlings to keep themselves out of jail.

That was in April. On May 2, a Friday night, Clifton and two of his assistants, Ed Hracs and Lou Dibari, were working late trying to assemble a set of Rockwell lease files. The office was empty. Everyone else had gone home. Hracs and Dibari finally found "the smoking gun," hidden away in the back of a transfile box in Steve Lichtman's office. Rockwell/Redwell Lease File 80–1, 80–2, 80–3: hand-written notes that looked suspiciously like drafts for reworked IBM bills of sale; pieces of paper listing IBM equipment, along with a number of "practice pages" apparently used for forging signatures of IBM representatives. One IBM bill of sale signed "M. J. Calderaro" appeared to bear tracings of the signature on the face of the bill of sale.

John Clifton: "You could tell by just looking . . . that someone was . . . working up title documentation right here at OPM."

Up until then, Clifton had been doing his best to believe there might be some way to explain the missing transactions. The right title documentation might just turn up somewhere. Myron might have some arrangement with Rockwell "allowing him to do it." Clifton knew something about "the Black Book" and he knew something about Myron and Sid Hasin. Maybe Rockwell had actual equipment out there they were letting him use as collateral to obtain short-term loans. But one look at these bogus invoices made it perfectly clear the equipment purportedly underlying these leases had never even existed.

Clifton: "After seeing this I knew it was just plain out-and-out fraud."

Clifton "became a little frightened." He rushed downstairs to the public pay phone in the lobby, for fear the phones at OPM might be tapped. He called his lawyer, Bill Davis, and made an appointment to see him first thing Monday morning. He made copies of all the "hot docs," retaining the originals to take over to Davis. Advice of counsel: "This is a serious problem but not much can be done about it until a fuller analysis of the problem has been completed." Davis advised Clifton to try to put together a clearer picture of what was really going on over there. Davis did say that his complete analysis might well end up with his paying a visit to the U.S. attorney.

Throughout May, Clifton put his men to work overtime tracking down the missing Rockwell leases, looking for absent records of payment, loose equipment receipts, for anything at all connected to the Rockwell leases, even loose scraps of paper. Especially loose scraps of paper. They worked at night and after hours, sorting through closets, chasing after distant leads, making copies of everything, covering up their tracks as best they could until the job was done. It took the team just under a month to put together a partial schedule of the bogus transactions. The minimum estimate of the fraud stood at $32 million, with only a portion of the files completed. Clifton knew what he had on his hands: "An absolute disaster."

By this time, Myron and Clifton had stopped speaking to each other. Myron had stopped talking to Clifton about the time Lichtman had started talking to him. Lichtman stopped talking to Clifton soon after that. Clifton could only imagine Myron had told Lichtman to keep his mouth shut. Clifton was working his assistants around the clock to finish up the fraud schedule. He decided to send Myron a memo requesting overtime payments as an opening signal that something was up. When Myron's response to Clifton's budget request was "not satisfactory," Clifton said to himself, "He's forcing me to meet with him. Okay, let's have a meeting."

That was the first week in June. Clifton brought the conversation around to the conversation they'd had in December, when he'd first warned Myron that any "problems" with the Rockwell transactions would be sure to come out in an audit. Now he had found "a number of inconsistencies" in the books involving Rockwell leases, with no Rockwell payments on certain deals, with all payments coming from OPM, with no title documentation to be found in the files.

Myron: "Don't worry. It's all taken care of. I know all about it."

Clifton wasn't having any. Not anymore. He told Myron he had been working on a schedule of bad transactions. That he had retained outside counsel to advise him on the problem, and on a proper course of action.

Myron: "I thought you'd been talking to someone."

Clifton: "I'm trying to do what is best for the company."

Myron: "Okay, you do what you have to do."

Clifton said he was doing just that; he was working up a "full analysis and in all likelihood I'll be resigning when it's done."

Myron: "Is there any other position in the company you'd be willing to take?"

Clifton: "I don't think so . . . none that I can think of."

Myron: "You know, if you'd stay on to help me clear this thing up, you could have any salary you'd want, you could name your figure." He offered Clifton a house, a car, a raise: up to $200,000 cash.

Clifton: "I'd like to help, but for my sake and my family's sake I just can't do it."

Myron wasn't acting angry. Just depressed. The fact that Myron did not explode, did not yell, did not deny, did not cry, made Clifton know he must be right. As soon as Clifton walked out of Myron's office, a lot of the tension he had felt over the past weeks just went away. No way could he help Myron now. Now the only question was, what is best for John Clifton?

His work sheets were finished June 7. He called Bill Davis. "There are massive amounts involved. What should I do?"

"Come over."

Davis's first question was, could OPM possibly survive in light of the size of the fraud? Clifton's answer was definitely not; not unless the fraud kept going. Myron had pulled off amazing things before to keep from going under, but this was the most amazing yet. A minimum of forty million down the tubes, probably a lot more. Clifton described OPM as a corporate junkie: it kept needing its "Rockwell fix" to stay alive. The fraud had to continue because the real business just wasn't there. Davis: "John Clifton did not think OPM could survive more than a couple of weeks in the face of what he had turned up."

In light of this, Clifton had a number of options. But one option was not open to him. He could not simply resign and forget about it. That way out did not afford Clifton sufficient protection, either from Myron or from the authorities. For Clifton to remain silent in the face of what he knew would simply put him "at Myron's mercy."

From Clifton, Davis learned that Myron was "a very sick and

verbally violent person who would scamper around arranging things to fit his personal need." Davis, from a background quite similar to Myron's, couldn't help but assume Myron must have developed "some very strange ability to ignore that background." It struck Davis as utterly anomalous for "a practicing Orthodox Jew to engage in these practices." Myron must be irrational, which made him potentially capable of doing practically anything to save his own skin. Fingering John Clifton was just one such possibility.

Davis's first advice was to go right down to the U.S. attorney's Office and tell them everything. A route that clearly afforded his client maximum protection from the authorities and minimum risk that Myron would try to nail him. But Clifton did not want to do that. He "did not want to be the one who closed OPM's doors": "I looked at the relationship which I had with Myron during the entire period. And although I guess most of what's on the record is negative, in my view the entire relationship was not negative . . . To me it was just one of those situations where Myron had chosen a way to go which I didn't think was correct, and I just couldn't go along with it."

For all Myron's occasional racist remarks, he had never once discriminated against him. Myron had given him "the opportunity to progress up the executive line from being just an accountant to gradually being a fairly high-up executive of a large company." He was grateful to Myron for giving him "an opportunity which I felt I would have gotten in very few other places." Myron had given him, a black, the chance to help run a predominantly Orthodox Jewish business. Clifton respected Myron for standing by him against the hostility of most of the "family members."

John Clifton loved OPM. He had grown up there. He had grown up as much because of Myron as in spite of him. When you had to find a million dollars to pay someone the next day and there was just no way you were going to find it, but you rammed a closing through and you found the money and saved the day, that was a feeling you didn't get very often at the average company. Myron made you believe you could do just about anything if you had to, though Clifton knew it was just that arrogant attitude that had gotten Myron in so deep over his head. Myron's impossible bullishness and willingness to take the giant step had been stressful, troubling, and confusing. At the same time, it had been contagious, seductive, and exhilarating. Clifton knew he had to walk now, because of what he knew. But he just couldn't live with the idea of forcing everyone else at OPM to take the same route.

He begged Davis to come up with some sort of "alternative protective strategy" that would keep him from having to "blow the whistle" on Myron, to "close OPM's doors." The only other possible way out would be for Clifton to inform Singer Hutner. To drop the ball in the lap of OPM's outside counsel, to wait and see "what the future might bring." Nothing else "would not involve him in active concealment and yet not require him to rat on his friends." If Clifton disclosed to Singer Hutner, it would be up to them to correct the problem. Their obligation to disclose the fraud would no doubt be constricted by the attorney-client privilege. But that was their problem, not Davis's or Clifton's.

Davis assumed five things would naturally flow from his client's disclosure of the fraud to Singer Hutner.

1. Singer Hutner would cease issuing opinions of counsel.
2. Singer Hutner would feel compelled to issue corrections of previous opinions of counsel they now knew to be incorrect.
3. They would persuade Myron to turn himself in to the U.S. attorney.
4. They would resign as OPM counsel.
5. OPM would close down.

Davis asked Clifton for the name of the OPM man at Singer Hutner.

"Andy Reinhard."

"Okay, he gets the memo."

Davis advised Clifton:

1. to prepare a memorandum on the fraud to give to Myron

2. to write a letter to Andy Reinhard enclosing a copy of the memo
3. to resign from OPM at the time of the delivery of the memo to Singer Hutner

On June 10, Clifton presented his last memo to Myron: "47 1979 Rockwell Transactions: Confidential."

Clifton: "Myron, I just don't know if I would have done what you've done."

Myron: "You know, the basic flaw in this whole thing is the equipment . . . You can document the heck out of everything else . . . but there's just no way from an accounting standpoint to show where we paid for the equipment."

Myron said he was "trying to do everything in his power to protect . . . other people involved in this." He asked Clifton to "hold off" sending his letter to Andy for a couple of days, until he had a chance to break the bad news to Andy himself. He said he was "going to work to pay off the fraudulent loans . . . and he was going to call [Clifton] and tell [him] as he paid off each one."

Myron: "Would you consider coming back to OPM after I paid off all these loans?"

Clifton had considerable faith in Myron's magical survival skills. But this time he couldn't imagine how they'd do the trick. Still, there was always that chance. With Myron you never knew.

Clifton: "I'd consider it."

20

Desperately looking for some way out of the box, Myron fell back on one of his oldest tricks: recruiting an external authority figure to impose "discipline" on him, to "sit on" him, to "watch over" him, to get him to stop. He needed a cure for his cash addiction that would not be worse than the cause. Mordy hadn't the head for it; Andy Reinhard never seemed to succeed; John Clifton had turned him down; Steve Lichtman wasn't strong enough for the job. Mendy Weissman was Myron's last hope for salvation, a potential angel of rational restraint. If Mendy gave up, or turned him down, that would be the final unforgivable defection.

By the end of April, Myron had decided to confess to Mendy, beg his forgiveness, ask for his help. He met with Mendy on the twenty-second and asked if it was true that Fox would need to confirm random leases in connection with its upcoming audit. Mendy said yes, that was part of any audit; without confirmation you didn't know if the leases were there. Myron was acting nervous. He asked if Rashba & Pokart might be willing to replace Fox as his auditors; they would have to forget about lease confirmations. Weissman refused. Goodman confessed to being involved in "illegal, improper, fraudulent transactions." Myron looked sheepish, boyish, unhappy, ashamed. Mendy simply looked shocked.

Mendy: "We'll have to resign."

It was Myron's turn to look shocked.

"Why?"

Mendy: "This is strike three. First the double discounts, then the check-kiting. Now more lease fraud."

Myron had been hoping for better than this from Mendy. Now Mendy was yelling and screaming and talking about quitting. This wasn't the idea at all.

Myron was getting more and more agitated and upset. He looked just about ready to cry.

Myron: "Please, Mendy, as a personal favor. Would you talk to Andy before doing anything?"

"What's the point?"

"Well, talk to him anyway. You know, to see if you really have to quit."

Mendy did not look forward to a discussion on this subject with Reinhard. But if Myron was going to put things on that basis, as a personal courtesy . . .

"All right. I'll talk to him." Myron had one of those fancy speakerphones with an automatic dialer. He didn't put the speaker on, so Mendy couldn't hear Andy.

Myron: "Andy, listen, Mendy has a problem . . . with one of his largest clients . . . he's thinking about quitting, but he'd like your input . . . That's right. Well, he'd just like to talk to you about it. That's all."

Myron was deliberately talking to Andy in such a way as to let Mendy know Andy knew. Andy didn't know Mendy was there. Myron didn't want Andy to know Mendy knew he knew anything.

Andy: "No way am I going to talk to him, Myron."

Myron: "There are going to be big problems if you don't."

Myron twisted Andy's arm. They ended up with a compromise neither of them was too crazy about: Mendy and Andy could discuss the problem, but only in hypotheticals, no names, no facts, no figures. According to Myron, Andy said that was a sham: "Trying to get around the problem without getting around the problem." The problem was confidentiality: what you had to tell. Andy, as a lawyer, had the attorney-client privilege. Mendy, as an accountant, did not. Andy didn't have it with Mendy because Mendy wasn't his client. Myron: "The whole thing was absurd."

Mendy: "By the end of the meeting it was clear to me that Reinhard knew what was going on."

Mendy felt anger, frustration, pain, and upset. Myron felt oddly optimistic: "We cleaned up the double discounts, we cleaned up the check-kiting. We can clear this up too." He begged Mendy to help him out, "assisting or suggesting methods . . . to raise funds to repay these debts."

Mendy: "Does Mordy know?"

Myron: "No."

Mendy: "How about Joe?" Joe Hutner.

Myron: "No."

Mendy: "You'd better tell them, Myron. You better make sure they find out."

Mendy went back to his office to confer with his partners about resigning his firm's largest account. Just doing "support work" for OPM, in the absence of an audit, had brought in over $186,000 in fees for 1979. The partners readily agreed that the firm had no choice but to resign. Mendy: "It was not a very formal meeting . . . I think we did it all standing up . . . on the run. There was no dissension." There was some speculation as to the nature and size of the crime. Knowing Myron, they assumed it had to be enormous for him to confess before getting caught. Knowing Myron's past, they assumed it must be some more elaborate and refined form of double discounting. They had to resign, but they agreed Mendy could do what he could for Myron as a friend, without remuneration, without Rashba & Pokart. In the opinion of outside counsel, they had to resign, but they didn't have to say why. Mendy suggested an appropriately vague formulation for the resignation: "There have been differences in concept with the company, with Myron Goodman in particular, as to the way they operate their business, specifically as to spending habits, as to the wasting of funds." Marvin Weissman: "We were concerned that if we informed anybody that a fraud had occurred . . . we were not [prepared] to prove that a fraud had occurred, and if a third party was so informed and had then damaged OPM, OPM could then turn around and sue us for . . . libel or slander . . . so we decided not to answer that we were informed that the company had committed a fraud."

Mendy and Andy had their little lunch at a "small place on the East Side, around Sixtieth Street." Singer Hutner was close by, at Fifty-ninth.

Andy: "I believe we have something to discuss."

Mendy said his "largest billing client," assuming Andy knew perfectly well who that was, had recently informed him that he was involved in a major fraud, after having been involved in two previous frauds. He and his partners had reached a final decision to quit. They were getting out.

Andy didn't seem too comfortable with this discussion. But Mendy says he supported Weissman's decision to withdraw, on the grounds that Mendy did not have recourse to the same privilege of confidentiality a lawyer had. Reinhard acknowledges Mendy told him a client had disclosed past wrongdoing. He acknowledges realizing Mendy was talking about Myron and OPM. But he maintains he merely suggested that Weissman should advise his client to see his lawyers, that he did not give a professional opinion on R&P's decision to resign. Reinhard says that when he told Myron about the lunch, Myron casually responded, "Mendy's making a mountain out of a molehill."

Myron couldn't count on Mendy staying on. But Myron could count on Mendy for wisdom. Mendy arranged a counseling session with Myron, as a favor, for free. He had hoped to see Myron quietly and privately in his office, but the confusion was so intense, with people running in and out and phones ringing and messengers ferrying letters back and forth, that Mendy finally said, "Myron, at the rates I'm charging I can't afford to waste time." They went downstairs to a coffee shop to try to sort things out.

Myron still had some assets to sell: the bank in New Orleans, the condo in New Orleans, a few securities. There were new lease deals being signed out of the country expected to generate a fair amount of cash. Mendy suggested that Myron take every penny he could spare and put it away in a special account, earmarked for the buy out. Mendy didn't know the size of the fraud, but he imagined it must be well under ten million, because when he suggested Myron sell the bank, Myron said, "Oh no, I don't need that much." Of course Myron could still play games.

One night late in May, Steve Lichtman called Mendy to ask if he could come over to his house. He turned up quite late, acting "very agitated, very nervous, very concerned." He knew Myron had told Mendy about the Rockwell fraud. Lichtman claimed it was only because he had been putting pressure on Myron that Myron had finally broken down and gone to Mendy for help. He said the fraud "involved leases that don't exist," that he was "deeply involved," that the problem was "pretty substantial," and that he wanted Mendy's confirmation that Myron was setting up a separate bank account to pay back the fraud. Steve begged Mendy to stay on top of Myron on this, to not let Myron slip out from under his pledges. Because Myron had a way of promising the sky and delivering dirt. Steve was there only a few minutes when Mendy's wife came downstairs to say Steve's wife was on the phone. Steve drove home, leaving that funny phrase sitting in Mendy's mind, "Leases that don't exist."

Mendy knew he couldn't take on this job alone. He needed help to help Myron. He needed Joe Hutner. "I had full confidence in Joe's ability and integrity whereas if he knew about this, he would delve into it and find out exactly what's been going on . . . he would do whatever had to be done . . . Joe was more objective as related to Myron Goodman than Andy was."

Mendy kept trying to push Myron to tell Joe. Joe was supposed to be looking for a buyer for the bank, and Mendy felt that created a perfect opportunity for Myron to confess, to ask Joe to sell the bank to pay back the fraud. June 2: Mendy and Myron met with Joe regarding the bank sale. Mendy kept waiting for Myron to open up. Afterward, Mendy told Myron he had better hurry up and tell Joe. Joe would know what to do.

Myron: "I know, I know, but I can't tell him yet. It's hard to tell him. I find it hard to tell him."

Mendy: "Either you're going to tell him, or I will. I'm giving you one last chance."

June 11 was the day John Clifton met with Myron to tender his resignation. Myron and Mendy met with Joe again, for three full hours at no charge to Myron. Mendy left Myron alone with Joe toward the end. He called Myron later.

"Have you told him yet?"

"No."

"I've got to see you, right now."

"Fine, come down to my office."

"No, I don't want your office. I want you to come to my house."

"Mendy, I can't just leave like that."

"You're going to come and we're going to have a meeting at my house because if you don't come I'm going to call Joe myself. Right now."

"I don't come to people's houses."

"To this one you're coming."

Myron came—to Mendy's house in Woodmere, in his limousine. Myron's driver took Mendy's kids off for a ride in the limo while Mendy took Myron upstairs to the back porch off the master bedroom. Mendy said Myron was going to call Joe and Mendy was going to watch. A month already Mendy had been waiting around. He was getting tired. Myron made excuses and promises. "I'll call him tomorrow. I'll call him next week."

He started pleading. Mendy started screaming. Mendy: "Myron doesn't scream at me. I scream at Myron . . . I'm probably the only one who ever did." Myron felt bad for Mendy getting so agitated. It didn't help Mendy's ulcer for him to get so excited. Myron wished Mendy would just calm down a minute for the sake of his stomach. But Myron was not going to give in without so much as a fight. Mendy: "There was a prolonged period of pleading on his part whereas if he tells Joe at this point he can't do any more business, I'm putting him out of business. All of that fell on deaf ears." Myron claimed if Joe knew about the fraud Singer Hutner would have to resign, and that would put OPM out of business. And if he couldn't do business, he'd never get the money to pay back the fraud. They kept arguing in circles, and Mendy would listen patiently and nod and say, "That's fine, okay. Now let's call." Mendy firmly believed in

Joe's ability to "resolve the Rockwell problem . . . to try and put it in perspective . . . to make a plan." He kept saying, "Come on, get Joe's advice. He seems to have some insight."

Mendy finally reached the end of his rope. He picked up the phone in his bedroom and dialed Joe Hutner's home number. Myron was sitting on Mendy's bed. Myron finally gave in. "On that night I thought maybe Joe could help . . . possibly try to undo some of what had been wrong." The phone rang in Joe Hutner's house around nine.

Mendy: "Joe? Listen, I'm sitting here with Myron, and he has something he wants to say to you." He handed Myron the phone. Myron held on to it for a moment, staring at it stupidly. He asked Mendy to step out on the porch. Having Mendy sitting there just made him nervous. Myron got on the line and started making all sorts of sobbing noises, not quite crying, more like strangling. He finally pulled himself together.

"Do you have any free time tomorrow?"

"I could make some available. Do you want to discuss this over the phone?"

"No."

They set up a meeting for the next day at Singer Hutner. Hutner knew just a few things. From the tone of Mendy's voice, Hutner knew it was serious: "It didn't sound as if I was about to get an invitation to a social occasion." It had to be something secret: "Not something that could be discussed freely in the supermarket aisles." It had to be some form of wrongdoing, and it had to be financial: "It was not going to be . . . some crime of passion . . . I mean if Myron had raped somebody I would have thought it highly unlikely he would have gone to Mendy. That was not as far as I knew his area of expertise." Since it must be financial, Joe wanted Mendy to be there when Myron disclosed it.

Hutner called a junior partner at his firm, Eli Mattioli. He asked him to do some fast research on the issue of attorney-client privilege, as pertaining to an accountant retained by an attorney as a financial expert, in furtherance of a service to a client. Mattioli was to prepare an engagement letter, to be signed by Marvin Weissman, that would "form an umbrella of privilege" allowing Mendy to be present during Myron's disclosure "without having any negative impact on the confidential nature of what would be imparted." Hutner called Mattioli back a few hours later.

"Have you done the research yet? Have you drafted the letter?"

"Can't you tell me what this is all about?"

"I don't know what it's about. How can you ask me that after what I've just told you?"

Mattioli drafted the engagement letter that night and brought it into Hutner's office the following morning, Thursday, June 12. Mendy Weissman came in to see Hutner and took the letter out into the hallway and read it. He came back a few minutes later, saying his outside counsel had advised him not to sign the engagement letter because his "prior knowledge" of Myron's activities would make any subsequent assertion of privilege problematical. Hutner thought that "quite an astute legal analysis." Hutner told him not to worry, Myron was expected to "tell all" that day anyway.

Myron finally turned up. Late, as usual. The meeting was confusing. It lasted the rest of the day. Different lawyers kept running in and out of Joe's office, spreading fat legal books out on Joe's desk, looking up various cases, looking over each other's shoulders, hemming and nodding, offering different opinions. The major issue that seemed to be stumping them was the attorney-client privilege: who had it, who didn't. They seemed able to agree Mendy didn't have it, so they kept shuttling Mendy in and out of the room, inviting him in one minute, asking him to leave the next. Myron: "They spent almost all the meeting putting Mendy in the room, putting Mendy out of the room." Andy Reinhard, Carl Rubino, and Eli Mattioli were all in and out. Joe was there all the time, Eli was there most of the time, Andy was there part of the time. There were some other lawyers, floating in and out.

Myron launched into his confession slowly, opening the clam up a crack.

"I have this problem . . . A significant problem . . . If I tell you what the problem is, if I describe the facts to you, that is if there were any facts, you know, the hypothetical facts."

"Yes, Myron, I understand."

"So if I told you something, who else would you have to tell?"

"It would depend largely on what you told me."

Myron clammed up.

"Well in that case, let's end the meeting now because I'm not going to tell you what the problem is."

They played with that a little bit. They didn't get too far. Myron kept acting peevish and childish. He refused to budge. But finally it was Myron who broke the deadlock. He proposed a game of charades.

"Why don't you ask me some questions and maybe I can give you enough information to give me an answer."

Hutner was willing to play softball, if that would help.

"Does this something you are going to tell me have to do with OPM?"

"Yes it does."

"Does it have to do with wrongdoing?"

"Yes it does."

"Is the wrongdoing substantial?"

Myron closed the clam again.

"Can this problem be solved by the payment of money?"

"Yes."

"Well if it can be cured with money, why don't you just sell the bank?"

Now Myron looked really upset. He didn't want to have to say this, but . . .

"It wouldn't be enough . . . it would have to be . . . millions more."

Hutner figured OPM could net at least five million on the sale of the bank, after repayment of the purchase loans. The fraud had to be more; from the way Myron was looking, it had to be much more.

Hutner tried to field Myron's questions one by one.

"I haven't had much reason to focus on rules relating to attorney-client privilege for some time . . . but I think at the very least you would have to tell Mordy."

"Why Mordy?"

"Well, you see, we're counsel to OPM and Mordy is a director of OPM. Beyond that he is also your business partner."

"That gives me a lot of trouble."

Andy stepped out of the room. Andy was also an OPM director. It was unclear if Andy's privilege of confidentiality might be compromised by his responsibilities as a director of the company.

"Do you have to tell Andy too? Does the whole firm have to know?"

"Since you give me the impression the matter is serious, it's probably not something I could appropriately withhold from my partners."

Myron kept staring at the floor.

Joe: "Is it some form of double-hocking?" Joe knew about double-hocking. Myron had mentioned it once to Henry Singer, his partner, in a taxicab.

"No."

"Is it over, this activity, whatever it is?"

Myron swore up and down it was over.

"Do you have to resign?"

"I honestly don't know . . . But I can't think of any reason off the top of my head why we would have to resign as long as it is completed."

"So who else would you have to tell?"

"Myron, I'm finding it very difficult to answer these questions in a void. Why don't you just unburden yourself to me the way you did with Carl Rubino, on the check-kiting?" Carl Rubino was one of Myron's favorite father figures. He had gotten Myron off on the check-kiting in March with just a small corporate fine. Myron had cried in court, "Carl, you saved my life." Carl had said, "From now on, Myron, you had better act like Caesar's wife." Myron had sworn to Carl, "From now on, I'll promise to be orthodox, in every respect." Myron worshipped Carl largely because he was always concerned about Myron's health, always recommending specialists. Myron: "Carl is a very compassionate individual." The father confessor role had worked well for Carl back in March in New Orleans.

"Myron, don't you remember how Carl helped you out? How you owed him your life?"

Myron wasn't buying.

"I'm very troubled about this Mordy thing. Are you sure about it?"

Hutner was quite sure.

"Well, I've really got to think on this."

"Does that mean you're not going to tell me?"

"That's right."

Myron went into "a long song and dance" about what a sensitive individual Mordy was, about all the emotional problems he had to deal with, about how he just couldn't see weighing Mordy down with one more problem with all the other burdens he had to bear. This particular problem Myron just didn't want to share.

Joe: "I think you're doing yourself a terrible disservice. To yourself, to Mordy, and to the firm."

Myron went off to the men's room. For quite a long time. When he came back into the meeting, he was holding an envelope. "John Clifton has resigned," he said, holding up the envelope. It was fairly bulky, more like a small package. Clifton had apparently written a letter to Andy Reinhard detailing the reasons for his resignation. This letter "made some reference to the facts under discussion . . . But the facts as set forth in this letter are fragmentary, and misleading." Myron announced that he had stolen the letter off Andy's desk, before he had a chance to read it.

Myron: "He never received it."

Joe: "Let me see that letter."

Myron cradled it under one arm.

"I'll take that under advisement."

When Andy came back, he told Eli Mattioli that "he had been holding the envelope in one hand and a letter opener in the other, and he was just about to open the envelope when Goodman burst in and snatched it out of his hand."

Myron, later on, would tell yet another story: on the way to the men's room, he had stopped in at Andy's office, just down the hall from Hutner's. Andy was sitting at his desk, reading the letter. Myron grabbed it out of his hands.

Myron: "You never read this." (Myron told John Clifton that Andy handed it over to him, saying, "I can't see this.")

Andy: "But I received it." The letter had been hand-delivered by an OPM messenger, so there was a record of the delivery.

Myron: "No, you never received it. I took it away."

They closed the door to Andy's office. Myron locked it. Myron read the letter through. They were both standing up. Andy wanted to finish it. Myron gave it back. Andy read it. Myron made a sharp left outside Andy's office and went straight down the hall past a large filing cabinet. On his way back from the men's room, he stepped back into Andy's office. He took the letter back and walked back into the meeting. According to Myron, he and Andy worked up the "purloined letter" story so Andy could say he never read this:

Dear Andy,
As a result of the Accounting Department's review of Rockwell transactions consummated in 1979, a number of issues have been raised which I believe should be brought to your attention . . . The major issues are:

1) Why isn't Rockwell making payments on the majority of transactions?
2) Why can't Accounting verify payments for $26,700,000 worth of equipment which the IBM documents available in the files indicate are paid?

Also enclosed are certain documents relating to IBM . . . which raise serious questions as to both the authenticity and the source of the IBM title documents finally submitted in connection with the financing . . . in addition to the inability to verify any payment by OPM for equipment . . . and the absence of Rockwell payments . . . I believe your attention to these matters is essential in order to see that the issues raised are properly resolved . . ."
Very Truly Yours,
John Clifton
Senior Vice President
cc. Myron S. Goodman

Friday, June 13, 1980: John Clifton was a bit shocked the next morning to see his letter sitting in plain view on the corner of Myron's desk.

Myron: "Why did you send that letter without telling me first?"

Clifton: "My lawyer told me to send it as soon as possible."

Myron gleefully admitted "stealing" it off Reinhard's desk. Myron was upset with Clifton. He said Clifton had "misunderstood" him; he hadn't wanted the letter sent until Clifton had gotten back to him to say it was on its way. Clifton said he had deliberately delayed sending it until the afternoon, so Myron could have a chance to tell Andy at the meeting that morning.

Clifton called Bill Davis later that morning. Now he sounded really upset. He had been "stunned" to see his letter to Reinhard on Myron's desk. Davis was stunned to hear it.

Clifton said, "in a sort of high-pitched eyes-squeezed exclamation," "Myron wants me to take the package back."

21

When Myron found Andy Reinhard in possession of John Clifton's letter, he became "absolutely petrified" Clifton was going to turn him in. Clifton had promised he wouldn't go to the authorities, but he had also promised not to deliver the letter to Andy without letting him know first. Now Myron didn't know what to do: Clifton might have gone to the U.S. attorney after all.

Myron claims he gave Joe Hutner some fairly explicit instructions: to talk to Clifton's lawyer, to find out if they were going to blow the whistle on him, to "explore the possibility" that there might be some way for Clifton to take the letter back, to not get involved in conversations with Davis about the contents of the letter. Myron did not want Hutner receiving any information about the letter outside the bounds of the attorney-client privilege.

Hutner denies following any such marching orders from Myron. He met with Bill Davis at Davis's office on Madison Avenue after 5 P.M., Friday the thirteenth. Davis was willing to attest to certain key facts: the "purloined letter" contained information disclosing Myron's "wrongdoing"; in Clifton's opinion, the problem "dwarfed New Orleans," meaning the check kiting; Clifton's opinion was that the fraud would have to be ongoing for the company to stay alive; OPM had provided Singer Hutner with false documents that rendered their opinions of counsel false and misleading.

Davis: "My client elected to disclose this information to you, instead of to the authorities."

Hutner: "What authorities?"

Davis: "Well, I suppose the federal authorities."

Hutner asked if Davis had an annotated copy of the U.S. Criminal Code handy. Davis pointed it out on his shelf. Together they read through Title 18, Section 4, the statute on misprision: "Affirmative Act of Concealment."

Davis: "Well, it does look like you have to have an affirmative act of concealment to be guilty of that."

Bill Davis did not impress Joe Hutner as being terribly "lawyer-like." He started out the meeting by going on about his show biz clients, pointing out various trophies and prizes hung up around the room. Hutner: "It was clear he didn't feel competent to deal with the issue . . . The whole thing was kind of absurd. Both of us leaning over his desk looking over the U.S. reports . . . like we were supposed to be collaborating on some sort of legal thesis."

Davis claims Hutner made it clear he did not wish to discuss the contents of Clifton's package: "I agreed I would not tell him what was in the package, if that was the way he wanted to talk about things. That was the way he wanted to talk about things."

Davis memorandum: "Hutner insists he not be told what [the contents of the Clifton letter] were."

Hutner: "From the way Davis was dancing around the letter, it seemed pointless to ask him for it, or for what was in it . . . to give me the letter would have been the most natural thing in the world . . . but here is a lawyer that recommends his client send a letter . . . and the letter is intercepted . . . Lo and behold the attorney arrives at his doorstep and he doesn't even offer me a copy."

Davis says he believed Hutner knew what was in the letter all along: "I found it hard to believe that he would talk about these matters of advising his most important client and not know what he was talking about." He claims to have been "stunned" when Hutner insisted he not be told what was in the package. He further claims he did not offer Hutner the letter because "I had visions of him clamping his hands over his ears and running out of the office."

Hutner: "If Davis assumed I was familiar with the contents of the letter, it is therefore an absurdity that I would have asked him not to reveal the contents I already knew . . . It would be laughable if it were not so outrageous."

Davis: "This meeting and the couple of meetings which followed it had an air of unreality about them . . . what John had put in the memos became suddenly tangential to the whole process that surrounded it . . . Nothing was fact, everything was possible . . . nothing was written in stone . . . The whole nature of the meeting was a kind of macabre dance around the issue."

Davis memorandum, June 13:

> Joe Hutner then went into a long and somewhat involved attempt to convince me that John Clifton should withdraw the material from Andy Reinhard (Myron Goodman?) and say nothing about it to anyone, leaving his resignation as the only event which would distinguish John Clifton from other persons at OPM.

Hutner: (Davis version) "Give us the opportunity to show you cases that show he will not have any liability if he takes the package back."

Davis: "Alright, you do some work and I'll do some work."

Hutner claims he was only asking for research on the question of whether Clifton had an obligation to go to the authorities with what he knew.

They agree they agreed to meet again on Monday.

Mattioli took a call from Hutner late in the day, around five, from Davis's office. He needed research done on what constituted legal "delivery" of a letter. Hutner believed if Clifton had sufficiently demonstrated an intent to disclose to a third party, it would be very hard for anyone to assert an "affirmative act of concealment" had taken place. Hutner called an hour later from Grand Central Station.

"Have you found anything out yet?"

Mattioli said he would be going into the office over the weekend. He'd call Hutner at home as soon as he turned up something definitive. Mattioli copied a few cases and called Hutner Sunday afternoon. Research seemed to confirm that an "affirmative act of concealment" was a crucial ingredient in this crime of misprision. Hutner asked Mattioli to bring his cases along to a meeting at Davis's office Monday afternoon.

Joe Hutner wrote in a contemporaneous chronology of these events, "Stop Davis."

Monday afternoon, Davis's office: Hutner showed up around six-thirty. Mattioli was already there, armed with weighty opinions asserting "something more than knowledge alone would be required to constitute an affirmative act of concealment." If forced to take a position on the Goodman interception, Davis was prepared to deem the Clifton letter "constructively delivered" to Andy Reinhard. Davis pointed out that since Clifton had formerly resigned on Friday the thirteenth, the attorney-client privilege would no longer hold if Clifton were to redeliver the letter, as Clifton was no longer an officer of the company represented by Singer Hutner. Davis was therefore not prepared to counsel redelivery of the letter. "As far as we're concerned, that letter has crossed the Rubicon."

Hutner maintained Mattioli's research indicated Clifton had not been legally obligated to disclose the problem in the first place: to Singer Hutner, to the authorities, to anyone at all. Since he had not taken any "affirmative steps to conceal the fraud," Clifton could very well have simply resigned and gotten off scot-free. Davis was willing to admit that his initial legal advice might not have been entirely accurate. But he still believed maintaining absolute silence would have been risky for Clifton, if not because of the authorities, because of Myron. For that same reason, he still believed "it would be fatal for John to take the package back . . . the man [Myron] was irrational . . . the man who would do anything to save his own skin . . . I didn't know what was going to happen out of this thing."

Hutner claims at this point he asked Davis for the letter. And that Davis refused to relinquish the letter "on the grounds that Clifton was no longer an employee of OPM . . . so the information would no longer be privileged . . . he did not proffer any explanation of why he did not give it to me on Friday when that objection would not have pertained."

Davis claims quite the opposite: that Hutner said Singer Hutner "might want to assert a lack of knowledge of the contents of the Clifton letter in the future." Davis: "It was patently incredible . . . that the package was delivered to Andy Reinhard's desk and somehow it left his desk and fell into the hands of Myron Goodman without anyone opening it and seeing what it was . . . That Hutner would admit receipt of the package by Andy and deny anybody knew what was in it was ridiculous." To Davis, "You can know something and yet not want to know it at the same time . . . not wanting it to be known that you know something . . . I didn't know what he knew . . . I could only guess what he knew."

Davis's own best guess, which he freely relayed to Clifton, was that Hutner knew "full well" what was in that letter, both from "the things Hutner asked . . . and the things he specifically did not want to know." Davis could only assume what Hutner was looking for was "deniability." Davis decided at that point, "I will play the game . . . If they want to claim they didn't get the package let them claim it." The point was that Singer Hutner was in "constructive receipt" of the letter, and his client had the messenger logs to prove it. The letter was Singer Hutner's problem. His client was off the hook.

Davis says he advised Hutner to "take your client down to the U.S. Attorney . . . you might get him some leniency." But he did not intend to advise his own client to do so. Neither Hutner nor Mattioli recalls receiving this free advice.

Hutner had to admit Davis's maneuvering on the issue was extremely adroit: "He didn't have to have his client go to the authorities . . . thereby exposing him to whatever trouble might be presented by following that course . . . He didn't even have to expose his client to the trouble of whatever questions might be put to him by Singer Hutner on the delivery of the letter . . . So 'mirabile dictu,' No misprision, no obligations for my client, no obligations for me."

Hutner says Myron told him, around this time, that he'd "taken care" of Clifton.

Joe: "So what's John planning to do?"

Myron: "He's thinking of setting up an independent accounting practice . . . I've given him a hundred thousand dollars."

Joe: "That's nice . . . how did you come up with that figure?"
Myron: "You know, one year's salary, to get him on his feet."
Clifton ended up accepting fifty thousand.

22

Carl Rubino, then in his mid-sixties, was a founding partner of a law firm which no longer bore his name. In 1971, when the firm was first retained as counsel to OPM, it had been known as Rapoport Rubino & Pincus. In 1975 it merged with the firm of Singer Levine & Singer to become Singer & Pincus. In 1976, after the departure of Meyer Pincus, Singer & Pincus was reconstituted as Singer Hutner Levine & Seeman. In 1971 it had twelve lawyers. By 1980 there were twenty-seven, and eleven partners. The firm operated, according to a former senior partner, "as a committee of the whole with respect to all significant matters of firm policy." Now that committee had to deal with the biggest crisis in its history: an admission of massive fraud on the part of its largest client. From 1977 through 1980, OPM provided from 60 to 70 percent of the firm's annual revenues: $2,284,675 in 1979; $2,663,628 in 1980.

Myron: "Singer Hutner was an extension of OPM. They were an arm of OPM. They were as if they were in-house counsel. The only reason they were not was because of Andy Reinhard . . . I could have had twenty attorneys in-house at OPM and forgotten all about Singer Hutner . . . But because of Andy and my personal obligations to him . . . they remained outside counsel and we paid those fees."

Even if Singer Hutner was little more than "an arm" of OPM, that didn't mean the body always got along swimmingly with the limb. Myron considered their fees outrageous. They never sent him an itemized bill; one of the senior partners would simply let him know what he owed. Hutner: "I always considered that an acceptable technique." At the end of 1978, Hutner asked OPM to pay the firm $50,000 a week to keep its accounts clear. But Myron kept falling behind. By the spring of 1980, Myron owed them over $700,000. Hutner did his best to press him, but Myron struck back the only way he knew how: "Any undue pressure by either you or any other member of the firm is only going to make the wheels of progress go backward. Let us all continue doing our jobs and continue on the assumption that the firm wants to maintain its relationship with OPM."

It bothered certain partners, and Myron had a pretty fair idea of who they were, that the firm relied so heavily on one client for more than half its income. In 1979 the partnership met several times to discuss the problem, addressing a growing concern that the firm was rashly overexposing itself to OPM. Hutner: "We were always owed money by OPM except for one brief moment in time." On more than one occasion, Myron bounced a check to Singer Hutner in payment of fees long past due. In 1979, OPM borrowed over $800,000 in short-term loans from its outside counsel. The firm was becoming well aware of OPM's never-ending cash crunch. Hutner: "Myron and I had an ongoing dialogue on the subject of fees."

Myron recalls the time he and Henry Singer were on an airplane, on their way to a bank board meeting in New Orleans on April, 1978. Henry told him the firm had decided to raise its fees retroactively to January 1. Myron: "It was a good thing we were on an airplane, because otherwise Henry would have been totally demolished. That really threw me for a loop." Myron paid the increase after a good deal of complaining. But he never got over finding out that the firm was charging him twenty cents a copy for photocopies. Myron: "That caused a big stink . . . I wouldn't talk to Andy for days. I stopped working with them." In 1979 Hutner chose to follow Henry Singer's example, rendering Myron a rather close accounting in an airport lounge on their way back from a bank meeting in New Orleans: "I thought it appropriate to discuss fees since I had a captive audience . . . his unpaid bill was big enough to get me unhappy and annoyed, big enough to drive me to pencil and paper." It was then that Hutner demanded Myron pay the firm

$50,000 a week to stay current. Myron would kick and scream, but he always paid up. He needed Singer Hutner, they needed him. Myron would later tearfully describe the relationship as "a bondage of the bookends."

Different people at Singer Hutner knew different things about Myron and Mordy: Andy Reinhard knew "everything," if you care to believe Myron, "either before the event, or after the fact." Joe Hutner and Eli Mattioli had heard about the double discounting, they say from Henry Singer, who was supposed to have been told about it by Myron in a taxicab. Singer himself does not recall the incident, nor does he wish to recall it. They knew about the check kiting; they knew about the cash-flow problems. They had plenty of reason to ponder OPM's financial condition, and Myron and Mordy's moral condition. But the bottom line was that Myron successfully projected only the murkiest image of OPM's increasingly shaky fortunes. The bottom line was that in the end Myron somehow always managed to pay off those gigantic bills.

Joe Hutner: "I was always a little mystified, frankly, by OPM's finances . . . There were so many conflicting signals. On the one hand, our bill would remain unpaid over long periods. On the other hand I would be asked to investigate and explore multi-million dollar acquisitions . . . it was hard for me to come up with a firm view." Hutner admits that the check kiting "certainly suggested they were having cash flow problems . . . but the amounts of the checks were really quite small . . . a few hundred thousands at a time . . . which in light of the kind of money OPM was able to generate on any given day seemed really quite minor." Now Myron was admitting to having committed fraud on a vast scale, considerably larger than the worth of the bank he had bought. Clifton's lawyer was claiming it "dwarfed New Orleans," meaning the check kiting. Clifton's lawyer had quoted Clifton to the effect that the size of the fraud made it highly unlikely the company could go on without it. OPM owed Singer Hutner nearly a quarter of a million dollars, with innumerable billable hours being put in every day, around the clock, closing OPM transactions. Now Singer Hutner, as a "committee of the whole," had to figure out what to do about all this.

Any final decisions, whether to resign, whether to stay on, how to deal with Goodman's pseudo-confession, would be ultimately decided by the partnership as a whole. But as a practical matter, Joe Hutner was the senior partner in charge of the OPM representation. Hutner naturally turned to Carl Rubino for advice, because he was a fine litigator, because he was a founding member of the firm, because he had a special relationship with Myron, because he had once been head of the Indictments Bureau of the New York D.A.'s office, because he was still quite active in the Bar Association. Hutner chose Eli Mattioli to help him because he was also a litigator, because he had a special relationship to Rubino, because he had worked on OPM deals, because he was one of the hardest-working lawyers in the office.

On June 17 Rubino and Mattioli met with Reinhard to talk about OPM. Hutner was out of town, at a meeting of the FNJ board in New Orleans. Rubino sagely announced, "We'd better get ourselves a good lawyer," quoting Mark Twain's well-worn admonition that "the man who represents himself has a fool for a client." Mattioli and Rubino were both graduates of Fordham Law School. They recommended an immediate, emergency consultation with Joseph M. McLaughlin, dean of the law school and a former professor of Mattioli's. McLaughlin was said to be learned in the area of attorney-client privilege. He was said to be a leading expert in the laws of evidence. He might be able to help them resolve their problems relating to the Clifton letter.

Hutner: "It was clear we had to get some sort of professional guidance here . . . We were way out of our depth. Rubino and Mattioli had come up with the tentative conclusion that McLaughlin was our man for the job. He sounded swell, and I didn't have the name of any other people at my fingertips . . . I had no reason to nix the idea."

On the eighteenth, Mattioli called McLaughlin at his office at Fordham Law School. He had a very complex "evidence problem" on his hands, a matter of great urgency. They arranged to meet the following morning at eleven. Hutner, Rubino, and Mattioli arrived at the dean's office in a "very distressed state."

McLaughlin: "They were obviously overwrought and I could tell whatever was bothering them was of some magnitude." Hutner did most of the talking, aided in his dissertation with occasional footnotes proferred by Mattioli. McLaughlin found the whole sorry tale full of odd twists and turns, including "a rather bizarre incident" involving a stolen letter.

The murk was made thicker by Singer Hutner's initial resolution not to identify the company or individuals related to the company. Hutner code-named Myron "Sam," Mordy "Harry," Clifton "Paul," OPM the "XYZ Corp." McLaughlin found Hutner's thumbnail description of the leasing business nearly impossible to follow, particularly when it came to a "possible knowledge" of an odd crime called "double hocking."

The "evidence problem," as McLaughlin understood it, was that their largest client had given them reason to believe he had committed some sort of fraud in the past. But now he refused to tell them anything more. They were reasonably suspicious a fraud had been committed; they were reasonably convinced that it was now over, largely due to the client's evident desire to "make a clean breast of the thing." He was apparently reluctant to divulge any "underlying facts" without ironclad assurances that his disclosure would be entirely privileged. He appeared ready and willing to confess, but "obsessively" concerned that his confession remain sealed in the confession booth. The issue thus turned on a question of evidentiary attorney-client privilege: when lawyers are able to disclose confidences, when they are not.

As he listened to the three distraught lawyers tell their story, McLaughlin began to realize this was far more than just an evidence problem. There were further considerations as to the future conduct of these attorneys if they were planning to continue to represent this client. It was really a matter of legal ethics, of professional responsibility. McLaughlin could not legitimately profess any particular expertise in that area. He had never taught it. In fact, he had never even taken a course in it. There was yet another problem, which he did his best to outline to his anxious guests: he was currently "in the throes of running for office." He was under active consideration for an appointment to the Second Circuit Court of Appeals.

But he might just know their man: Henry Peter Putzel III. Pete Putzel had taught professional responsibility and legal ethics at Fordham. He had been an assistant U.S. attorney for four years. He was out of teaching now and had recently reentered private practice full-time. McLaughlin would be pleased to take on this representation if Pete Putzel were available to assist him. McLaughlin claims he tried hard to make it clear to these men that he would be available to offer his services only in a "somewhat avuncular role . . . as a kind of Lloyd Cutler hanging around in the wings . . . I wasn't about to get into the nitty-gritty of this thing." Not only was he running for the Second Circuit, "I had a school to run."

None of them had heard of Pete Putzel. They had heard of Dean McLaughlin. They would be happy to consider his stipulation, but they would be "far more comfortable" if "the Dean" were willing to stay in the picture.

Hutner: "Joe McLaughlin was very anxious to take on that representation . . . If he had said to me, 'I'm awfully sorry, Joe, this ain't my field . . . But I've got this character you've never seen who may be able to help you,' I would have said, 'Well, thanks a lot, but I can find people whose field it is and I don't need your recommendation.'

"But what he said was, 'I'd like to take this on, and it doesn't look like something that should take a long time . . . But I'd like to have a back-stop and his name is Pete Putzel.' We sat in his office for hours . . . and again in my office, for hours . . . Why wear ourselves out for hours giving all these details to a man who is not in a position to assess them?"

McLaughlin called Putzel at his office on Sixth Avenue that afternoon: "Three lawyers have been to visit me . . . in a high state of agitation . . . with a complex matter involving difficult questions of professional responsibility." After checking his calender, Putzel called back to say he would be happy to help. McLaughlin gave some additional background. Putzel took notes:

Client is a poor kid from Brooklyn . . . who has grown up the hard way and become very successful in business . . . he is a young man in desperate physical shape . . . has gone from rags to riches . . . two successful young millionaires from Brooklyn in a very big industry . . . details very confusing.

A meeting was arranged at Singer Hutner for Friday, June 20. Putzel and McLaughlin; Hutner, Rubino, and Mattioli. Hutner briefed them in greater detail: The client is thirty-three years old and in fragile health. His business is in great difficulty. He bought a bank for ten million dollars. He promptly kited over four million in checks through it. He wears a pacemaker, but he also plays softball. He has "fifty pairs of shoes and a bizarre taste for expensive wines and predilection for helicopters." He lives "in an absurdly high fashion" on the old Wardwell estate out on Long Island. He has a "morbid fear of criminal prosecution," which surfaced during the check-kiting trial, at which time he had gotten off with a corporate fine and a light slap on the wrist.

Hutner then related, according to Putzel's notes, "a bizarre set of facts involving a letter which had been sent . . . and then stolen in some way." The letter had been sent by the company's chief financial officer, who had since resigned. "Paul" had been advised by his attorney that he was "under no obligation to go to the authorities . . . or to recover the letter." Meetings with "Paul's" attorney had produced a conclusion that "to do nothing would not constitute misprision on Paul's [Clifton's] part." Hutner said he did not trust Davis, he seemed like "a sleazy person." But so far they had kept to their word not to disclose what Clifton knew. Clifton was giving out as his reason for leaving "that the company was living too high, and the client wasting his money."

Their "problem" had all begun a week before, when "one of the two principal shareholders" had come to see them and said: "If I told you something I have done, which is wrong, would it be privileged? And if I were to tell you what it is, would you have to tell my partner, and will you have to tell anyone else?"

When off the top of his head, Hutner had said, "Yes, I would have to tell your partner and I would have to tell my firm," the client had refused to say anything more.

Putzel tried to isolate the main issues now facing the firm:

1. Andy Reinhard's "dual role" as a director of the company, and a member of its outside counsel. Reinhard's resignation from the board seemed unavoidable.
2. Did Singer Hutner represent the client personally, or the company? This was plainly a conflict of interest, because the client was defrauding the company. The client was the "principal perpetrator"; the company was "the victim." The client clearly had to retain his own counsel, immediately.
3. What is the law firm's obligation to disclose the client's confession? What is privileged here? What is not?

Hutner said they were inclined to believe the client's claim that the fraud was over. Why else would the man be in "a confessional mood"?

Hutner: "Since he has come to us with the apparent intention of making revelations . . . only a maniac would telegraph his punches to his lawyer."

Putzel: "A lawyer is supposed to assume that his client is telling the truth, unless he has evidence to the contrary."

Hutner did mention that John Clifton, "Paul," had told his lawyer he believed the fraud would have to continue "for the company to survive." The entire issue of privilege hinged on the question: Is the fraud still going on? Was it over? If the fraud was indeed over, the firm was obligated to preserve the attorney-client privilege. If the fraud was ongoing, the firm had a clear obligation to restrain the client from continuing, and if that attempt was not successful, to disclose the fraud to third parties.

Disciplinary Rule 7–101 B:

> When a lawyer receives information that a client has perpetrated a fraud . . . he shall call upon his client to rectify the fraud. If the client refuses to do so, he shall bring the matter to the attention of

the appropriate person or tribunal . . . unless the information is obtained through a confidential communication.

Canon 4:

Communications made in furtherance of a future or ongoing crime are exempt from the privilege.

Putzel: "If Goodman had said, 'I am in the process of robbing banks,' that would not be privileged."

Putzel and McLaughlin concurred in recommending Andrew M. Lawler, a graduate of Fordham Law School and former assistant U.S. attorney for the Southern District of New York, as Myron's personal attorney. McLaughlin: "Andy and I were pretty good friends." His private practice largely consisted of defending clients accused of white-collar crimes. Myron clearly fit into that savory category.

Putzel and McLaughlin urged Myron's retention of his own attorney as the first step toward obtaining a fuller disclosure of the "underlying facts."

Putzel: "The worst disservice an attorney can do to a client is to coax from the client information under the umbrella of privilege, and then turn around and say, 'That isn't privileged.' . . . The privilege would only have extended to the corporation, not to Goodman individually."

Putzel: "The whole premise of the attorney-client privilege is to create a 'sacred space' [within] which the client can fully inform the attorney of what he has done."

The firm adopted an "interim device," on the advice of Putzel and McLaughlin, as suitable protection that the fraud was indeed over:

1. Encourage Goodman to retain his own counsel.
2. Accept representations by his counsel that the fraud was not ongoing.

The retention of a man of "such high standing at the bar" should, in Putzel and McLaughlin's opinion, give the firm "considerable comfort."

At the close of the meeting, Mattioli showed Putzel and Mc-

Laughlin an anonymous postcard received by Andy Reinhard and Alan Jacobs back in April:

> Your conniving machinations and subterfuges are despicable, a disgrace to the firm per se, and to the legal profession at large. Your cunning is not fooling anyone."

Neither Putzel or McLaughlin felt confident rendering a professional opinion on the postcard.

23

From their very first conference with Putzel on June 20, the Singer Hutner lawyers "made it clear that they were prepared to walk away from the client if that was their obligation . . . It was also made clear that if it was ethically permissable, they would like to continue to represent the client." What was not made clear was that the client still owed them $700,000, and if they walked away from Myron, their chances of ever seeing any of that money would be pretty slim. They did tell Putzel that OPM was the firm's "largest client by far," that it represented from 60 to 65 percent of the firm's revenues, that to resign would undoubtedly cause the firm a good deal of hardship. Hutner predicted that resignation would undoubtedly bring about OPM's downfall within a matter of weeks. Putzel advised that as long as the firm was convinced in good faith that the fraud was actually over, they were not ethically obligated to withdraw from the representation. Putzel: "You had a bunch of very jumpy lawyers who were very concerned about whether they had to abandon this client."

Since they clearly wanted to stick it out, the overriding question became, What were they obliged to do? Putzel warned they could not "simply stick their heads in the sand" and ignore what they had been told. But since what they had been told lay largely in the realm of conjecture, their first obligation toward their client, the corporate entity, was to "press for the underlying facts." Now they had been put on notice that something was wrong. But in the absence of actual knowledge of what that wrongdoing was, they were obliged to "service the client as they had before," while keeping up the pressure on Myron to tell all.

The firm was strictly prohibited from aiding and abetting or in any way becoming a tool of the fraud. Disciplinary Rule 1–102 (A) (4): "A lawyer shall not engage in conduct involving dishonesty, fraud, deceit, or misrepresentation." This placed a clear obligation of "due diligence" on the firm if it elected to continue to represent the client. Putzel advised that suitable "prophylactic measures" had to be taken to protect the firm from being used to further an ongoing fraud. Putzel: "I was not at all versed in the financial matters of the company. I gave general advice to Singer Hutner: 'You have to be good and satisfied that every transaction you are handling is a proper transaction. If it is a proper transaction there is no ethical impediment to your closing a transaction you are satisfied is proper.'" According to Putzel, there is no obligation set forth in the code for a lawyer to "investigate his client." In fact, such close checking of a transaction could well prove a disservice to the client, if construed by a third party as a sign of mistrust. The ethical question, "When does a lawyer have an obligation to disbelieve his client?" had a clear answer in Putzel's opinion: "A lawyer is entitled, in fact, obligated to believe [a client] absent evidence to the contrary."

Putzel: "The fundamental concept is that the attorney is not the policeman of his client. He or she is an agent of the client and a representative of the client. Now that doesn't mean the attorney can put blinders on and do whatever the client says. But it does mean that absent evidence to the contrary the attorney is entitled to believe representations made to him by his client."

The use of "prophylactic measures" did imply a certain obligation to play cop. On June 23, Mattioli, Hutner, Rubino, Jacobs, and Reinhard met with Putzel to discuss possible due diligence procedures. The optimal form of police-protection in this case would have been "third-party verification" of transactions: calling up the equipment vendor, such as IBM, to make sure the equipment existed and that the title documentation matched that on the lease, and calling up the lessee, such as Rockwell, to ensure that the lease had been properly executed, and the lease terms sent to Rockwell matched those on the lease being supplied to the bank. In theory, quite simple. In practice, according to Alan Jacobs, who handled the closing of these transactions, "a logistical nightmare . . . worse than unwieldy." His reasons were fairly persuasive: closings were run on a rush basis, information and lease terms varied up until the very last minute, lease rates and interest rates fluctuated daily. Coordination among the various people involved would be a "tremendously cumbersome procedure."

The "interim device" advised by Putzel was for Myron to sign "officer's certificates" confirming the authenticity of all transaction documents. Carl Rubino was not too keen on the idea. "To ask an alleged wrongdoer to certify that documents are authentic" struck him as hardly an effective prophylactic, in view of Myron's past history. When the issue was put to a vote of the full partnership, Joel Hasen, Myron's nemesis at the firm, commented off the record that "Goodman . . . is a bad person . . . nothing good will ever come of him." When it came time to vote, Hasen abstained. "It's all news to me." Rubino did not attend, but when Mattioli called him with news of the positive vote, he agreed to "defer to the opinion of outside counsel," while repeating his own private opinion that such a measure could be only of "questionable effect."

Two Rockwell leases were due to close in the next few days: Rockwell 0–39–80 and 0–42–80. Both were permanent loans with the Rhode Island Trust Company, totaling approximately five million dollars. Tuesday, June 24, midmorning. Eli Mattioli and Carl Rubino were in Joe Hutner's office. Alan Jacobs came in with a question about the upcoming closings, How had OPM been able to make five million dollars in equipment purchases without borrowing any money? According to the title documentation submitted by Myron, the equipment had already been purchased by OPM. Jacobs knew of no recent "interim" financings that would have generated that kind of cash. In view of Myron's recent admissions, Jacobs couldn't help wondering whether the IBM bills of sale and invoices might not be real.

Hutner: "Let's take a look."

Jacobs went back to his office to get them: three photocopied sets of bills of sale and invoices. Mattioli noticed something "very strange" about one of the signatures.

Mattioli: "I recognize that handwriting."

Jacobs: "Whose is it?"

Mattioli: "It looks like Myron's."

Carl Rubino and Joe Hutner were standing there, looking over Jacobs's shoulder. They examined the signature, "Frank Chartier, Vice President." Rubino: "I think we'd better get a handwriting expert to take a look at these."

A "squawk box" was turned on to call Putzel. Jacobs had the documents hand-delivered to Putzel's office the following morning. Expert opinion: "There is some question as to the ethicality of having a handwriting expert make a determination on the basis of copies." Mattioli's suspicions might just have been an "overreaction" to what had been going on. Seeing things that "aren't there . . . seeing ghosts." Mattioli was casting aspersions on the integrity of his own client, possibly even slandering him, libeling him. Putzel: "For the firm to engage a handwriting expert at this time is neither advisable or necessary."

Wednesday, June 26, late afternoon: Joe Hutner called Myron to tell him the firm had retained outside counsel, and that Myron was going to have to sign officer's certificates attesting to the authenticity of all future deals.

Myron: "No problem."

Myron was also going to have to get his own personal lawyer because it would be a conflict of interest for the firm to represent both Myron and OPM.

Myron: "No problem."

Myron was going to have to make a "full disclosure" to Mordy.

Myron: "That's a problem."

Myron agreed to come over to Singer Hutner to meet Andrew Lawler. Lawler came first, Myron came late. Lawler announced he had a "clear calender" and was fully prepared to devote himself to Myron's "best defense . . . at an intense level." Myron had not yet made up his mind about retaining personal counsel. Lawler said if Myron was willing, he would be willing to continue their discussion in private in an empty room down the hall. An hour went by. Rubino: "Gee, I wonder if they're still there." Mattioli took a trip down the hall. Still talking. Putzel and Rubino left around eight-thirty. Hutner and Mattioli remained behind, determined to stick this thing out to the end. A little before ten, Myron and Lawler emerged from isolation, having been in constant conference since five-thirty. Myron announced his retention of Lawler. Mattioli handed him an officer's certificate to sign, attesting to the authenticity of title documents submitted by him for the Rockwell leases due to close the next day.

Myron: "I'm only vouching for my own personal knowledge when I sign this?"

Eli: "That's right."

Myron insisted on inserting a phrase to that effect: he was not vouching for the knowledge of any third parties. He looked over at Lawler: "Okay, I'm going to sign this thing." Lawler nodded. He signed several, with a flourish, two or three certificates each to certify each deal.

On June 27, Alan Jacobs and Singer Hutner used the suspect photocopied title documents in closing the Rockwell leases. All the title documents and the leases that they supported were fake; the transactions they purported to verify were fraudulent.

Myron: "I knew the title documents didn't look good . . . Andy knew they weren't good . . . Alan Jacobs I gave a song and dance to." When Alan and Eli thought the bills of sale looked fake, Myron says he had to put pressure on Andy to get the deal closed. Myron broke down and admitted to Andy these deals were not real.

Andy: "You *putz*."

24

Pete Putzel was visibly "heartened" when Myron retained his friend Andy Lawler. He took "considerable comfort" in Lawler's personal and professional integrity: "I knew darned well that Andrew Lawler would never permit his client to perpetuate a fraud while he was representing him—I continue to believe that." Carl Rubino went even further: he requested assurances from Lawler that the fraud was over. Lawler could not provide any absolute proof, only his word that he had no knowledge of a continuing fraud. As far as Putzel was concerned, that promise was just going to have to do.

Putzel believed, at first, that Lawler's presence on the scene should put additional pressure on Myron to come clean: "I felt we were working our way toward getting disclosure . . . and that is what we wanted." But Myron's retention of Lawler ended up slowing things down. Lawler was now advising Myron as to whether or not it would be in his best interest to disclose what he had done, when, and to whom. Lawler presented a barrier between Myron and Singer Hutner; whereas it might have been in OPM's and Singer Hutner's best interest for Myron to disclose the fraud, Lawler could well decide that it would not be in his client's best interest to do so.

Myron and Mordy were spending the Fourth of July weekend together at Grossinger's in the Catskills. On July 2, Myron told Joe Hutner he had decided to tell Mordy "all" over the weekend. The next day, Myron called Eli Mattioli, wanting to know whether he "should disclose the underlying matter to Mordy." Mattioli was caught off guard: Wasn't that Andy Lawler's job, not his? Mattioli got in touch with Lawler and put Carl Rubino on the line.

Rubino: "Where do things stand with Myron?"

Lawler: "I'm not in favor of Myron disclosing to Mordy just now."

He asked for a meeting on July 9 to "structure" the disclosure in such a way as to maintain the attorney-client privilege against all possible challenges.

The order of events was carefully scripted to unfold in the following sequence: (1) Reinhard would resign his directorship; (2) Myron would "tell all" to Singer Hutner; (3) Singer Hutner would tell Mordy. The big day of disclosure was set for July 21, early afternoon. Myron turned up, without Mordy. Mordy "had to attend to a medical problem," after which he was going out to California; between taking care of his medical problem and his business trips he was going to be all tied up. He also apparently had various undefined "obligations in Upstate New York." Myron asked for another extension, to give Mordy more time to "tie up loose ends." Putzel agreed that disclosing the fraud to Mordy so soon after treatment of the undisclosed "medical problem" might well distort Mordy's emotional reaction to the news. There was a risk of an overly "negative reaction . . . he might even do something irrational." Putzel had not yet met Mordy.

That afternoon, Lawler called Mattioli to discuss a list of questions concerning the impending disclosure:

1. What would the attitude of the firm be toward a "very general" statement by Myron as to the underlying situation? To what extent would the firm feel obligated to ask further questions?
2. What is the firm's position on the disposition of the Clifton letter? Will there be a demand by the firm for the letter? If the demand were refused, what action would the firm take?

Mattioli: "The firm would not find a "general statement" sufficient . . . The firm is actively seeking the letter and we consider it a crucial detail in any full disclosure."

As to the question of Myron's making a merely general statement, Hutner's response was much more specific: "Bullshit . . . and I made sure that was communicated directly to Lawler."

Lawler: "Well, I think Myron is being overly optimistic about being able to fulfill his obligation to tell the board."

The firm had been advised by Putzel that to issue new opinions of counsel on past fraudulent deals would constitute a new fraud. Singer Hutner was required to issue periodic "updates" on its opinions, certifying that the equipment on lease was still operating at the same location as specified in the lease documents and was unencumbered as of that date. Putzel advised that to issue such updates on past fraudulent deals would constitute a new form of fraud. Lawler had asked Alan Jacobs to prepare a list of all deals on which updated opinions were due, so that he could find out from Myron which deals were real, so at least the updates could be issued on those. But wily Myron had other ideas: he wanted updated opinions sent out on all deals, good and bad, reducing the chance that someone out there might start smelling a rat.

After the abortive "disclosure" meeting of July 21 broke up, Myron sat in his chair until everyone but Joe Hutner and Eli Mattioli had left. They refused to talk to him, and he got the message. That night, Myron called Mattioli at home.

"So what did you and Joe talk about after I left?"

"About that explosion in Murray Hill where all those people were killed."

"No, come on, I mean what did you talk about about this thing?"

"Myron, you have your own lawyer now. You deal with him on that. Don't worry about how you're being represented. If you want to know that, don't ask."

"Okay, okay, but listen: will you see to it that Alan gets out those updated opinions, right away?"

"Listen, Myron, I don't know why you're calling. I don't understand the purpose of this call at all. Talk to your lawyer, okay? I don't want another word."

"But listen, Eli, I've got to talk to you."

"This conversation is over."

Myron slammed down the receiver. Mattioli called Carl Rubino. Rubino said he'd bring these "pressure tactics" up with Putzel the following morning.

Myron: "They asked me to make a full disclosure. I said no. They threatened resignation but then they would back off because they didn't get paid yet." He says Joe Hutner "really stuck it" to him: "You pay the bill and we will continue representation. If you don't pay the bill we're not going to continue, we will resign right now." But Myron had an effective response prepared for that: "Not if you want me to pay you. You do that and you're not getting a penny." Myron: "That kept them in line."

Myron says his friend Andy Reinhard loyally kept him "abreast of the conversations they were having with Putzel . . . which attorneys were for what and against what."

Putzel: "By late July we had spent a lot of time putting gentle pressure on Goodman and Lawler to make a disclosure. And we were getting nowhere . . . It had been a month since the Dean and I had been retained . . . and we were within a week of my projected vacation and we had gone along for a period of time without disclosures and I was getting incredibly unhappy about the situation."

On July 22, Mattioli told the group about Myron's phone call of the night before. Hutner decided he was going to have to deliver an ultimatum. This charade had dragged on long enough. He was finally getting mad at Myron, and disenchanted with Lawler: "The nature of Lawler's questions for the first time suggested that Lawler's involvement, rather than being productive of prompt and full disclosure, might indeed have produced the opposite result." Hutner picked up the phone. It was early evening by then. Myron had been fasting due to some religious holiday and was in something of an emotional state even before he took Hutner's call.

Putzel: "There was the worst lightning and thunderstorm I have ever seen in New York over the East River . . . and it coincided with some of the most melodramatic aspects of the call . . . there was wild lightning and claps of thunder."

Hutner delivered his ultimatum: "If you don't tell Mordy Weissman by this coming Monday, I am going to call him and tell him myself."

Myron immediately lost control. "You are trying to drive a wedge between me and Mordy! You're trying to put me out of business! You're going to make me do something you'll never forget!" On and on and on.

Putzel: "Hutner was pleading with Goodman to be rational and Goodman was threatening Hutner and remonstrating that Hutner was trying to ruin him . . . He took it all very badly."

Hutner's voice suddenly, sharply shifted in tone: "Myron, please, don't say that . . . Myron, please, now, don't do that." Hutner turned to the group: "Myron is up on the windowsill."

Myron's office was nine stories above lower Broadway.

Myron: "I'm going to go out the window and I'm going to die and my blood is going to be on your hands!"

Hutner: "I couldn't help but get the feeling that the suicide threat was meant to be implemented forthwith."

Hutner kept trying to calm Myron down. Standing, sitting, stalking around, pleading, cajoling, scolding, soothing, trying desperately to make Myron see reason. Myron kept up the suicide threats, the death threats, every sort of threat he could think of. Joe Hutner finally backed down: Myron could have overnight to get ahold of himself and do some hard thinking about his future. The effect of Hutner's yielding was nearly miraculous. He went calm. He made sense. He kept quiet. He climbed down off the sill.

Steve Lichtman had been called to the scene by Myron's secretary, who was convinced Myron was really planning to do away with himself once and for all. Lichtman could hear Goodman screaming through the closed office door: "I am going to leave behind a letter that will send all of you at Singer Hutner to jail!"

To Lichtman, later, Myron explained his bizarre behavior, "I had to do something to keep those lawyers in their place."

25

Somehow, and for some reason, Myron had managed to persuade himself that Mordy knew nothing about Rockwell. He claims to have forgotten by July of 1980 Mordy's original work forging IBM invoices. He still believed "Mordy did not know about it. And I believed if he had known about it, he might not have gone along with it." More than once Mordy stumbled upon a fraud team emergency huddle called behind Myron's closed doors. But if Mordy ever so much as wondered what was going on, Myron would say, "You really don't want to know." Mordy would obligingly wander off, knowing not to ask any questions.

Mordy never once asked Myron about the Rockwell deals. He knew about the early terminations, the buy outs, the endless, enormous, and never-ending obligations of OPM. There were lists, and he had seen them. Myron would occasionally ask Mannes or Steve, "Where does Mordy think all this money's coming from?" But Mordy never came out with "Myron, where are we getting all this money?" No, he left well enough alone. He knew what was good for him. He wanted out anyway.

Now Myron had to tell Mordy. Or Joe Hutner would tell him. At least Myron wanted the privilege of telling his partner himself, in his own way. Myron preferred, if possible, to set his confessional scenes on airplanes, for privacy in midair. He and Mordy were booked on a California conference flight July 29. As usual, the discussion began on the plane and wound up in an airport lounge. Myron had a list prepared of all the bad deals to help him with the disclosure: "I had to make sure everything that had to be told to him was told to him . . . in the right way . . . to try and soften the blow . . . why I hadn't told him before."

Myron told Mordy he had something important to say. A certain item on the agenda he hadn't wanted to tell him about, but finally had to. He had financed from fifty to sixty million dollars worth of bad Rockwell leases. Myron waited patiently for Mordy to react, to yell, to cry, to lose his cool. But Mordy, under practically permanent emotional control, maintained his cool to the end.

"So?"

"So Joe Hutner tells me to make the disclosure at a board meeting next week."

"Why a board meeting?"

"Because you are the rest of the board of directors, and the board of directors has to be told."

Mordy displayed no anger, pity, or fear.

"No problem. I'll resign from the board. I don't have to know. I don't want to know. I want to resign anyway." They worked up a plan: they wouldn't say they had talked, Mordy would resign at the board meeting, Myron wouldn't have to talk, they would make a settlement, Mordy would leave OPM. At this point, Myron was willing to go along with just about anything. He says Andy Reinhard "knew exactly what was going to happen."

Andy: "Who knows, try it, maybe it'll work."

Myron: "This was a very depressing period . . . who knew anything anymore." Through it all, Mordy stood by him: "He wasn't angry at me, he was very sympathetic."

August 6, 1980: the conference room at Singer Hutner. Present: Myron, Mordy, Andy Lawler, Andy Reinhard, Joe Hutner, Eli Mattioli; Putzel was away on vacation. Mordy opened with an important announcement: he intended to sell his partnership interest in OPM to Myron; he would continue on for "an indefinite period of time as a marketing consultant." This should not imply any falling out with Myron; the final decision had been reached between them after long, hard deliberation. It had always been Mordy's personal plan to retire by age thirty-five. There were other things in life more important to him now than work, or OPM. He had decided to divorce himself from the company and devote himself to travel, family, relaxation, reflection. He and Myron had always disagreed on how to grow the company: Myron had wanted a big operation with a large staff while Mordy had been content to keep things small and spend more time with his family. This moving speech was interrupted by a message: an urgent personal "phone call" for Mordy. Mordy dashed out to take the "call," leaving behind an unbroken silence. He finally drifted back in, looking positively pained by the whole proceeding.

Joe Hutner resolved to treat all this as "little more than a charade" until he received evidence to the contrary.

"Be that as it may, the true purpose of this meeting is for Myron to make a disclosure." Reinhard conveniently broke in with a document to hand around: his resignation from the OPM board, effective immediately. Hutner had just begun his recitation of events leading up to this impasse, when Mordy interrupted.

"Why are you boring me with all this? Wait a minute. I don't understand. I'm telling you I'm selling my interest in this company. This matter is no concern to me. You're telling me I'm just going to sit here and listen to something that's going to make my stock in the company worthless?"

Hutner elected to ignore this comment. No matter what might take place in the future, as of this moment Mordy was still a member of the OPM board of directors, and thus entitled to a disclosure. Mordy did not leave the room. Hutner: "Mordy looked as if I was putting him to sleep. He didn't act like he cared what was being said or that he'd even heard it."

Hutner asked if Mordy would care to tell him what Myron had told him. Mordy: "No, Joe, why don't you tell me what you know?"

Hutner went into the old "After you, Alphonse," routine. He gave a brief recitation. Mordy looked terribly tired.

"Yeah, Joe, that's about it. So?"

"So, Myron, please proceed, and give us all the facts."

"I'm sorry, Joe. I'm not prepared to do so at this time."

"Myron, we have been waiting a long time for this meeting with the understanding that you were going to make to us a full disclosure. Will you please come forward and make one now?"

Myron: "Mordy has resigned from the board. Andy has resigned from the board. So now we don't have to have this meeting because I know what is happening."

Hutner repeated the firm's demands, reminded Myron of his commitments to the firm, urged Andy Lawler to urge Myron to keep his commitment. Hutner "looked beseechingly over at Andy Lawler . . . and got just a stony glance in return."

Hutner, Rubino, and Mattioli walked out of the meeting.

Rubino: "This is getting more and more difficult all the time."

Hutner: "Putzel is supposed to have some sort of relationship with Lawler . . . what in hell is going on?" It was hard to tell from Lawler's behavior when Myron was stonewalling whether Lawler had been expecting him to come forward or not. When Myron refused to say anything, Lawler had not looked very surprised.

Putzel was on vacation that first week in August. But he heard about the abortive board meeting.

Putzel: "A good deal of posturing was going on . . . it was very difficult to determine exactly what was the truth between Goodman and Weissman . . . there was a considerable feeling at the firm that Goodman was going along with a pre-arranged charade to insulate Weissman . . . I was deeply concerned that we had made no substantial progress . . . I certainly believed it was necessary to press onward with the demand for disclosure . . . We were trying to devise a strategy for getting this man to give us the information we needed to make ethical judgments."

In the meantime, Singer Hutner continued to close OPM deals on the bare basis of Myron's certificates.

26

Myron had plenty of problems on his hands: now it was Coopers & Lybrand. They had convened a special meeting for August 7 at OPM with Lou Moscarello, a Coopers partner named Tom Walther, Bob Lage, the engagement manager, and Joel Peck from Lehman Brothers. Myron was terrified they might have stumbled across something involving Rockwell; he didn't trust Marty Zelbow not to go snooping around sticking his nose into things that weren't any of his business.

Lou Moscarello opened the meeting by saying that a member of his management survey staff had come across a situation at OPM with which they were "extremely uncomfortable." Myron had brought Michael Weinberg, one of his senior in-house counsels, along to the meeting. Weinberg interrupted, stating OPM's position that whatever they might have uncovered would be more appropriately raised with Mr. Goodman "in private."

Moscarello: "Privacy is all very fine with me, but I feel duty bound to bring this matter to the attention of Lehman Brothers, and I'm going to tell Lehman Brothers whether you like it or not."

Goodman: "Well, alright then, I'm going to tell them myself." He positively "flew" into his inner office to call Alan Batkin.

Myron: "I'm here in my office with the Coopers' people and they've got some 'dramatic disclosure' they're planning to make. I don't want it done out in front of everybody. What should I do?"

Batkin: "Why don't you tell everyone except the Coopers'

people to step into your office so Lou Moscarello can tell you privately."

Myron: "Okay, that's really terrific."

Batkin: "Why don't you give me a call afterwards and tell me what the problem is."

Myron strode back out to issue a statement.

"I have given Coopers & Lybrand full access to all my books and records but this matter must remain confidential. I am the only person who will make the decision as to whether anything discussed in this room is to be passed on to Lehman Brothers, or to anyone else for that matter."

Joel Peck, Steve Kutz, and Andy Reinhard stepped into Myron's inner office while Lou Moscarello, Tom Walther, and Bob Lage stayed behind to confront Myron.

Moscarello: "I am making no specific allegation . . . we have not conducted an audit . . . but I am very uncomfortable with a certain situation we have uncovered and until I get a satisfactory explanation this engagement is going to have to be suspended."

Myron sat waiting, peering over the edge.

Moscarello related how a Coopers & Lybrand employee, not Marty Zelbow, had come across some ledger cards disclosing over five million dollars in unexplained "advances to shareholders" at a time when the company appeared to be on the brink of insolvency.

Myron could have kissed Moscarello. Shareholders advances? Five million dollars? He couldn't care less if Coopers resigned. He only cared if Lehman Brothers abandoned him because of it. Now he could lose Coopers once and for all. Now he could finally get rid of Marty Zelbow.

Myron: "What do you mean by uncomfortable?"

Moscarello: "I'm uncomfortable with the implication of preferential payments to shareholders from an insolvent company." He explained that Steve Kutz had predicted "a substantial loss" for the company as of year-end 1979. Michael Weinberg countered that as far as they knew, most of the money in question had gone to buying the FNJ bank. Moscarello said that was only seven out of ten million, which left three million over and unaccounted for.

Myron: "What do you mean by suspended?"

Moscarello: "We choose not to be associated with situations like this. Questions of improper withdrawals at a time when the company might very well have been insolvent . . . Unless you are able to come up with an explanation which will satisfy me, we will have to consider this engagement terminated."

Myron: "They didn't formally resign at that meeting. They said, 'If you want to do anything about the problem you get back to us. Otherwise we are not going to get back to you.'"

Myron had no intention of getting back to Coopers: "It was a blessing in disguise." Now he could forget about Coopers doing an audit. There would be time to spend looking for new accountants. Time he could put to good use.

When the Coopers people left, Myron stepped back into his inner office disguising a tremendous sense of relief. He started barking instructions to Steve Kutz, to the other members of his staff, that "this is what we are going to do . . . we are going to get detailed information to produce a response to this point they have raised." All this for the benefit of Lehman Brothers. Myron called Joe Hutner with the news; Joel Peck called Alan Batkin.

After the meeting, Moscarello also called Batkin.

"I don't like to be associated with this crap."

The withdrawals made by Myron and Mordy might well have been made in anticipation of bankruptcy.

"I just don't trust that guy."

Batkin tried to point out that Myron and Mordy were owners of their own business. It might have been prudent or imprudent, but they had a right to do it.

Moscarello: "Maybe they don't own their own business. Maybe the creditors own the business. This whole thing is beginning to smell like another Continental Vending."

In the 1960s, two senior C&L partners had been convicted of knowingly certifying false financial statements of Continental Vending Machine Corporation after an officer had withdrawn a good deal of cash from the company in anticipation of an imminent bankruptcy.

Batkin tried to point out some key differences between the two cases:

1. Coopers & Lybrand wasn't auditing OPM. They were doing a management survey.
2. The Continental Vending case had involved a sophisticated scheme to hide the improper withdrawals. In this case, there had been no attempt to conceal the officer's loans; they were reported right on the ledger cards where they could easily be found.

Moscarello admitted maybe it wasn't the same. But he just didn't want to work for Myron anymore. His confidence in the man, which had never amounted to much to begin with, had been seriously eroded.

Batkin asked if there was anything Myron could do to satisfy him. Moscarello thought for a moment.

"No, I don't think so. I really can't envision anything."

Moscarello did not tell Batkin that Nick Bluhm, the man who found the ledger cards, had written him a rather lengthy memo detailing the officer's loan problem but prefaced with a summation of certain suspicions along the lines earlier raised by Zelbow. Moscarello finally got the message. Now he had something more substantial to hold on to than pure speculation. A clearly improper act that gave him the excuse he needed to withdraw without offending Lehman Brothers.

Marty Zelbow had not been terribly shocked when Bluhm found those ledger cards. Five million dollars unaccounted for didn't seem like much compared to what he now suspected was going on. The day John Clifton resigned, Zelbow went down to Clifton's office to say good-bye. Clifton looked tired. He said he had been with the company a long time and had helped build it up to its present size, but now he wanted to be doing something else. Zelbow asked if his departure might have something to do with Rockwell leases.

Zelbow says Clifton responded: "In part."

Clifton says he didn't answer.

It didn't matter anymore. Zelbow could go home.

Myron still had to smooth things with Lehman Brothers. When Batkin informed the Lehman Brothers operating committee of C&L's discoveries, they directed him to perform an analysis of the shareholder's account. Myron obligingly trotted right over to Lehman Brothers with his ledger cards and books, determined to prove that of the approximately five-million-dollar increase in the account since year-end 1978, over three million had gone to buy the bank stock. Of the rest, OPM had been "very liquid" on the dates the other two million were withdrawn.

Nearly 1 million was attributable to Myron's and Mordy's "personal worth." The other 1.3 million was broken down as follows:

- $650,000 in a brokerage account at the firm of Herzog, Heine, Geduld
- $300,000 to purchase stock in the name of Lila Goodman
- $200,000 to a discretionary account at Drexel, Burnham, Lambert
- $100,000 charitable contribution to Yeshiva University
- $40,000 loan to Steve Lichtman, to buy a house
- $65,000 loan to Myron's sister, to buy a house

The rest of the money, about half a million, had gone into Myron's basement, to build a movie theater, discotheque, and ballet room for his daughters.

David Sacks: "There was a great deal of discussion at Lehman Brothers about how you spend $500,000 refurbishing a basement. No conclusion was reached."

The Lehman Brothers operating committee elected, once again, not to abandon OPM. They decided instead to suspend all placing of OPM debt until Myron found himself new accountants. Not simply to replace Coopers, but to do a full audit. They couldn't be just any accountants, but a reputable firm approved by Lehman Brothers.

Myron meekly agreed.

27

Now Myron needed new auditors or Lehman was leaving. Alan Batkin: "Unless we get new auditors in here right away and show them we're moving ahead, Lew is not going to be happy. We have to do our due diligence, Myron, don't ever forget about that. And we're not talking about six months from now, we're talking about right now."

Myron heard him and tried to reassure him: "Don't worry, we're talking to Ernst & Whinney." Myron's plan was to get Ernst & Whinney in, and get them lost in the utter confusion of OPM for a minimum of six to eight months. Pretending he wanted an audit as badly as Lehman Brothers did was "all just a delaying tactic to get Rockwell off the books." And Lehman off his back.

Myron's "apparent alacrity" in meeting Lehman's demand to retain a Big Eight accounting firm gave Joe Hutner a faint brief wisp of hope. Myron might even be on his way toward cleaning up his financially fouled nest. He could hardly consent to a new audit otherwise. But Myron's apparently cooperative attitude created new problems for Singer Hutner: Putzel advised that if new auditors were to be retained, it would be impossible for the firm to allow Myron to mislead them. If Myron did not reveal the facts to the auditors promptly after their retention, the firm would have an obligation to tell them. Putzel: "This audit cannot take place."

All through August, Myron continued to keep Singer Hutner in the dark as to the details of the fraud. Hutner was away on vacation from the seventh to the twentieth; Putzel was also away a good part of that time. The focus of disclosure had shifted from Myron's telling Mordy to Myron's telling Singer Hutner. Hutner would call Lawler, Lawler would call Myron, Myron would call Hutner and continue to stonewall. Hutner would press for "the facts"; Myron would pop back: "Alleged facts," or "facts if there are any facts." Hutner would get fed up: "Myron, please, just to shorten these discussions, just say 'facts' and you can have my word I'll read that as 'alleged facts.'" The situation might have been laughable if it were not so completely outrageous.

Hutner decided to retain Mendy Weissman as his "eyes and ears" to watch over Myron, to keep him honest. "If it appeared that Goodman was going to attempt to mislead the auditors he would be in a position to tell us what was happening." Retaining Mendy would keep "any information which came into his possession . . . privileged, because he would be acting as our agent." On September 4, Mendy went along with Joe Hutner to a meeting with Harry Manchar, a senior partner at Ernst & Whinney.

Hutner: "It was a very delicate thing. We had to make sure as long as we were still in there that a new auditor not be misled. On the other hand, we couldn't broach an attorney-client confidence . . . It was a nightmare . . . The whole thing was a nightmare . . . I was going crazy trying to figure out what to do." Mendy was not comfortable taking on this assignment to find out if Myron was telling the truth to his new auditors, but he did it all for Joe: "If Joe wants it, I'll do it."

When Joe said Myron was planning to retain Ernst & Whinney, Mendy couldn't help but think nothing good was going to come out of that, nothing but trouble for everyone. He was even more upset when at the meeting with Manchar nothing was said about the fraud, or even about the check kiting. Mendy felt downright embarrassed for Joe putting himself in such a position. He was particularly concerned that out of personal loyalty to Myron, Joe might go and let himself be used as a tool.

Harry Manchar's office was in the Citicorp Center on East Fifty-third. Joe could tell Mendy was bothered as they came down in the elevator. Mendy could tell Joe was upset, frustrated by the whole situation. Mendy felt bad for Joe. He purposefully led Joe over to sit down at one of the little marble tables in the atrium "out of the hearing of everybody."

"Joe, what are we doing?"

"What do you mean what are we doing?"

"Well you know, this is just terrible."

"I don't know what you're talking about."

"This whole thing, Joe. I mean, what do you think you're doing here? How can we lead a sweetheart like Harry Manchar into a goddam hornet's nest? What are we getting them involved in this thing for? Why don't we quit? Why don't you get out?"

Joe just sat there looking miserable. Mendy leaned forward and started to whisper.

"Joe, the problem is much larger than I ever thought . . . You know whatever it is Myron is still holding back on? I had a little talk a while back with Lichtman, and it's much, much worse than we thought."

"Lichtman knows about this?"

"Lichtman is in on it. And he asked me to guess how much was involved . . . So I said, 'How about ten million,' and he said, 'Keep going,' and I said, 'Twenty million,' and he said, 'More,' so I said, 'Thirty million,' and he said, 'No, you're not there yet.'"

Joe was looking a little pale.

"Holy shit."

"So now I assume you understand why we quit."

Hutner: "I did understand, in part."

Myron was in Boston. Hutner got hold of him right away and demanded a meeting that night. Myron kept telling himself flying home on the plane, "I have to tell him. I just have to tell him." But he kept trying to figure out some way to cop out of it. Myron knew it was either that or resignation. He couldn't cope yet without Singer Hutner.

Hutner met Myron at OPM.

Hutner: "Look, Myron. We have been after you for two months now to tell us what is going on. You know these new accountants are going to be engaged soon in this thing. Why don't you just let us know what this is all about, so we can figure out what to do."

Myron could see Hutner was "in terrible shape." Hutner told Myron "what a terrible dilemma this was and how they really hadn't figured out how to handle it." Hutner said they were all desperately hoping Manchar would turn down the job.

To Hutner, Myron seemed in a "semidrugged state" that night. He was "very rambling and slow, floating in and out . . . at times he was incoherent, but never really irrational . . . there were times when he got vaguer or slower but Myron was really a very sharp guy . . . A lot of people would have been happy with his level of slowness . . . He was more tired, worn out, than anything else." Punchy as he was, Myron finally came out with jagged bits and pieces of the crime. For the first time, he described the problem as "a fraud on the Rockwell leases." Myron had the distinct impression this was no news to Hutner.

Myron's outline was loose, rambling, disjointed, a sort of stream of consciousness. But as Hutner sat there listening to Myron unwind, he was finally able to fix an image of what went on over there. He gathered Myron had "induced Singer Hutner to transmit false financing documents to banks . . . and separate versions to Rockwell."

Joe: "Has it stopped?"

Myron: "Yes."

Joe: "Since June 12?" The date of the Clifton letter, Myron's partial confession.

Myron: "No, before that."

He pressed the point.

"Are you sure the firm has not been defrauded along with the others?"

Myron: "You know I wouldn't do that."

Hutner had little choice but to believe him. Hutner called Putzel. They arranged to meet for lunch at the Yale Club the next day. Hutner needed advice on what to do now, "saddled, not armed, with this new information."

Hutner sat with Putzel in the dining room overlooking Vanderbilt Avenue. He gave out his gleanings from Myron of the night before.

Hutner: "I can't imagine now why we didn't see it." He seemed "surprised at the simplicity and the obviousness of the thing."

Hutner now knew there was a fraud, that it was massive, that Myron had altered documents supplied to the firm. As far as he was concerned that was quite enough.

"I want to get the hell out. I'm disgusted and I want your acquiescence."

But it was not enough for Putzel. Putzel readily agreed that the firm had been used as "an unwitting and innocent instrument of the fraud." Resignation was therefore "permissible," perhaps even "desirable," maybe even "appropriate," but by no means "mandatory." As Putzel explained, it was unfortunately not altogether so easy to simply get the hell out. The firm's ethical obligation under Disciplinary Rule 2–110 (A) (2) was quite clear and persuasive:

> A lawyer shall not withdraw from employment until he has taken reasonable steps to avoid foreseeable prejudice to the rights of his client, including giving due notice . . . allowing time for employment of other counsel . . . delivering to the client all papers and property to which he is entitled.

And so on and so forth. In short, Singer Hutner could not just "drop Goodman like a sack of potatoes." Any withdrawal from OPM would have to be accomplished gradually, not precipitously. Putzel preferred to think of the process not so much as a blunt resignation, as more of a genteel "unwinding." The point was the firm could not "injure its client unnecessarily." OPM could not stay in business more than two days without a law firm to close its transactions. Neither Putzel nor Hutner was particularly eager for the firm to become "the proximate cause of the downfall of OPM." It was up to Singer Hutner to stick by OPM, until such time as Myron was able to effect an "orderly transition" to a new firm. In the meantime, Putzel agreed to contact Lawler to arrange for Myron to make an "orderly disclosure" of additional facts to the firm.

28

Myron spilled more beans the night of the ninth. To Hutner, Rubino, Reinhard, and Mattioli at Singer Hutner. He outlined the mechanics of the fraud: how they had altered documents by substituting new signature pages, and inflated lease terms and rentals so the banks would lend money based on false numbers. How when there was no lease at all, the lessees' signatures were simply forged on bogus lease documents requested from Singer Hutner, transmitted back to Singer Hutner, and presented at the closing with the bank. How they would alter documents "in the dead of night" and simply restaple the cover pages.

Joe: "Which lessees are involved?"

Myron: "Only Rockwell."

What about Rockwell's in-house counsel? Myron: it was easy to get signatures from Rockwell, they would "just walk the document through" on the West Coast. They would sign "just about anything" out there. Myron had them "bamboozled."

"Did Mordy know?"

"No."

"Anyone else?"

Under pressure, Myron named names: "Steve Lichtman, Mannes Friedman, Marty Shulman, Allen Ganz."

"Sid Hasin?"

Myron looked shocked.

"Sid doesn't know."

"Anyone at the banks?"

"No."

Joe wanted to know more about the banks. Which ones had

been hit. He was hoping not LaSalle National Bank, because Merle Bushkin, a private investment banker and a friend of his, had helped OPM find financing there. He was hoping not Philadelphia Saving Fund Society, because he had great respect for their counsel, a man by the name of Ralph Clover.

Hutner: "In both cases, my hopes were dashed."

Myron explained that OPM would make the lease payments directly to the banks on the "shortfall" between the real and fictitious versions of the leases. He estimated the amount of this "shortfall" at something like thirty million.

Could Myron conceivably make restitution?

Myron launched into a brief, and to Hutner, "patently unrealistic" accounting of how these losses could be covered in eighteen months or less.

Hutner: "Whatever it was . . . it was not an honestly held view."

Joe had no choice but to call him on it.

"Myron, I don't know much about your leases, but I know most of them are not shorter than four years. How can you say it can all be paid off in under two years if your leases are at least twice that long?"

Myron managed to look suitably crestfallen.

"You're right, Joe, it's true. I don't have any eighteen months leases, so you say it can't be done. But have faith, Joe, just have faith. I can do what I say."

Hutner did not want to hear any more of this gibberish. Myron kept it up for a while. Carl Rubino mercifully cut him off:

"Myron, get us a spread sheet."

Myron acted downright insulted.

"A spread sheet? You mean an accounting? I can't even do that on my good deals."

He looked around at his old friends, incredulously. They weren't buying his act anymore.

"Okay, okay." He relented. "I'll get you one in a couple of days."

Myron limped out on his cane. He had broken his leg playing softball, and the bones were not mending well. Hutner said something about calling Putzel. Mattioli looked down at his watch: nine o'clock. He took a quick look down the hallway. Myron was gone.

Mattioli: "Well, he did seem a little contrite."

September 10: Rockwell/OPM 0–42–82 was closed by a Singer Hutner associate at the Crocker Bank in San Francisco. Assisted telephonically by Andrew Reinhard in New York. The transaction was utterly fraudulent; no third-party verification. The Singer Hutner associate in San Francisco was not aware of the revelations of the night before.

A full partnership meeting was held on the fifteenth. On the agenda: What to do now? Hutner came out roundly for resignation; enough was enough. Putzel repeated his view that although the firm was fully entitled to resign, it had to do so "in a manner least likely to inflict injury upon the client."

Henry Singer wanted to know "whether or not under the circumstances we don't have the option to blow the whistle on Myron."

Putzel: "You absolutely may not . . . the rules on attorney-client privilege specifically bar us from speaking to third parties."

Howard Chase: "Given the state of the firm's awareness, isn't it time to just go down to the authorities? What can possibly happen to us if we do that? How can that be wrong?"

Putzel: "You have to understand, this information is privileged . . . it cannot be disclosed except to prevent a future fraud."

Mort Levine: "Why isn't it fraudulent . . . to continue as counsel to OPM?"

Putzel argued that it would not be fraudulent to continue the representation. In fact, it could even be argued that as long as OPM was making lease payments on the bad loans, that some form of "restitution" was in fact being made. To resign abruptly would put a halt to that payback, put OPM out of business, and ensure that the banks would never see any more of their money.

While they were debating the issue of alerting new auditors, a call came in from Harry Manchar as if on cue. To Hutner's intense relief, Manchar explained he felt he had to turn down the engagement not because of the fraud, but because of the check kiting. Hutner hadn't mentioned it at their meeting; Manchar had wormed it out of Lehman Brothers. Hutner walked back into the meeting stunned at Myron's continuing good fortune: "Myron has gone and done it again. He's dodged another speeding bullet." Myron was beginning to look impregnable. If not quite a sinister Superman, at least a latter-day Lex Luthor.

What Hutner didn't know was that Mendy Weissman had headed them off at the pass. On his own recognizance he had approached Harry Manchar, and told him that OPM had been Rashba & Pokart's largest account and that they had been forced to resign in April. He didn't need to say any more; Manchar and his partners got the message. The check kiting provided the proper excuse. Mendy had saved Manchar from the hornet's nest just in the nick of time.

Myron showed up late with Andy Lawler. Without a spread sheet, but with a smooth assurance that "a list is being prepared." Hutner still wanted the Clifton letter. Lawler promised to get it. Hutner wanted "all the facts." Myron responded "cryptically": "You substantially have all the facts." In what struck Hutner as "a final fling of chutzpah," Myron tried to claim that "the thievery was not going to have an adverse effect on his financial statements." Because "we haven't booked the phoney assets, we've only booked them as liabilities." Hutner: "Some cockeyed thing like that."

A question arose as to whether an "early revelation . . . might result in some leniency from the U.S. attorney." Lawler was "inclined to resist an early revelation" on the grounds that there would be little to be gained by it. An "early revelation" would inevitably result in an early bankruptcy. As long as Myron stayed in business and out of jail, there was still some faint glimmer of hope he could "make good on his debts."

Andy Reinhard: "Myron has succeeded before in the face of dire financial circumstances."

Hutner, Rubino, and Mattioli voiced their contrary belief:

"The writing is on the wall for Myron." It was looking a little late for miracles, even for Myron the Magician.

Putzel reiterated his view that there was still no "compelling" reason for the firm to resign. If Myron continued to comply with the firm's demands for a complete disclosure, including a detailed accounting of each phoney transaction, there was as yet no "ethical obligation to withdraw." But Putzel did finally advise the firm to cease relying on Goodman's certificates. They must insist from now on on "third-party verification" of leases.

Putzel: "The firm should continue only on such terms as we believe absolutely adequate to prevent further frauds."

Hutner: "Verification is the best way to make sure any further deals will not be tainted with fraud."

Rockwell E.S. 0–52–80 was due to close in four days. Eli Mattioli called Myron to tell him that the firm could not proceed without verification of key terms with Rockwell.

Myron: "That's impossible, you can't do that!"

Myron resisted, insisting such verification would undercut his credibility, look like his own lawyers didn't trust their largest client, lead to a public discovery of the fraud, force him out of business, ensure that the money would never be paid back.

Myron: "Well now you and Mr. Putzel have held this thing up so long it doesn't even make sense to think about it anymore. It's too late to get the deal closed on time anyway. You've done real well."

Mattioli took this as a peculiar means of relenting. Singer Hutner prepared a one-page verification form. Andy Reinhard prepared a cover letter instructing Sid Hasin to sign the form, telecopy it back to Singer Hutner for the closing, and mail the signed original back to him immediately.

Myron, Mordy, Steve Lichtman, and Mannes Friedman were all in Chicago on the eighteenth. Myron called Andy Reinhard on the speakerphone. Myron couldn't talk on a regular phone because he "only had one ear and that would create pain." Andy created a much bigger pain by saying he'd already sent the confirmation form out to Sid Hasin.

Mordy came rushing into Myron's room, wanting to know if

Myron was all right. No, Myron was not all right: he was going bananas. Mordy tried to get Myron to calm down, without success. Myron was acting like the roof had fallen in. Mordy knew enough not to ask why.

Myron hadn't told Andy this was a bad one. Myron: "Andy didn't want to know about the fraud. I only told him when there was no alternative but to bring it out to him. If I would have told him every fraud I would have had bigger problems."

Myron did manage to browbeat Reinhard into telling him the letter had been airfreighted out to Rockwell by night courier. He even got the name of the courier service: Bor-Air. Myron didn't have much time. He dispatched Lichtman and Friedman out to California that night, with orders to intercept the letter at all cost the next morning. Mannes and Steve turned up at Seal Beach well before Rockwell opened for business. They didn't have long to wait. As if on cue the courier walked into the lobby to give the letter to the security guard, who would ordinarily have it sent right up to Sid. This time he rang up Sid's office, probably because the letter was marked "Confidential." Sid's secretary came down to pick up the letter. Mannes and Steve looked at each other. Lichtman did most of the talking.

"We asked Singer Hutner to send us some material and we didn't know what hotel we were staying at. So we asked them to send it out care of Sid. It's very important we get it immediately because we have to get right back to Myron."

She looked at the letter, addressed to Sid Hasin. She looked at Mannes and Steve. She shrugged and gave the courier permission to hand over the letter to the nice boys from OPM. While Lichtman drifted upstairs to engage Sid in a conversation on his favorite subject, the best place for lunch, Friedman forged Hasin's signature on the verification form, snuck into Rockwell's telecopy room, and telecopied the form back to Reinhard.

They still had the original, which had to be mailed back to New York. Friedman forged Hasin's signature one last time, and together they rode out to the airport. They had to mail the letter from L.A. or else it would look pretty suspicious. They decided to mail it from a box at the airport just as they got on the plane. They were petrified: the whole caper had the ominous look of a Myron-hatched plot to get the two of them implicated in the fraud. By going out to Rockwell without Myron, by sending Singer Hutner a letter that would live on in their files forever, they were leaving a paper trail that could be easily traced back to them. Myron had sworn up and down he'd take the rap for everyone if any of this ever came out. But even Myron would have a hard time explaining this last deception as solely his handiwork.

They stood by the mailbox in a state of anxiety. They were in this thing together. There wasn't much left they could do about it. Each held a corner of the letter as they jointly dropped it into the box.

29

Lehman Brothers was leaving. Not because of the fraud, but because of the cause of the fraud. OPM was dying, and Lehman Brothers didn't want to be around after the fall.

In 1978 the headache of OPM had been a bargain. OPM had been looking for financing on long-term leases, typically six to eight years, which involved the placement of long-term debt in the three- and four-million-dollar range. By 1980 the average lease had shrunk to under four years; the average deal had retracted to under a million. Which meant more work for less money, which meant bond salesmen and traders were no longer eager to keep pushing OPM deals. As if that wasn't enough, OPM demanded an inordinate amount of unpaid financial advice; Lehman Brothers began to see itself as running a runaway company for an irresponsible, tyrannical child; there was the check kiting incident and now all this inexcusable stalling on the audit. For the fees they were now pulling in, it all just didn't seem worth it.

Lew Glucksman: "The business was getting smaller. The deals were getting smaller. The amount of time, the endless time, all these conversations . . . When we talked of who said what to whom . . . I do not like to get involved this much. My time is valuable. I didn't want to get involved and have to call this guy and that guy . . . the clock was running out."

Glucksman felt bad for Myron. He didn't want to "leave him in the lurch": "So I began to explore some method or find someone who could handle the work for him because I thought that was the decent, honorable thing to do . . . So I wouldn't have all the aggravation and we wouldn't have all the aggravation of the calls and everything going back and forth." Glucksman thought he knew just the man for the job: a former Lehman partner just setting himself up as a consultant, who had at one time been active in lease financing. It looked to Glucksman like "an ideal way to help [him] get started and to supply very professional services to Goodman."

Myron had other ideas. Since the beginning of the year, in anticipation of a possible Lehman pullout, Myron had been financing deals through a private investment banker, Merle Bushkin, an old friend of Joe Hutner's. Hutner and Bushkin had lived in adjacent apartments in White Plains in 1960. Hutner: "Bushkin was a one-man band . . . he had ingratiated himself with Goodman by placing ten or twelve million in deals with LaSalle National Bank practically overnight." This one-man band was going to be Myron's replacement for Lehman Brothers, if Myron had anything to say about it.

On September 16, Alan Batkin called Myron to report that the Lehman Brothers operating committee had voted to resign by the end of the month unless new auditors had been engaged by then. That was the end of the line for Myron; he'd rather lose Lehman Brothers than face the risk of an audit right now. On the eighteenth, Myron called Joe Hutner "in a highly emotional state" to ask him to meet with Bushkin in Chicago.

This threw Singer Hutner into a tizzy. Here Myron was asking Joe Hutner to meet with his old friend Merle Bushkin to place debt on financings Hutner knew full well might be fraudulent. For a week Hutner had known Myron had placed a fraudulent Rockwell transaction through Bushkin: LaSalle National Bank, closed May 16, 1980, for $1,820,674. Now Myron was proposing Bushkin take over for Lehman Brothers. Myron's desperate request put Hutner in a lousy position.

Putzel: "You cannot under any circumstances . . . apprise Bushkin of what you know . . . At the same time, you may not, under any circumstances, allow Myron to actively mislead Bushkin at that meeting."

Hutner: "If Myron is going to say something deceptive to

Bushkin, I am going to have an obligation, or at least a right I intend to exercise, to call my client a liar to his own face."

Putzel: "I'd rather you didn't do it."

Hutner: "I'm not terribly pleased by the prospect myself."

Against the advice of counsel, and with enormous misgivings, Hutner decided to go. He told Eli Mattioli: "Myron sounded so distressed over the phone . . . so out of control . . . so desperately needing someone to hold his hand at the meeting." He felt it impossible to turn him down, out of "humane considerations" more than anything else.

Hutner: "I didn't want to be there . . . I was very conflicted about it . . . It made me uncomfortable and I resented it. On the other hand, I had been put on notice Myron was going to be there and I didn't want him misleading Bushkin . . . The lesser of two evils was to go out there . . . my main worry was that Goodman was going to get his hooks into Bushkin." He had a pretty fair idea where that might lead, having been there himself.

The night before the meeting with Bushkin, Hutner called Myron at his Chicago hotel.

Joe: "You're taking a big risk having this meeting with Merle . . . if you say anything I think is misleading I'm going to have to point it out."

Myron: "Don't worry about it. You won't have to do anything. All you have to do is sit there . . . You won't have to say a thing."

Hutner: "Putzel and I worked out a script . . . We decided it would be better if I didn't speak . . . but rather I would tell Myron what would be permissible to say and what not . . . I told Myron what he could say and what he couldn't say . . . But then Myron didn't follow the script . . . he was smarter than Putzel and me put together."

The meeting took place in Myron's limousine, between the Marriott Hotel O'Hare and LaSalle National Bank. The script called for Myron to do all the talking, and for Hutner to stop him, correct him, edit him, revise him, if he went astray. But the meeting began with Myron turning innocently to Hutner, asking him to give Bushkin a recitation of recent events.

Hutner: "Myron outfoxed me. I was miffed. As meticulously as I could I gave out what I thought of as unprivileged material."

Hutner took notes of the meeting a few hours later, on the plane home:

> OPM and Lehman Brothers are about to part company as a result of demands Lehman has made . . . that it hire auditors who would do a two-year audit . . . and communicate freely with Lehman during the course of their work.
> I traced the hiring of Cooper's and Cooper's quitting because it felt 1.7 million in officer's loans might have constituted a bleeding of OPM when insolvent . . . I reported the comment of a Cooper's partner . . . that he "didn't trust" Myron.
> I reported that Ernst & Whinney . . . had backed off because of "bad public relations" with respect to the New Orleans plea bargain.

Bushkin recalls Hutner's "meticulous" debriefing quite differently: Lehman Brothers was leaving because OPM had not met certain conditions, but the conditions were not mentioned; Coopers had left not because Myron might have been "bleeding the company while insolvent" but because of "personality clashes" between Myron and the Coopers partner-in-charge; a "major accounting firm" had decided against performing an audit, but he recalls no particular mention of Ernst & Whinney.

Bushkin subsequently arranged debt financings on two bogus OPM/Rockwell transactions for a total of $4,353,674 with LaSalle National Bank.

While Myron was coaxing Hutner to help him bag Bushkin, the fraud was beginning to falter.

September 18: Robert L. Clare III of White & Case, representing Bankers Trust Company, wrote a letter to Alan Jacobs of Singer Hutner, wondering why OPM was paying a number of banks directly on several Rockwell leases, when the closing documentation explicitly stated that Rockwell render lease payments directly to the financing institutions in question. Clare politely inquired as to the reason for this discrepancy, and suggested that if the practice were to continue Singer Hutner should consider obtaining formal consent from the financing banks.

On September 22, the Singer Hutner partnership met to discuss resignation. Jacobs showed Putzel his disturbing letter from Clare; Hutner brought up his traumatic meeting with Bushkin. Both situations pointed up the increasing difficulty of trying to represent their client's best interests while protecting its confidences. Putzel advised once again that Singer Hutner could not allow Myron to mislead innocent third parties, or mislead any third parties themselves. But under no other circumstance could the firm possibly compromise the attorney-client privilege. Reconciling the two dictates was not turning out to be easy.

Putzel advised Jacobs to ignore the letter from Clare, for now. If Clare called to follow up, he was to say he could not discuss the matter. If Clare asked why he could not discuss the matter, Jacobs would just have to say he could not discuss the reasons why he could not discuss the matter.

Putzel: "The position of the firm should be not to respond and not to say why it can't respond."

Continuing to represent OPM in full knowledge of the fraud was becoming embarrassing, dangerous, awkward, and unbelievably time-consuming for Singer Hutner. With all partners present, the firm voted unanimously to resign. As the issue was so clearly critical to the firm, they agreed to hold a second and final vote the following morning.

30

September 23, 1980, 8:45 P.M. With all partners present, the firm voted again in favor of withdrawal. Reinhard tried to abstain. Hutner insisted the vote be unanimous. Reinhard changed his vote to a reluctant "in favor," expressing a desire to give Myron "an adequate time period" in which to retain new counsel. Pending deals should, above all, not be threatened. Putzel readily concurred, citing Disclosure Rule 2–110: "Obligation of a lawyer not to withdraw from representation in a way that will cause unnecessary harm to his client."

Myron turned up promptly at noon for news of the verdict. He knew the firm had resolved to resign once already, but they had not yet let him go into limbo. They kept telling him they were waiting for a "fuller disclosure" but he didn't quite buy it. Myron: "They were playing good guys so they would get paid the rest of their money . . . that seemed to be a prime concern . . . all this 'unwinding' was supposed to be because we were nice guys and they were nice guys." Myron knew these guys a bit better than that.

Myron was still all worked up over Singer Hutner's "abandonment." He did what he had to do: he stayed up all night, on all sorts of painkillers, writing an eleven-page double-spaced letter. It was rambling, emotional, vindictive, pleading, threatening, bitter, and utterly heartfelt. He hid the letter in his pocket at first, waiting for the right time to let fly with his parting shot.

Hutner took him aside to tell him the bad news: "Having decided we wanted out . . . we want to get out as fast as possible . . . if the house of cards is going to collapse . . . we want as much distance between us and you as possible." Myron could hardly argue with that; he was telling it straight from the hip. But Myron did not respond directly to Hutner. He waited for Reinhard and the other partners to join them, and launched into his soliloquy: "It appears the time is right for me to review . . . certain matters and problems which I feel either the firm or OPM must resolve so we can move forward in a productive manner . . . and maintain the relationship which commenced approximately ten years ago with a telephone call to my dear friend, Andrew B. Reinhard."

The partners glanced around nervously at one another; he was sounding like an after-dinner speaker at a testimonial dinner. With all his lavish gifts to charity, Myron had attended more than his share. "As you know, contrary to the belief of one or two of the firm's members, I am a sincere and dedicated individual. My only basic requirement from a professional relationship is that I be treated fairly, professionally, and a mutual personal relationship develops . . . Most of you know me to be fair and generous with people I develop a close personal bond with . . . However, that close and personal bonding can only remain solidified if both ends of the bookends feel that the bond is true, sincere, and not false."

Here Myron paused solemnly, as if waiting for a smattering of applause. With none forthcoming, he plunged on into stormier subjects: "I will not allow, subject to forces beyond my control, that relationship to become unbound because of problems and/or matters which if reasonable individuals sit down and discuss, and discuss, and discuss, as an infinite item, it can be resolved."

He didn't have to look right at Joel Hasen and Howard Chase during the next item. "Never once have I not defended the firm when outsiders have taken potshots at the firm in general or individuals specifically . . . Sadly, I cannot say the same for every partner at Singer Hutner . . . More than once have I been informed by reliable sources, who have absolutely nothing to be gained by creating fictitious matters, that at least one if not more than one members of the firm have made derogatory remarks about myself and the future of OPM."

He widened his remarks to encompass the partnership as a

whole: "I would think that the firm could act in a much more discreet matter when it comes to protecting its own ass . . . at least have the courtesy of not acting without thinking . . . I do not want to see another John Clifton, Hoby Shapiro, or Lehman Brothers . . ."

The mild after-dinner remarks were turning rancorous. He continued to fulminate against those who had dared to betray him, to deny him the fealty to which he was personally due: "On a more personal note (I know you are wondering what everything above was) I feel deep down with many hours of thought behind it . . . that an individual or individuals who never heard of OPM, who never heard of the leasing business, who did not even try to understand the relationship which exists between OPM and Singer Hutner, who are obviously 'white-shoed and ultrafascist attorneys,' should not be in a position to determine the future of OPM and Singer Hutner."

He didn't have to roast Putzel and McLaughlin by name. But his bitterness could blast only so long before wallowing back into bathos: "Sometimes in one's life, we must put aside 'the book,' and look deep into each one of our souls, and determine what is proper in a given situation, irrespective of 'the book' . . . Maybe I should have looked out for myself rather than other people. I didn't. Whether that is good or bad, G-D only knows . . . There is no question in my mind that your counsel is representing you 'by the book.' Let me just say, that I thought a little 'bending of the book' might be appropriate in this matter. Especially when I did what I did (if I did anything so terrible) because of other people . . . and Singer Hutner was one of those persons, or more appropriately, firms."

Hutner: "Perhaps he had a paperback in mind."

There was a silence. A general intake of breath. Was Myron going to be done before dinner? Myron still had the floor, and was not one to take verbal shortcuts: "We have come a long way together. Through the ups and downs of the American business community . . . To break 'the bondage of the bookends' now would be a disgrace, and would lead to a personal depression by I am sure the majority of the firm and myself. Let us not allow this to happen. Remember, the reason OPM grew to where it is today is because of the blood, sweat, and a lot of tears . . . It would be a disgrace, a shame, and sinful, if we do not act on these matters and others . . . to resolve in our minds that we will either be kept bonded as bookends or sever our relationship . . . It would be very, very sad for me to have to ask Singer Hutner to resign."

Joe Hutner broke the long silence: "Can I have a Gelusil break please?"

Carl Rubino sat there sadly shaking his head, a disillusioned father finally forced to give up on an errant son.

"Myron, since money is tight. Save yourself the cost of a stamp. Don't bother sending that letter."

The partnership meeting broke briefly for dinner and reconvened after eight. The vote was taken one more time, to resign. Hutner told Goodman the firm would send him an official termination letter the next day. "We will thereafter continue to think of any alternative whereby we might resume." Myron nodded sadly. The bondage of the bookends was broken. For now. Myron never said never.

Goodman, Hutner, Rubino, and Mattioli walked out of the conference room straight down the hall. A spiral staircase wound down from the second floor library to the reception area below. Myron halted at the top of the staircase. The group stopped short behind him. Myron turned on them, suddenly savage, a foul look crossing his face. Raising his cane, he let out a high, strained howl:

"If you do this and bring down this company I will bring down this firm! You can't do this to my grandmother and my parents! I will bring down this firm!"

Myron was trembling. He held the cane high in his hand. The staircase was carpeted but the floor below was paved in stone. With all his strength he hurled the cane down; it broke into two on the floor.

The partners stood their ground in a stunned circle. Myron ran down the stairs. He flung open the door to Andy Reinhard's room and dashed inside, as if for somewhere to hide. Mattioli and Rubino ducked into Alan Jacobs' room, just down the hall. And Reinhard dashed after Myron. Mattioli was shocked to see

Mordy Weissman standing silently in the doorway to Reinhard's room. When had Mordy come in? Why was he here? It was like seeing a ghost.

Rubino took a seat in Jacobs' office. Mattioli sat down. Rubino: "Well, let's just see if they need us for anything." Mattioli could hear Myron shouting at Andy, on and on, louder and louder, berating him at one point for his "association with reformed Jews." After a while, Andy came in, looking like he'd fallen down five flights of stairs. Andy said Myron had been saying "all sorts of insane things." Andy sat still for a minute, collecting his thoughts, and finally let out a sigh: "I've got to go back there," he looked just a little afraid. Myron was clearly a very sick man.

Mordy came in, looking bashful, withdrawn, his usual shadowy self. He gave out an odd little shrug: "There must have been a lot of meetings around here these last couple of days." He let out a chuckle. It was all "so terribly ironic," he said, OPM's business had never been better. Its prospects were so excellent: "I've been working on some very rich deals," he said. The lawyers could not do more than look at each other: Was this the same OPM Myron was running straight into the ground?

Mordy went on, encouraged by their lack of response: it was all "highly ironic" to him that he should come in here to find Myron in such a state of emotional collapse while business was booming so phenomenally. More than anything else he needed a functioning Myron to help him keep the show on the road. The main object in his mind at this moment was to do whatever he had to do to keep Myron on the beam. He kept reciting, by name, a whole slew of "rich deals" he had on the burner, as if by some magic incantation he could make all the rich deals come true.

Mordy left as he came in: like a shade, or some apparition. Andy came back, looking subdued. "They're going to be leaving soon," he said in a sort of stage whisper. Mordy appeared in the open doorway, with Myron leaning against the doorframe beside him. Myron seemed to be under sedation. He was just barely able to stand. The two of them stared vacantly into the room. Mordy held Myron up by the shoulder, speaking softly, as if to himself:

"I'm worried about him. I'm taking him home."

31

Singer Hutner might have decided to quit, but that didn't mean they were through. The painful process of "unwinding" still had to begin, which would last until Myron replaced them. The terms of resignation still had to be worked out, and more important, the language of disclosing the split to third parties had to be settled. Myron had not yet come through with his "spread sheet." Singer Hutner had not yet been paid.

The lawyers met late in the afternoon on September 25. They made a belated decision to get tough. Concerned Myron might still try to stiff them, they decided to demand a retainer for continuing work and prompt payment for past services rendered. Not willing to be put off by anything less than a full accounting, they would refuse to go on "unwinding" without it. If Myron was going to permit verification on all future deals, they were going to have to demand confirmation letters be sent out before any closings went forward. Andy Reinhard was assigned the thankless job of "grabbing Myron" after Temple on Saturday night to prepare him for the new dispensation.

According to Myron, things weren't quite as tough as they sounded. The immediate issue was to set the terms of resignation, and the reasons given out for the split. Myron: "Putzel wanted 'resignation.' I wanted 'agreement.' Singer Hutner wanted 'mutual determination to terminate the relationship.'" Myron claims Putzel was pushing for resignation because "he was to the right of fascist . . . he wanted everything to be totally against the relationship between OPM and Singer Hutner . . . Singer Hutner was leaning to the left of center, in favor of me, in favor of OPM." Myron held on to the only trump card he had left for all it was worth: "Singer Hutner wanted to make things as easy as possible on OPM because they wanted to get paid . . . if they had been at all hard they never would have got paid." Being soft meant basically being agreeable: the termination would be "mutually agreeable"; they would refuse to discuss the reasons for the split with third parties; they would continue to close deals until he found successor counsel. Business as usual, with a clear end in sight; that was Myron's idea of "unwinding."

Singer Hutner hand-delivered two letters implementing the new "get tough" policy to Myron's house on Saturday, September 27. One letter demanded $500,000 no later than Monday, for past unpaid and future services rendered during the transition period. The other letter demanded that Myron permit "immediate and independent verification from third parties" on all deals closed during the transition period, defined as sixty-five days. The letter contained a list of all transactions due to close during that time, along with a number of deals on which update opinions were due. The list included seven bad Rockwell deals financed over the summer.

Myron magnanimously wrote back to Reinhard ("the only person I still recognized at that firm"): "In the spirit of cooperation and for the benefit of OPM I authorize you to verify leases . . ." with the notable exception of the seven bad Rockwell deals. Coyly, he added: "I have not included the entire listing . . . I want to thoroughly think through whatever ramifications there might be, as relate to specific lessees . . . I was led to believe this would be a one-shot verification . . . true, there were murmurs and rumblings about independent verification, but formally there was never any such request made." Independent verification would certainly not mean very much if Myron kept calling the shots.

There was still the outstanding matter of the "spread sheet." At various times Myron says he had considered giving the firm an incomplete accounting, but Andy Reinhard had advised he had might as well "give it to them all at one time." The moment of reckoning had finally arrived: the firm was not going to play ball anymore without it. But Myron couldn't resist holding out to the end, stringing them out to the limit. It wasn't so much a question of handing them a total as letting them know he had been lying to them for over three months. The fraud had not stopped in June. It had been going ahead full speed all summer. He had no idea what this revelation might do to his formerly airtight privilege. He was just going to have to find out.

Monday, September 29: Myron was driven uptown to Singer Hutner in the late afternoon, ostensibly packing his "Blue Book" of all the bad deals. He brought along his Bible instead, which he had decided might make better reading. Thursday, September 25 had marked the commencement of Sukkoth, the Feast of the Tabernacles, the traditional Jewish ceremony in celebration of the fruits of the harvest.

Myron opened the meeting by reminding the group that he was "observing the religious season." He thought it only appropriate to read them certain selections from Ecclesiastes, which is customarily read during Sukkoth. The lesson for today, which he intended to support with elaborate scriptural allusion, would be: "Sometimes the legitimate purposes of a man's activities are not apparent to those around him . . . at such times the people about such an individual must have faith in the legitimacy of his purposes."

Myron was thirty-five years old, deaf in one ear, afflicted with tunnel vision, walking with a cane, suffering constant pain from twin pacemakers alleviated only by massive doses of painkillers. In Ecclesiastes, the aging King Solomon reflects on a long life dedicated to toil and pleasure, wisdom and foolishness, profit and loss, youth and age, and despairs of ever finding his way toward God through a world shrouded in fog, rife with inequity, full of folly, wracked by confusion. Where fools prosper and poor wise men are "despised and their words are not heard." Where good and evil are indistinguishable in the gathering darkness.

> Who is as the wise man? and who knoweth the interpretation of a thing? . . . For who knoweth what is good for a man in this life, all the days of his vain life

which he spendeth as a shadow? for who can tell a man what shall be after him under the sun?

The dying king is forced to conclude:

> I have seen all the works that are done under the sun; and, behold, all is vanity and vexation . . . Then I looked on all the works that my hands had wrought, and on the labour that I had laboured to do: and, behold, all was vanity and vexation of spirit, and there was no profit under the sun.

A man is only as good as the spirit of his time:

> For man also knoweth not his time: as the fishes that are taken in an evil net, and as the birds that are caught in the snare; so are the sons of men snared in an evil time, when it falleth suddenly upon them.

The ways of men cannot be judged by men, but only by God:

> For there is not a just man upon earth, that doeth good, and sinneth not . . . Lo, this only have I found, that God hath made man upright; but they have sought out many inventions . . . For God shall bring every work into judgment, with every secret thing, whether it be good, or whether it be evil.

Myron closed his reading with a high-powered pitch for their understanding, and a promise that if the firm would just stick by him a little longer, he would be able to make "full restitution."

Jay Seeman: "Where is the spread sheet? When are we going to see it?"

Myron: "It's coming, it's coming. Don't worry. I'll have it by tomorrow. Everything takes time."

"Well, at this point, can you at least give us some more definite idea of the amounts involved?"

"Well, I'd have to say, in the range of eighty to ninety million."

Seeman: "Could it be more than that, Myron?"

Myron: "I don't think so . . . I'll know by tomorrow."

Hutner: "Myron, I think you'd better start looking for new counsel."

Myron: "Well, whether it's logical or not, Mordy and I have concluded we'd like to stay with Singer Hutner for now."

Hutner: "On that I'd have to agree with you, Myron. It is illogical."

September 30, 1980: the time of reckoning was now at hand. Henry Singer, the firm's financial expert, was to perform the cross-exam. Myron came at last, armed with his notorious Blue Book, updated monthly by Steve Lichtman and Mannes Friedman so that anytime Myron would know the total figure he owed. Myron carried a reduced photocopy version of the Blue Book everywhere he went, which he viewed as a sign of his intention to pay his illicit debts.

Ecclesiastes 5:5: "Better is it that thou shouldest not vow, than that thou shouldest vow and not pay."

Myron had reason to be anxious about Henry Singer's Spanish Inquisition: "Henry was a born fascist." He was not only a fascist, he was a fascist with a head for numbers: "What Henry had in his pinky about accounting I didn't have in my entire head." Singer had always been one to see through the "purported to be accurate" accounting methods used by OPM: "He understood it was all a sham." Singer had never had much in the way of illusions as to soundness of the Kutz method: "He knew what it was—basically a device." Singer had always urged Myron to "take in his income on a conservative basis and see what the true values were." In spite of Henry's natural skepticism, Myron always felt Singer retained a certain faith in his ability to pull through: "He always argued against my optimism but the bottom line was that he believed me . . . because there was nothing else really to do but believe me."

Now Myron handed his interrogator two blue folders, with documents bunched together in three groups: "Bridges to Nowhere," "No Underlying Lease," "Altered Leases."

Singer: "How much is the monthly debt service on all your bad deals?"

Myron took a wild stab: "$2.5 million, give or take a few hundred thousand."

He neglected to mention an additional $25 million he would need to repay bad bridges coming due in less than three months.

Myron insisted he would be writing twenty-five good deals a month in the next year, which would generate $15 million a month, based on an estimate of 3 percent positive cash flow on total equipment cost. Singer knew enough about OPM deals to dismiss this claim as absurd. Myron further claimed he would be closing $40 million worth of new deals in the month of October. Under duress, he grudgingly conceded he owed $800,000 a month on the Rockwell sublease agreement, $500,000 a month on early terminations, $150,000 debt service on the FNJ bank loan, $500,000 general costs, and $400,000 in equipment maintenance. To offset that, he estimated that OPM Europe should bring in monthly revenues of $415,000 along with another $2 million from leases of used peripherals. The actual fact was that OPM Europe was going broke at about the same rate as OPM U.S. In conclusion, Myron grandly projected: "We should be able to make full restitution in well under fifteen months."

Singer thanked Myron for his cooperation and asked him to step out while he discussed these latest revelations with his partners. Singer announced that Myron's assertions as to his ability to pay back the bad deals was "not supportable . . . even using these unsupported figures he is giving us." Assuming the ninety-million-dollar total was correct, and there was no reason to assume it was, a buy out was utterly beyond his capacity within any foreseeable stretch of time.

Myron already knew he had blown it. He could tell by Henry's expression: "He kept trying to justify it, but he could never get to justifying how the company could stay in business unless some astronomical numbers were written." At midnight, Eli Mattioli introduced a resolution: "We advise the client we adhere to our letter. We advise him to inform Lehman Brothers, Merle Bushkin, and others as appropriate."

Andy Reinhard was against voting at all: "It's very late, we're all very tired, Myron has made a good faith effort to respond to all the questions asked of him . . . Why not defer this important decision until tomorrow morning?"

Reinhard's objection was overruled. The vote went one last time against Myron. Jay Seeman, Eli Mattioli, and Andy Reinhard were sent down the hall to get him.

Seeman: "We have discussed, at length, everything we have learned tonight. The firm has nonetheless resolved to adhere to our termination letter, as it was originally sent."

Myron took it all remarkably well:

"I know the firm has seriously considered the matter, and though I can't say I'm happy with the outcome, I'm willing to resign myself to it."

The partners said good-bye. Myron did not say good-bye. He would be seeing a bit more of them in the future than most of them would have liked.

Myron might have rendered Singer a list of all his bad deals, but the firm didn't catch on immediately: Myron had been misleading them all, all summer, when he claimed that the fraud was over. A few days later, Alan Jacobs and Henry Putzel compared Myron's spread sheet with the list of deals they had closed in the preceding months. They were shocked to find that "virtually all certificates given us by the client were false." Myron had pulled the wool over their eyes, and now it was too late to do much about it, in the expert opinion of esteemed outside counsel.

Putzel advised that the ongoing frauds of the summer were past frauds now, therefore entitled to the same protection under the privilege as any other past crime. The firm was still "ethically barred" from disclosing the fraud, from blowing the whistle, and "in spite of your understandable chagrin that the client had lied to you . . . from acting in a manner detrimental to his interests."

Ecclesiastes 1:15: "That which is crooked cannot be made straight: and that which is wanting cannot be numbered."

Ecclesiastes 5:3: "For a dream cometh through the multitude of business; and a fool's voice is known by a multitude of words."

32

While Singer Hutner was unwinding, Lehman Brothers was resigning. October 1: Myron was summoned to Lew Glucksman's office at 1 William Street for the last of their heart-to-heart chats.

Glucksman: "We have reviewed this account and made a decision to terminate the relationship . . . I simply can't afford to put time into this anymore."

Myron knew this was not going to be a subject for debate; the debating was all over now. He was appropriately ashen-faced but did Glucksman a final favor: he refrained from crying.

Glucksman: "We at Lehman Brothers still have consideration for the relationship."

He mentioned in passing the former Lehman partner he thought might be able to help him.

Myron: "Thank you, I do appreciate it. I'm very grateful to you for all your help . . . I know there have been surprises from time to time, and problems, but I hope you don't look too unfavorably upon the entire relationship."

Glucksman: "We still feel kindly toward you . . . Feel free to call us at any time about the business. Keep us posted on how you're doing."

Myron promised to do just that, though he knew if Glucksman really knew how he was doing, he would have eaten those last words for breakfast.

Like Singer Hutner, Lehman Brothers agreed to help conclude any deals still "in the pipeline." Myron was grateful for small favors. There were a number of rather large fraudulent bridge loans coming due any time now: Rockwell E.S. 0–30–80 for $650,000, Rockwell E.S. 0–48–80, 49–80, and 50–80, for $10,000,000, both financed with First National Bank of St. Paul; and three more Rockwell bridges financed with the Crocker Bank in the total amount of $13,871,302. Myron needed those bridges "rolled over," their terms extended, or he was going to go belly up in no time.

Singer Hutner was justifiably concerned that Myron might try to "pull off an end run" and induce Lehman to help refinance those bad bridges. On October 10, they prepared a letter to Goodman advising him that they intended to inform Lehman of "pertinent facts" if he were to try such a thing. They demanded that Myron send Lehman a letter forgoing any intention of refinancing those deals, and to provide the firm with a copy of the letter he sent them. Myron happily signed the letter reflecting his agreement to abide by their terms, but never sent Lehman its letter.

Singer Hutner wrote Myron several more times, but he never responded to their satisfaction. Finally, they sent him a letter chastising him for misleading Lehman, noting that "the closing of the transactions . . . are imminent in spite of your knowledge that certain of them could not be closed lawfully." Singer Hutner demanded that Myron sign a letter that read, in part: "With respect to the Rockwell transactions listed . . . they are currently on bridge loans and OPM does not intend to refinance them in any manner." They asked Myron to return the letter to them, for transmittal to Lehman Brothers. Myron signed the letter and returned it to the firm, which sent it to Lehman Brothers by messenger.

The Lehman partner to which it was addressed never received it. All the fraudulent financings were extended by St. Paul and Crocker. Eli Mattioli saw an article in the New York *Times* noting that Lehman Brothers was moving from its old headquarters at 1 William Street into new offices nearby. He and Hutner idly wondered whether the messenger might have delivered the letter to 1 William Street, just as Lehman was moving, causing the letter to be somehow lost in the shuffle.

Singer Hutner believed that keeping Lehman Brothers from

arranging the refinancings would prevent Myron from doing it, even though they knew Lehman had resigned as OPM's investment banker. Myron wrote Lehman a letter advising them that Singer Hutner was handling the fraudulent transactions. Three days later, OPM issued notes to St. Paul extending the maturity of the bad Rockwell bridges until March 1, 1981. Against considerable odds, Myron had pulled off the end run they had all been worried about. He had played his last bluff hand against Singer Hutner, and won. Luck still hung in his favor.

With Singer Hutner and Lehman Brothers now out of the picture, Myron was hoping to do more deals in-house, using his own legal and debt placement staffs. A few months before, he had hired thirty-two-year-old Gary Simon, a former associate with Donovan Leisure Newton & Irvine, and former in-house counsel for Lever Brothers. He asked Lehman Brothers if he might hire Max Greenberg, a twenty-nine-year-old corporate analyst at Lehman who had worked on the OPM account. Greenberg's Lehman Brothers superiors advised him to take the job, and Greenberg successfully negotiated a $45,000 salary from Myron, roughly twice his Lehman pay. With Simon and Greenberg on hand, Myron felt he had the internal resources to generate, finance, and close deals on his own, fulfilling his long-frustrated ambition of "controlling his own destiny," at least in that vital department.

In September, Gary Simon started having trouble contacting lawyers at Singer Hutner. They were always closeted in "partnership meetings" and would not be disturbed. Simon went to see Myron.

"I think the partnership might be splitting up . . . I can't get a hold of anyone over there."

Myron seemed unusually tired that day. Simon knew he had been working particularly long hours in recent weeks, a good deal of those hours at Singer Hutner.

"Gary, don't worry, they're not splitting up. But we are having discussions about the possible termination of our relationship . . . It's going to be a very difficult transition period, with a lot more work for you."

Simon noted he was slurring his words worse than ever; he seemed done in by strain, pain, and medication.

The first week in October, Myron called Simon back in. He was even more woozy this time.

"We're splitting with Singer Hutner."

"I know, you told me that two weeks ago."

"Did I?" Myron had no recollection. "Well, in any case, over the next few months you and I are going to be the most important people in this company . . . and I'm not too sure in which order."

Myron took Simon by the arm and led him into the enormous conference room, where every key company executive was waiting: thirty, maybe forty people. The room was buzzing; no one knew what was up.

Myron stood in front of the giant movie screen that moved up and down at the flick of a switch.

"There has been a mutual determination between ourselves and Singer Hutner to terminate our relationship. There has also been a mutual severance of our relationship with Lehman Brothers. On the advice of counsel, the reasons for both separations may not be discussed. The two incidents, by the way, are entirely unrelated; they are simply a coincidence of time."

Allen Ganz pantomimed jumping out the window.

Myron went on for quite some time, quite eloquently, on the subject of OPM's having to "control its own destiny." Outside people were no longer necessary, even convenient: the company had grown far too big for that. The plan was to build up the in-house legal staff, and the in-house debt placement staff. It would be all for the better in the long run, though over the next few months things might get a bit difficult. Singer Hutner, he didn't mind saying, "just couldn't cut it . . . they weren't big enough, or prestigious enough, for a company of our weight and worth."

Gary Simon had trouble swallowing this. He kept badgering Myron for something a little more realistic; he knew OPM was Singer Hutner's largest client and they wouldn't resign unless there was no other choice. But Myron would only stick to his own party line: "They couldn't handle the peaks and valleys;

their fees were outrageous; they wouldn't give me itemized billing." Finally he admitted at the end of one of these sessions: "If you have to know, some of the lawyers over there think that our selling tax shelters is a sale of securities, and that requires filing with the SEC, and we refused to do it." So, Simon thought, it's a securities law problem. That at least made some sort of sense. He asked a number of Singer Hutner partners about it, and they told him they couldn't discuss it. Simon was forced to be "satisfied that the securities law problem was the only problem; everything else was just business."

After Simon closed his first transaction, a legitimate Rockwell financing, he took Rockwell's closing package down to the mail room to have it sent out to Sid Hasin. He asked Lichtman on the way if this was the proper procedure. Lichtman said, "No, you shouldn't be doing it that way at all. When you do a Rockwell closing, you give everything to Myron, and Myron will take it from there."

Singer Hutner made a concerted if ineffectual effort to protect Gary Simon. On October 13, Putzel advised them: "We have an obligation to make sure the chief legal officer is not placed in the same position we were placed in." In blunter terms: "[We] must insist [Myron] tell [Simon] or we tell him or we quit." But Singer Hutner depended upon Myron to tell him, which Myron had no intention of doing, because he knew that Simon would quit. Myron made it plain he wasn't going to tell Simon anything; so as to avoid having to tell Simon themselves, they resolved to warn him indirectly, with a memorandum telling him to follow certain "due diligence" procedures on all Rockwell deals.

The draft memo explicitly advised Simon to follow some rather specific "essential procedures" on all Rockwell transactions. But Myron wasn't having any; he claimed that the reference to Rockwell was "tantamount" to exposing the fraud, which they were not permitted to do under the attorney-client privilege.

Myron: "I'm against it."

Singer Hutner went along with Myron. They took the teeth out of the memo. They dropped all mention of Rockwell, and though they did advise Simon to verify leases, they suggested verification with OPM, not the lessee. They suggested Simon use only original documentation, but that struck him as something "any lawyer would do." Singer Hutner felt it was still dropping plenty of "red flags," sufficiently conspicuous to warn Simon, but Simon simply thought the firm was being "obstructionist" and "obnoxious," attitudes he attributed to "sour grapes" over losing their largest client.

Putzel interpreted Simon's "willfully defiant attitude" quite differently: he speculated that Simon "knew everything and was just going to proceed, willy-nilly."

Putzel: "A careful lawyer who received the communication that he had been given . . . would have proceeded very differently from the way he proceeded . . . It did not seem likely . . . that he would receive these rather strong documents and do nothing . . . ask no questions."

But Simon did ask questions. He asked Eli Mattioli, "Look, if something is wrong with these deals, I want to know it today." Mattioli, on the advice of counsel, said nothing. Meanwhile, Simon kept closing Rockwell deals. On one such deal, the closing counsel for the bank asked him for an opinion that the equipment was "located at the equipment locations specified." Simon asked Allen Ganz about it.

Ganz: "If that's where Myron says it is, that's where it is."

The equipment was not at that location. It had no location. It didn't exist.

From December 1980 to February 1981, the OPM Legal Department under Gary Simon closed six bad Rockwell deals worth just over $13 million.

For all his brave talk about OPM "controlling its own destiny," Myron knew that Gary Simon and his embryonic in-house legal staff would not be able to handle the flow of OPM transactions all by themselves. When he asked Gary Simon to recommend outside counsel, Simon suggested Kaye Scholer. Myron got "very excited about the prospect." When Simon was badgering him for reasons for the Singer Hutner split, Myron had accused them of not being able to handle his "peaks and valleys." With 150 lawyers, the twenty-fifth largest law firm in the United States, Kaye Scholer could hardly be accused of being too small for the job. Mannes Friedman had a brother-in-law at the firm: Sidney Kwestel, a litigator. Kwestel set up a meeting with Myron to meet the head of the firm's banking department.

Myron arrived in grand style, with an entourage consisting of Friedman, Lichtman, and Simon. According to Kwestel, his presentation was "superb." As he breathlessly described OPM's booming business, his arm deftly shot up to the ceiling: "We're going up, up, up!" He looked like a carnival barker, but the performance was undeniably masterful. He carelessly dropped the enticing fact that he had been paying Singer Hutner $50,000 a week. When he promised the firm a minimum weekly fee of just over half that, the show was just about over. Myron went home terribly impressed with himself: he had these smart lawyers right where he wanted them; the old OPM bag was still holding out.

Peter Fishbein, a partner at the firm, was a friend of Joe Hutner's. Hutner: "We were close friends. We went on vacations together. I ran for Congress in 1966 and he helped with the campaign. We live in adjacent communities. We saw each other socially."

Hutner asked Putzel what to do when Fishbein called.

"I'd like to say, look, Peter, don't ask me any questions. Just don't do it."

Putzel: "Oh my God, that is precisely what you cannot do."

Putzel explained for the ten thousandth time that such a warning would constitute a direct violation of two central professional precepts: (1) not to betray a client confidence, and (2) not to cause your client "unnecessary hardship." Hutner had heard all that before, which didn't make him feel any better: "This was not a conversation I looked forward to with pleasant anticipation."

Fishbein called Hutner at home a few days later to ask if there was anything his firm should consider in taking on the OPM representation.

Hutner: "The only way I can answer your question is to tell you what I'm sure Myron told your partners: namely, that the decision to terminate was mutual and that there was a mutual agreement that the circumstances of termination would not be discussed."

Fishbein: "Then I guess we'll accept the representation because I assume you would alert us if anything was wrong."

Hutner: "I have nothing to add."

The second meeting between Myron and Kaye Scholer was more like a party. Gary Simon: "It was half social and half business that day, because they were happy about getting a client that was going to give them a couple of million dollars a year, and we were happy about getting one of New York's best law firms to represent us."

Myron called Alan Batkin at Lehman Brothers to tell him the good news: "We've just retained Kaye Scholer . . . I feel a sort of 'ethnic closeness' to them. Did you know they've even got a daily 'minyan' over there, just like OPM? That makes me feel very comfortable."

Batkin was happy to hear it.

Fishbein called Hutner again, with a special request. He wasn't sure he had enough associates on hand to handle a client of "OPM's magnitude." He was wondering if Hutner might have let any of his young lawyers go recently. Having just lost the OPM account, Singer Hutner had indeed been forced to contract rather sharply. Hutner saw this as a golden opportunity to warn Fishbein off the engagement without disclosing a confidence.

"Yes, Peter, as a matter of fact I have . . . five or six."

"Oh good, are they available?"

"As a matter of fact, they're not."

"Oh? Have they all gotten jobs?"

"No, as a matter of fact, none of them have gotten jobs."

"You're saying none of them are available, but none of them have gotten jobs?"

"That's exactly what I'm saying, Peter."

"Well that is very curious."

"Eureka!" Hutner thought to himself. His friend had finally gotten the message. But Fishbein simply took Hutner's remarks to mean his lost associates were looking for "opportunities" somewhere else than in the law.

Sidney Kwestel was Mannes Friedman's brother-in-law, and a friend and neighbor of Andy Reinhard's. He called Reinhard to ask about staffing up for OPM. Reinhard said he hadn't really worked much on OPM transactions, that his chief legal function on the account had been as Myron's "hand holder." Kwestel asked him the real reason for the termination.

Reinhard: "Don't press me on it."

Kaye Scholer represented OPM for four months. It closed one fraudulent Rockwell transaction, to the tune of $2.4 million, while working closely with the OPM in-house staff to close another $13 million in bad deals.

Hutner: "This specific thing caused me more personal pain than anything . . . including learning that Myron Goodman was a thief."

Later on Fishbein told Hutner that if he had been in Hutner's position, he would have said something.

Hutner: "He was understandably annoyed . . . he referred to it as my 'little faux pas' . . . his firm did lose $600,000, which may have colored his mood on the thing."

33

By November, Robert Clare of White & Case had still not been given a satisfactory explanation as to why OPM should be making monthly payments on Rockwell leases when the closing papers explicitly stated Rockwell should be paying its lenders directly. When Clare called Alan Jacobs at Singer Hutner in October, he had been given the runaround:

"Don't be concerned . . . Rockwell is OPM's largest customer, they have a large number of transactions with them, and as an administrative convenience Rockwell pays OPM, and OPM passes the money on to the lenders."

As far as Clare was concerned, he was "simply trying to comply with the closing documents, which provided for a direct flow of funds from the true credit in the transactions." The "true credit" was of course the lessee, namely, Rockwell. As it was, the thing was clearly being handled the wrong way: if OPM wanted to pay the banks directly, why didn't the closing documents stipulate that, and have done with it?

Clare restrained an urge to call Rockwell "because of the business relationship between OPM and Rockwell . . . I was reluctant to jeopardize that." He tried other routes: he called Alan Batkin at Lehman Brothers, who promised to look into it. Clare heard nothing from him either. Something strange was going on, and no one seemed too concerned about it. On November 3, Clare finally put aside his reservations about jeopardizing the sacred OPM/Rockwell relationship. He called Dan Byrnes at El Segundo to request "further assistance in clarifying the matter." Clare pointed out Rockwell's failure to pay monthly rentals directly to the banks and mentioned, hardly in passing, that OPM had been frequently late in meeting the payments themselves.

Byrnes sounded surprised. He couldn't understand it; Rockwell always made its payments on time. Clare read to Byrnes a list of lease numbers, including Rockwell E.S. 79–26, E.S. 80–1, and E.S. 80–2. All three were phantoms, with no underlying leases at Rockwell. Byrnes kept no list of Rockwell leases in his files; that function was concentrated in Sid Hasin's department. Byrnes promised to check into it. The numbers, as such, meant nothing to him.

In November, Bankers Life Company of Des Moines became concerned over the same issue. They wrote to Sid Hasin declaring Rockwell in default on six OPM leases. All six leases had been altered by the OPM fraud team. Bankers Life demanded immediate payment on the delinquent leases and direct payment from Rockwell from now on. Attached to the letter were copies of consents and agreements purportedly signed by Rockwell, which reflected the bank's inflated lease terms. This was what Myron had always worried might happen some distant day. Rockwell being given a look at the "other side." Hasin claims he did not notice the enormous discrepancies in equipment value, monthly rent, or lease terms. He did not bring the matter up in conversations with a Bankers Life officer. Instead, Sid called Myron at home.

"Myron, are you sure there's no problem here?"

"Of course not, Sid. We'll take care of it. Don't worry, we'll get you whatever you want, whatever you need."

Sid: "Myron was 'very sweet' about the whole thing."

Myron went into his daughter's room to sit down and think. It was all he could do not to panic. Bankers Life wanted direct payment. Direct payment meant Rockwell had to see the lease. Rockwell didn't have a lease, not with those numbers.

Myron: "The world was coming to an end."

Myron called Sid back to stall, giving him his usual long song and dance: "It's all a mistake, if there's any problem don't worry. It'll be bought out. We'll take care of Bankers Life, no payments are going to be late, everything's going to be okay."

Sid might have gone for it, but Myron couldn't sit easy with those documents reflecting the inflated lease terms preserved for posterity in Rockwell files. Goodman, Lichtman, and Friedman flew out to California that night to try the old switcheroo. While Friedman "kept chickie" at his door, Myron snuck into Sid Hasin's office and stole the consents and agreements and the Bankers Life letter right off the desk. They substituted phoney ones from their own lease files.

Bankers Life was insisting on direct payment on Rockwell leases from now on. A long-term solution was desperately needed to avert the collapse of the fraud. When in doubt, Myron turned to Marty Shulman. The two veterans of countless criminal crises put their heads together, with nearly miraculous results. The ultimate solution was predictably brilliant: to open a bank account called the OPM/Rockwell Special. All future payments to Bankers Life were to be made through that account. The wire transfer slips would read: "OPM/Rockwell Special." Who could tell which company had the account, OPM or Rockwell?

They opened the account at LaSalle National Bank. They promptly paid Bankers Life through it. Myron had Marty Shulman call Sid Hasin, pretending to be a Bankers Life official, and explain that their last letter was "in error," the mistake was theirs, kindly disregard the whole thing.

The concept worked like a charm: Bankers Life wrote back to Sid Hasin, withdrawing their threat of legal action on the condition that "Rockwell make timely payments to Bankers Life in the future."

They had dodged "another speeding bullet."

Thanksgiving of 1980 Allen Ganz spent over at Myron's house. An extremely depressing scene. Myron, for one thing, was a physical wreck. He was getting more and more deaf all the time, he walked with a cane, he could only see you in front of his face because of his tunnel vision. He was not rational most of the time. He never slept at night. He fell asleep during meetings, during conversations, during Thanksgiving dinner. He was definitely on drugs during dinner. He could have opened a drugstore and supplied an entire country with what he carried about on his person. Myron was getting to be a deranged personality, and this was becoming a sick situation.

Myron kept promising it was all going to end soon. Allen had long since given up hope. Myron was not going to stop until they all ended up in the jail, or just as likely the loony bin. Myron kept saying he'd protect everyone, but Allen knew what to make of his promises. Steve Lichtman was easily as miserable as Allen, and Mannes Friedman was, if possible, even worse off than Steve.

The only one really enjoying himself was Marty Shulman. Shulman was the fraud team cheerleader; only a few days before he had been urging the demoralized team on: "Let's go for Vesco's record!" Vesco had made off with about two hundred million. Ganz had no idea how far behind they were, but they were closing in on the last record fast.

Ganz had been sure the whole thing was all over in March, but they had been saved in the nick of time by the Passover Plot. The Philadelphia Saving Fund Society was getting nervous about constant late payments on fifteen OPM/Rockwell leases. A PSFS guy named LeRoy McClellan had called Bill Neely, Rockwell's treasurer in Pittsburgh. McClellan read him a whole list of serial numbers and the amounts of money delinquent. Neely called Sid Hasin and read the numbers to him. Myron, Lichtman, and Friedman were in California, so Hasin showed them the list. Hasin couldn't understand it; according to his records, Rockwell's lease payments were current. Myron told him not to worry, it must be some "computer error" on the part of PSFS. Those rental numbers couldn't be monthly payments, they were much too large; they had to be unamortized note amounts on the financings. Hasin accepted this gobbledygook and let Myron take it from there.

Myron flew back to New York and packed Sam Ganz onto the next train to Philadelphia with the full payment, to be paid to McClellan in person. But Hasin told Allen Ganz that Bill Neely was still upset about PSFS accusing Rockwell of welshing on its obligations. Neely was not going to be satisfied hearing from Hasin that the problem had by now been solved. Neely wanted to hear McClellan eat his own words; he expected nothing less than a full-dress apology.

Again, Marty Shulman's fraud team effort went way beyond the call of duty. He volunteered to call Neely himself, to impersonate McClellan on the phone. Myron might even have done it himself except for it being Passover. He was strictly prohibited by Sabbath law to hold conversations by phone. Shulman was not so observant.

Marty called Neely, identified himself as LeRoy McClellan, advised him they must have been "in error," apologized for the inconvenience, and asked him to disregard his previous letter. Neely had talked to the real LeRoy McClellan several times that week. Either Shulman was an amazing impersonator, or Neely didn't have much of an ear. Neely accepted the apology gracefully. The speeding bullets were flying all over, but none had yet hit on target.

The fraud team was relieved at a disinformation mission accomplished, but the whole incident just made Allen even more depressed. It all struck him as "very sick, very sad." Particularly when his father had been put on that train to pay PSFS in person. Then he had said to himself, "Okay, now it will end. Now it will crumble. This is totally tragic." He was sick to death over it; he couldn't bear to talk about it; he couldn't even bear to think about it.

By this time Myron was paranoid. He could hardly speak to anyone at Rockwell, or to any of the banks. He was usually so out of it anyway he couldn't have if he wanted to. Mannes Friedman became the Myron impersonator. The perfect, together, rational Myron. A better Myron than Myron. Except half the time he didn't have the faintest idea what he was talking about.

One time Friedman had to call Paul Kazunas, treasurer of PSFS, as Myron. Mannes didn't know very much about leasing, while Kazunas knew quite a bit. Friedman dialed the number about twenty times until he got such a terrible connection Kazunas could hardly hear him. This was supposed to sound like he was in Belgium, where the real Myron was at the time.

Friedman planned to hang up if Kazunas asked him anything he couldn't answer. He could always blame the poor Belgian connection, he had been cut off, whatever. Kazunas didn't delve into details. Friedman followed the script perfectly. After that, Mannes had no more problems enjoying the importance of being Myron.

Mannes really got into it. He got so he could do a matchless Myron to people who had talked to the real Myron less than an hour before. Everyone got quite a kick out of it. One time Mannes was talking to someone as Myron, and that person asked to speak to Mannes. Mannes had to get Lichtman to say Mannes couldn't come to the phone. Sometimes Lichtman would pitch-hit for Mannes and turn into a passable Myron. Myron's secretary, Ruth Holloway, once caught Lichtman's Myron-on-the-speakerphone act with Myron sitting right there beside him, egging him on.

Holloway: "It was very humorous to observe."

Ganz: "This convinced me, as if I needed convincing, that this was a loony bin and it all had to end any day now."

But now it was Thanksgiving, near the end of a second felonious year, and the fraud was just not about to be stopped. It had looked all over the day Lehman Brothers and Singer Hutner resigned, October 6. Allen had made as if he was going to jump out the window at the meeting that day. He was the last one the fraud team was supposed to call in a crisis, because he was supposed to be the first one to bail out, possibly straight down to Broadway.

December 1: Robert Clare telecopied consents and agreements for Rockwell E.S. 80–1 and E.S. 80–2 to Dan Byrnes at Rockwell. The documents listed the date of the leases and the number of monthly payments. They did not list the rental amounts or the equipment description.

The responsibility for "archiving" Rockwell leases had been finally taken out of Sid Hasin's hands. John Hayes had been given the job of keeping track of all leases. Hayes started searching through Rockwell lease files, looking for any documentation pertaining to the material Clare had recently sent Byrnes. No matter where he looked, how he looked, or how hard he looked, he could find nothing in ISC files having to do with E.S. 80–1 or E.S. 80–2. Sid Hasin's only suggestion was that Clare must be confusing those leases with E.S. 0–01–80 and E.S. 0–02–80. But Clare's leases had been signed and executed nearly a year before the leases Hasin was talking about. It was as if the leases had vanished into thin air, or had never been there at all.

December 5, 1980, Myron spent getting his teeth fixed. Gary Simon spoke to Sid Hasin that morning about a certain Rockwell deal without talking to Myron first. It happened to be a bad deal, on which the equipment numbers jibed, but the lease terms and rentals did not, by a long shot. Sid called Lichtman and gave him the numbers, which was enough to set off another team panic. Mannes and Steve dashed over to the dentist's office and broke the bad news to the boss just as he was coming out of the ether. Myron just about lost it that time; he was rapidly approaching the end of his rope.

"What are you waiting for? You idiots! Get Sid on the line right away!"

Lichtman called Hasin to tell him it was all "a mistake." Gary had the wrong numbers; don't worry, forget about it.

Hasin once again went for it. But too many people were calling up too many people; bad connections were starting to be made. Myron had Gary Simon install a "Rockwell hot line" in his house "so Sid could contact him any time . . . so Gary would know that Sid was calling . . . so he could decide whether to take it or not." Mannes and Steve thought the hot line was not such a hot idea; all Gary had to do was talk to Sid about one more bad deal and the whole thing was going to blow. It was as if Myron didn't care anymore. He wasn't even minding the fraud.

Myron: "This was a period of total chaos. I would do anything without even thinking about things. I was flying very high at this time, on tremendous quantities of drugs."

34

January 23, 1981: Robert Clare of White & Case was in the midst of closing an OPM/Rockwell transaction, financed by the Paul Revere Insurance Company, when he called Dan Byrnes at Rockwell to say that Paul Revere was "very anxious" that lease payments be made direct to them by Rockwell, not OPM. That seemed perfectly fair and reasonable to Byrnes; he hoped OPM wouldn't mind. Four days later, Clare sent Byrnes more copies of consents and agreements from earlier OPM/Rockwell deals, as a step toward resolving the "payment flow" issue. The material sent by Clare referred to one phantom lease and two altered leases. Byrnes relayed it to Robert Hayes to compare with the documentation in his files. Hayes was still trying to track down the two earlier leases, E.S. 80–1 and 80–2, without success. Hayes finally asked Rockwell's bookkeeping department to call OPM for copies of the leases from their files.

Late January, 1981: Allen Ganz's assistant Jeff Resnick heard a "loud groan" coming from Allen Ganz's office. Allen was moaning, groaning, and cursing, which wasn't his typical style. Before Resnick could do anything, he was shocked to see Myron Goodman and Marty Shulman come trooping double-time down the hall. They disappeared into Allen Ganz's office. The door stayed closed a long time.

When they finally left, Resnick went in to find out what was going on.

Allen: "You don't want to know. I'll take care of it. Please, don't bother me."

Resnick was pushy. He wouldn't leave well enough alone. After a while, Ganz couldn't take saying no anymore.

"We've been putting signature pages into Rockwell leases and changing the lease terms and rentals."

Resnick was not entirely surprised. Most of last year he had spent preparing Rockwell lease documentation, and at some point he realized he was preparing certain leases in pairs that didn't always quite match. He detected a pattern, but not a purpose.

"How long has this been going on?"

Allen looked sick to his stomach. "I don't know, about two years." He dated the trouble from when he started his ulcer.

Allen explained all the moaning and groaning: he had discovered that the signature pages on two versions of a Rockwell lease were not identical. A new signature page had to be forged, and he needed Myron and Marty for that.

Ganz: "Can we count on you?"

Resnick: "I guess so."

One of Resnick's first lease-manufacturing jobs was to create versions of the two phantom Rockwell leases Robert Hayes was looking for out at Seal Beach. This had to be a bang-up job because Rockwell was looking for copies. If Rockwell was looking for copies of leases that didn't exist, someone must have alerted them that the leases had been financed somewhere. The cover story was going to be that the phantom leases had gotten "lost in the shuffle" at OPM, which anyone familiar with OPM's bookkeeping might accept as not utterly farfetched.

The problem was that these particular phantom leases had been financed for so much that the idea of their simply getting lost, even at OPM, might be a bit hard to swallow. So they tossed in some peripheral bits of equipment Rockwell had actually received but OPM had never bothered to put on a lease. Resnick dutifully worked up the new versions of E.S. 80-1 and 80-2 on the OPM Vydec word-processing equipment. The fraud team supplied copies of real Rockwell signature pages from Lichtman's private collection. Myron was originally going to courier the leases to Hasin, but at the last minute changed his mind. Mannes Friedman, just back from vacation in Florida, and Sam Ganz, the preferred personal courier, were sent out on a rescue mission, to pull a last fast one on Sid.

Unfortunately for them, Sid wasn't the archivist anymore. Now it was this new man, Hayes. Hayes had been talking to someone at Bankers Trust a few days before, when he realized they should be able to provide him with copies of the leases he had been looking for all this time. Bankers Trust was happy to oblige. They sent Hayes their versions of E.S. 80–1 and 80–2, which had been financed nearly two years before. The leases arrived at Hayes's office on February 10. Sam Ganz and Mannes Friedman were due to arrive early the following morning.

Mannes and Sam showed up at Seal Beach with their freshly minted phoney leases. Hayes took the Bankers Trust version from his desk and headed straight down the hall to the meeting. Friedman and Ganz handed over their leases; Hayes took a long cool look at his. The OPM team members were forced to squirm in their seats as Hayes's gaze wandered slowly, painfully, from one to the other, his widening eyes finally beginning to focus on the matter of monthly rentals:

Bankers Trust E.S. 80–1: $25,566 a month;
OPM E.S. 80–1: $231 a month
Bankers Trust E.S. 80–2: $32,321 a month;
OPM E.S. 80–2: $352 a month

The speeding bullet had finally hit. On target: a direct hit. Hayes demanded an explanation.

Friedman boldly spoke up.

"These leases are for add-on equipment for a computer in Jackson, Tennessee. They're both part of E.S. 88, so they should have been called 88–1 and 88–2. There must have been a typo somewhere, the 8 became a 0, see? That's why they're 80–1 and 80–2, instead of 88–1 and 88–2." Friedman had been fast on his feet; Hayes was definitely wavering.

Hayes called Rockwell's facility in Jackson, Tennessee. They did indeed have the equipment in question. Which did at least seem to explain the existence of the OPM leases with the low rent. But what about the Bankers Trust versions? To what equipment did those two belong?

Here even Friedman was stumped. He excused himself to call Myron in New York, to "investigate" the situation. Myron himself was finally at a loss. How could they come up with a real Rockwell computer at those rents when there wasn't one to be found in the world?

"Mannes, listen, I've got to think. Call me back every fifteen minutes, okay? Tell them I'm still looking into it. Tell them anything; keep stalling."

Two hours went by, and four more calls. Myron was still "checking into it." Myron finally came up with a sufficiently convoluted explanation for the discrepancy: he had once asked Sid Hasin to let him take a motley collection of minor add-on equipment and put it all together onto two large leases. The two large leases could be financed at a considerably lower rate than a whole slew of smaller ones. Sid had okayed it, on the condition that Myron would cancel the smaller ones once the large ones were successfully financed. But the smaller leases, "by mistake," had never in fact been canceled. OPM had never invoiced Rockwell on the large leases and had been making the payments themselves. Which explained why Rockwell had no material in its files relating to the two larger leases.

Mannes and Sam and Hayes went out to lunch. Friedman tentatively tried Myron's story on for size. Hayes listened politely and ate slowly. Friedman did his best to reassure him:

"Of course, now we know what's going on, we'll buy out those leases immediately."

Sid Hasin happened to be sitting right there, across the room, eating his own lunch with typical gusto. As Hasin strolled out, Hayes stopped him at the door to ask if he remembered anything about what Friedman had just told him. A proposal to consolidate a number of smaller pieces of peripheral equipment onto two large leases, to bring the rate down?

Sid: "It sounds familiar, I don't recall the details exactly." Myron had in fact proposed a similar arrangement quite recently, only a few months before. But not back in 1979, when these two leases had been financed.

None of it quite came together for Hayes. The typos, the add-ons, the low rates and high rates, the financings "by mistake," the phone calls every fifteen minutes, the convolutions, Sid Hasin's face, Mannes Friedman's face; the whole thing didn't quite jibe. After lunch, Hayes headed back to his office with one thought in mind: to take another look at those leases. Something odd caught his eye: the Rockwell signatures on the Bankers Trust versions of the leases looked downright peculiar. The signature of Robert C. Peterson, Rockwell's procurement officer, was just not right. It was not just the signature itself, which looked pretty shaky once you stared at it a while; the title was wrong: that was it! Hayes was no handwriting expert, but he knew Peterson's position in the company: Director of Material. This lease identified him as Vice President, Lease Acquisition.

Hayes called Hart, a senior Rockwell attorney. Hart called Peterson. They arranged a meeting to examine the documents on Friday, February 13. It didn't take long for Peterson to confirm that those were clearly not his signatures. Tuesday, February 17: Hart called Clare. He and "some other Rockwell people" wanted to come out to New York right away, something urgent was up.

The Rockwell delegation arrived at White & Case the following morning, carrying their versions of the Rockwell leases. The two groups compared groups of documents. Not only were the two leases Clare had been concerned about clearly fraudulent, but a large number of "gross discrepancies" turned up on a number of other OPM deals. Hayes called California, to ask them to compare as many OPM leases as possible with versions supplied to them by the banks. A string of fraudulent transactions was quickly uncovered, including one that had closed just a week before.

That afternoon, counsel for Rockwell and Bankers Trust paid a visit to the U.S. Attorney's Office. A grand jury was convened the next day. The day after that, subpoenas were served on OPM and four OPM officers. The lid had blown off this fraud at last.

35

While Rockwell and Bankers Trust were meeting with the U.S. attorney, Sid and Myron were meeting in Myron's hotel suite at the Hyatt at LAX. They had plenty to talk about, as usual. In fact, they had more to talk about than usual. At fifty-seven, after eighteen years, Sid was leaving Rockwell at last. He was coming to work for OPM.

The whole thing was settled. Sid had signed a consulting contract with OPM on January 26, at an annual salary of $125,000, more than twice what he had been earning at Rockwell. Sid was to become president of OPM Data Services, a new subsidiary specializing in equipment refurbishing, time-sharing, and various and sundry other data-processing activities.

Sid had always wanted to be an entrepreneur, and this was his last big chance. The worst thing about his present job had always been that at best he could save money, he never could make it. Sid's happiest times at Rockwell had been spent selling Rockwell computer time on the open market: "I personally enjoyed it. I liked selling time. I like making money." But when the B-1 Bomber and the Space Shuttle came through, Rockwell had no excess data capacity left over to sell. Rockwell withdrew from the market, but Sid maintained a lot of valuable connections in the time-sharing industry.

He had made two great friends who brokered time, Bob Madariaga and Bill Graham. They had a company called Worldwide Network Systems they hoped to sell to "these very successful people from New York," OPM. Sid considered the concept synergistic; he knew Myron had always wanted a refurbishing business. A data-processing service would be an excellent place to dispose of computers building up in OPM's inventory. He took the idea to Myron, who was intrigued. Sid hoped to head up the whole thing, with Bob and Bill working for him as salesmen. Myron dispatched Joe Hutner to California to look Bob and Bill over.

Bob and Bill wanted to sell OPM a data-processing center and a marketing service. But they had already sold their customer list to another company, which left only the center with a whole collection of aging computers on unprofitable leases from Itel. The center turned out to be actually owned by California Life, a small insurance company, which was looking for someone to take it off their hands. So Bob and Bill didn't own the center either. It was unclear just what they owned.

Hutner: "These two fellows . . . wanted to be compensated on the basis of some theory that absolutely eluded me . . . they believed they were entitled to a commission on the sale of a company they no longer owned to a third party . . . they wanted a lot of money, a million or two million . . . and they wanted to be hired as executives and salesmen to be compensated on some astronomical basis."

For confirmation, Myron sent his trusty lieutenant and self-styled data-processing whiz, Marty Shulman, out to meet Bob and Bill. Shulman: "Myron was attracted to the idea because it was his dream to own half the world and control his own destiny . . . Sid wrote a great picture . . . I thought it was a pipe dream." Shulman's conclusion came close to Hutner's for once: "These salesmen basically had nothing to sell . . . a customer list maybe, but then again, the customers didn't even have to go with you." They reported back in July of 1980 at a "cabinet meeting" convened by Myron at Grossinger's to discuss the project. A decision was reached. Myron: "Bob and Bill were connivers . . . it would be a disaster to buy it."

Myron felt personally bad for Sid. He felt so bad he decided the only way to break the news would be to do it over good food. He flew out to California the next night to take Sid to dinner at his favorite restaurant, the International at LAX. Sid took the decision philosophically: "What is best for Sid Hasin is best for

Sid Hasin, forgetting about Bob and Bill." Sid really appreciated Myron's coming all this way to tell him in person; he sadly put Myron on the ten o'clock red-eye back to New York the same night. Sid went back to the drawing board to propose a new program, retaining some of the same ideas, sans Bob and Bill.

Now Sid wanted Verl Rosenow to go in with him on the venture. Verl was OPM's man in L.A. Sid and Verl were truly close. Myron: "Sid felt his relationship with Verl was true father/son." They went bike riding together. Sid was closing on sixty and he wanted Verl along so if he fell and hurt himself, Verl would be there to pick up the pieces. Sid's next proposal was for a salary of $150,000 a year, plus a hefty commission on sales. Myron worked him down to $125,000 plus a Seville, though Sid said he really preferred a Continental Mark IV, the car Verl Rosenow had. In the end, Myron told Sid he didn't care what car, as long as it was not German-made. Sid and Verl went biking all around Orange County looking for a building to buy. They finally settled on a building in Irvine, close by Sid and Verl's houses, for a bit under a million. Myron took out an option to buy it for $180,000. Sid signed the consulting contract January 26 and presented his retirement letter to Larry Manly on the thirtieth. Sid was home free at last.

Myron: "As our discussions went on, before I offered him the job he had moved his desk and worked for us for two years . . . It wasn't a question of if Sid was coming to OPM, it was a question in Sid's mind of when Sid was coming to OPM."

Sid was leaving Rockwell in ten days. He and Myron were just hashing out the final details, at their usual leisure, when a call came in for Sid from his office. Sid came back into the room, looking extremely upset.

"They've impounded my files. I don't know what's going on." His secretary, Mary Kyle, had just told him all his files had been moved into the audit room at Seal Beach.

Myron did his best to maintain. He didn't seem at all disturbed.

"Well, you have so many important files they probably just want to make sure they've got everything under control before you leave."

Mannes Friedman and Steve Lichtman kept wandering aimlessly in and out. Mordy was somewhere around too. Myron had to run off to lunch with Maury Dahn, head of ISC, and Dalton Davis, ISC's controller. Sid wasn't going along; he was no longer in the picture. Myron was worried about the Hasin impoundment, but he left for lunch in a fine mood. They seemed to have bought his outrageous explanation for that mix-up on E.S. 80–1 and 80–2.

Any concerns Myron might have had were allayed by Dahn and Davis over lunch. At length, they launched into an enticing description of Rockwell's expansion plans. The "long-range combat aircraft," the B-1, was definitely on its way back; the Space Shuttle program was starting to gear up; they had all sorts of huge aerospace contracts on-line. They were going to be needing to build up an enormous computer capacity in the very near future.

They expected to be making forty million dollars worth of new lease awards in the upcoming months. Myron could expect a hefty chunk of that business to be coming his way. They even hinted around that OPM might be considered as the "sole source" for computer procurement at Rockwell, the prize Myron had always dreamed of in vain, that Sid had been pushing at Pittsburgh for years. Now it was all finally coming true, despite Sid Hasin's departure.

Dahn and Davis hoped Myron could do them just one more small favor. There was a certain IBM 370/168 they had subleased to OPM. It looked like they'd be needing it back. Would Myron kindly sign a release form for the "F" machine? They would be happy to work out the precise lease terms later. Myron was so pleased with the upbeat mood of the luncheon he signed the release form then and there. He was driven back to the Hyatt as close to ecstatic as he had been in some time. It looked like he'd finally "arrived" at Rockwell, even if Sid would no longer be there.

When Sid returned to his office at lunch time, his office door was locked with a lock to which he had no key. He headed straight for Maury Dahn's office. There, Dahn's secretary, Linda Holman, told him that Myron, Maury, and Dalton were still out to lunch, but that Mr. Dahn had left word he would be back shortly and would personally explain everything. Mr. Hasin should realize that this unusual measure in no way, shape, or form was intended as a reflection on him. Above all, he shouldn't blow up until he heard the full explanation; at that time he would be free to decide whether the drastic steps taken had been justified under the circumstances. Linda got a phone call just then from the International; lunch was going to go on longer than expected. Mr. Dahn had an afternoon appointment, but he would be happy to see Mr. Hasin in his office the next morning at eight o'clock sharp.

Thursday, February 19, 8:00 A.M.: Maury Dahn was as "elated" with the lunch of yesterday as Myron Goodman had been. Maury gleefully told Sid he had "secured" the release of the "F" machine and had promised Myron "all sorts of sole source procurement" awards to get it back. He was acting just like a little kid who had made off with someone's toy truck.

Sid: "But Pittsburgh will never approve."

Sid and Maury had proposed making OPM the sole source back in September, but it had been turned down by Bob DePalma: "Competition is healthy. It's the American Way." Now Maury was looking at him strangely.

"Of course they would never approve."

It came upon Sid like a flash: Maury had deliberately tricked Myron into giving up the machine!

Maury was quite delicate about it. The reason Sid's files had been removed and sealed in the audit room was that there was "a distinct possibility of improper deals involving OPM and OPM leases." He said he was not at liberty to discuss the matter further. He had scheduled an appointment for Hasin to see Hart at nine-thirty the next morning. Sid left Maury's office in something of a daze. Myron called him that afternoon from the offices of SoCal Edison.

"Do you know what's going on over there? Should I stay here until this thing is fixed up?"

Sid didn't know what to say.

"No, I really don't know what it's about yet. I hope to find out something a little more concrete soon."

"Okay, call me if you hear anything."

The "F" machine was impounded by Rockwell that day in Circle, Illinois. The truck was stopped, physically, from delivering it to a non-Rockwell location.

36

Thursday, February 19, 5:15 P.M.: Craig Barony was on the flight back to New York alongside Myron and Mordy. Craig had been working for OPM only a couple of months, as Mordy's main gofer. Craig graduated from BU in 1977 and put in a year at Baruch Business School; he heard from various people he knew from the Catskills that "OPM was a good opportunity to get into." He met Mordy at Grossinger's over the July 4 weekend. He sent him a resumé. A few months later, Mordy hired him as Assistant to the President, at a salary of $20,000 a year.

Craig spent most of his time on the road, taking messages, screening calls, handling baggage and travel arrangements. Mordy never seemed to make a move without extensive consultation with Myron. They traveled together at least once a month, usually just to talk. They would meet on the plane, work on the plane, get off the plane, and go their separate ways. Marty Shulman once said to him: "Those two guys were born joined at the hip."

Myron and Mordy traveled first-class. The entourage always went coach. Craig spent a good deal of his time with Mannes Friedman and Steve Lichtman, two extremely nice guys. Lately, morale had sunk to an all-time low. Steve was always depressed. People said he was planning to quit, but Myron wouldn't let him. Mannes had taken over most of Steve's responsibilities, handling day-to-day dealings on the Rockwell account.

Myron took his whole office with him everywhere he went. Memos, leases, ledgers, working papers, calculators, office equipment. With the airlines, Myron was notorious for trying to take too much on the plane. Certain airlines had started refusing to book seats under his name. Craig's job was to lug everything on and off the plane, to make sure nothing was lost. The only item he never touched was Myron's "personal bag." A small maroon leather job he wore wherever he went, on a strap across his shoulder. Some people said he kept drugs in that bag. Other people said money.

Now they were heading home for the Washington's Birthday weekend, happy to be through on the Coast. Myron had come back from his last meeting with Rockwell high as a kite; they were letting him in on these "top secret" projects, forty-million minimum, he said. No one else would even be told; there wasn't going to be any bidding. Mannes had flown back to New York the night before. Craig was left to handle the luggage alone. They were sitting on the plane, just starting to taxi down the runway, when an announcement came over the loudspeaker:

"Will Mr. Myron Goodman please step to the front of the plane?"

Naturally, all three of them went forward. The stewardess handed Myron a message:

"Mr. Goodman should not take this flight home. Mr. Weissman may, if he must."

Myron turned pale as he turned toward Mordy. Mordy was already hopping out the front hatch. They went off to phone New York. Mordy got back on the plane. He told Craig to get the bags off the plane, something important was up.

Craig: "Is this a personal or a business matter?"

Mordy: "Strictly business."

Craig went to collect their tickets from the stewardess and arrange for the bags to come off. He went to look for Myron and Mordy. They had disappeared.

Craig had them paged. No response. He called OPM in New York. Myron's secretary said they had just checked into the Hyatt. She gave him the number. Craig called. Mordy picked up.

"Take the next plane back to New York."

Craig did what he was told.

Gary Simon was in his office when he got a call from Preston Baptist, the OPM office manager. Bruce Woods, a U.S. postal inspector, was standing right there in front of his desk, having just served a subpoena on the company and four OPM officers. Simon rushed down to Preston's office to take a look at the subpoena. It named Allen Ganz (Contracts), Joel Klein (Equity), Hoby Shapiro (Accounting), and Pete Cimino (Finance). Simon had Ganz, Klein, and Cimino paged; he gave Woods Shapiro's last known home address. Simon called the other three into his office.

"You and the company have just been served with subpoenas. I have no idea what this is about other than that it appears to seek information related to OPM's dealings with Rockwell. I advise you not to discuss this matter until further notice."

Simon had to locate Myron and Mordy. They were supposed to be coming back that night on the red-eye, but nobody knew for sure. He asked Myron's secretary to track them down. They had just boarded an earlier flight. Simon had her pull them off. Myron came on the line.

"Myron, you and the company have just been served with subpoenas requesting all documents related to Rockwell."

He sounded "sullen" at the other end. He was probably stunned. "Don't go home yet. I'll get back to you."

Myron hung up. Then fell apart. He nearly passed out. He became incoherent. It was all Mordy could do to get him to a room at the Hyatt to assess the situation. Myron finally pulled himself together. He asked Mordy to leave the room. He called Andy Lawler and Andy Reinhard.

Andrew Lawler called Simon. He identified himself as Myron's attorney. He had to have a copy of the subpoena immediately. Simon had never heard of Lawler. He'd have to confirm that with Myron before he could respond to any such request.

Mordy called. Lawler had been retained by Myron "over the summer," he didn't know in reference to what. Simon should do whatever Lawler asked. Myron got back on the line.

"Gary? Can you get us a private plane? We're very upset. We don't want to fly home commercially."

Simon arranged for a chartered plane to pick them up. They couldn't be served with a subpoena on a private plane.

Between four and five that afternoon, Allen Ganz took a call from Preston Baptist. Allen told him it would have to wait. Then he heard the loudspeaker paging him, Klein, and Cimino. Allen ran into them at the elevators all going upstairs to see Preston. In Preston's office, the gentleman from the post office handed each of them a subpoena. Allen stalked straight into Mannes Friedman's office.

"I've just been served with a subpoena."

"You're kidding." Allen was a great kidder.

"I'm not kidding. This is for real. This is it."

Suddenly there was a lot of running around. People being summoned on the loudspeaker into Myron's area. Myron calling from California, wanting to speak to different people, separately. A lot of back and forthing in and out of Myron's office. People talking privately to Myron. Everything very hush-hush.

It was getting on toward six when Mannes Friedman came to find him. He'd just been speaking to Myron in person, on a non-OPM phone: wiretaps. They were to gather up all Rockwell files and take them directly to Myron's house. Mannes headed back upstairs to get his Rockwell things from the ninth floor; Allen and Jeff Resnick took everything they could from the eighth.

They loaded about ten large transfiles into Myron's limousine. Danny Ascher, Myron's chauffeur, drove Resnick and Friedman to Lawrence. Allen and Marty Shulman followed immediately behind in Allen's leased Buick. The four of them arrived at Myron's house in a state of total panic. Mrs. Goodman was at home. She had no idea what was going on. She didn't ask any questions. All she knew was that four OPM men were sticking document boxes in her $500,000 basement.

Friedman and Resnick started routing through the files. Allen had to go back into the city to pick up his wife from her class at NYU. They were looking for any internal memoranda, handwritten notes, pencil drafts, transmittal letters, anything that might link Lichtman, Friedman, Shulman, or Ganz to the Rockwell fraud. Myron had told them all along he would take the rap for them if it broke. They had to make sure he could make the claim stick. They stayed in the basement until after ten, before giving up for the night.

Myron and Mordy checked into a midtown Manhattan hotel around midnight, under assumed names. They needed to stay "invisible" for a while. They needed time to talk.

Myron met with Andy Lawler the next morning, who told him that any Rockwell material responsive to the subpoena would have to be returned to OPM immediately. Myron issued the order for Danny Ascher to bring the boxes back, but not before Allen Ganz had a chance to go through them again. Early the next morning, Allen combed through the boxes and took out one entire box full of bad paper. Lichtman gave him strict orders to burn it all in his fireplace, but he couldn't stand the idea of crouching over a bonfire in his living room, burning evidence. He brought the box home and hid it in the crawl space under his house.

They had to destroy anything at the office that might link them to the leases. Marty Shulman threw out two IBM Selectric typing balls he'd used to create phoney title documentation. Jeff Resnick found the Vydec word-processing disk containing Rockwell leases fabricated since the fall of 1980. He cut it up with scissors and flushed it down the OPM toilet. Danny Ascher had the ten file boxes left in the basement, purged of evidence, back at OPM by nine in the morning.

Myron was in his office at seven-thirty. Mordy didn't come in. Myron told Gary Simon he still had no idea what was going on. At the entrance to his office sat seven transfile boxes marked "Rockwell."

Myron: "That will be all you're going to need to answer the subpoena." Then, almost as an afterthought: "It's all going to be business as usual."

Simon: "It's not going to be business as usual for me. I'm not signing any more opinions-of-counsel until I know what is going on here."

Myron shrugged. "Suit yourself. Do what you have to do." He looked tired from the flight. "I'm going up to Lawler's office. I'll be gone for the rest of the day."

Simon set about trying to be responsive to the subpoena. He had the seven transfile boxes moved into his office, and with his four staff attorneys started routing through them. He went to all the logical files: Ganz's, Resnick's, Myron's. He had no reason to believe they had been tampered with. But they looked far from complete. Simon decided to build an extra door downstairs in the file room, with a special lock. They would store all the Rockwell material in there and seal off the area.

37

In late September, on the twenty-fourth, Myron had had dinner with Allen Ganz, Mannes Friedman, and Steve Lichtman at Schmulka Bernstein's restaurant on Essex Street. Myron promised he would take the rap for all of them if anything should surface.

"I am putting aside fifty grand for each of you to use, to cover legal fees if anything should happen."

Marty Shulman never showed up. Lichtman told Shulman that Myron was going to cover for them.

Shulman: "Tremendous. How's he planning to do that?"

Saturday night after the subpoenas came in, Myron took a briefcase out of his bedroom closet. He'd been hiding it in there for five years. In the briefcase were documents on all the bad deals Mordy had a hand in since the beginning. He took the briefcase over to Mordy's house. He and Mordy made a fire in the fireplace. They dropped the documents in the fire and watched them burn.

Sunday, February 22, Mannes Friedman's house: A meeting of the key conspirators. Shulman, Friedman, Lichtman, and Ganz. Allen was assigned the role of devil's advocate, of cross-examining the others. How would you answer this or that question. In the end, of course, everything was going to have to come down to Myron.

Lichtman and Friedman had handled only Rockwell's version of the leases. They had nothing to do with the inflated versions financed at the banks. Allen Ganz handled only the financed versions, he never saw the Rockwell side. So the story was that the left hand never knew what the right hand was doing. Which was pretty much the case at OPM anyway. Resnick and Shulman were going to say they did the same things with the bad leases as they did with the good leases. They were just following orders.

The whole story swung, of course, on Myron's character. He was a tyrant and irrational, and "you would just jump through hoops to get things done." There was never any time to ask questions. You did what you were told. As Allen Ganz saw it, it all made sense:

"He had Singer Hutner people duped. He had Lehman Brothers people duped. Why couldn't he have OPM people duped?"

Sunday, February 22: Sid Hasin called Myron at home. He wanted to hear from "Myron's own lips" if what they were saying about him was true.

Myron: "Talk to my lawyer."

The following Tuesday, Sid passed a personal note to Myron through Verl Rosenow: "I will no longer have anything to do with OPM or any person connected with OPM from this moment forward, including OPM Data Services."

Dave Lesnick was married to Myron's sister. He had known Myron ten years. Dave was a teacher at Shellbank Junior High School at Avenue X and Batchelder in Brooklyn. Mordy was a teacher too, before he went into business. Dave met Myron through Mordy. In 1972 he worked at OPM during his summer vacation.

David helped Mordy lease minicomputers. At the end of the summer, Mordy said, "Why don't you stay on and leave education? Because you are doing just phenomenally."

It was a tremendous decision. Dave was not only teaching junior high. He was assistant principal at the Howard Bay Jewish Center. And he was a rabbi.

But Dave had a medical problem: a kidney stone. Mordy suggested a compromise: Why not take six months' leave of absence from the Board of Education, have his operation, and work part-time at OPM while he got back on his feet?

He worked with Mordy in sales. He saw Myron in services Saturday nights. He saw Mordy at work. They spent time together, running all around the city. Sometimes to Boston or Washington. They had a fine time.

By 1980 Lesnick was an OPM vice president earning $75,000 a year. Sunday after the subpoenas arrived, Myron came over to the Lesnicks'. He seemed upset, disturbed.

"I've received a subpoena but it didn't say why. I don't know why I've been subpoenaed. But there may be things in the papers . . . different things."

He came in and sat down. He was unusually agitated, even for Myron. He wanted to know if David and his wife would be willing to go with him over to his parents' house. He didn't want his parents to worry. They might see certain things in the papers but he didn't want them to get excited. His father was just getting over a heart attack and he wanted him calm and collected.

Myron's parents had company. Myron called them away from their guests. He took them upstairs to talk in private. David's wife went with them. David stayed downstairs and talked to Myron's grandmother.

Myron told his parents: "I've just been subpoenaed. Don't get excited. Don't get all worked up. I don't know what it's about but if you should see things in the papers, just realize the papers always exaggerate."

He said people were always trying to get at OPM because they were jealous. Remember that *Business Week* article back in 1978? That had been a terrible article and it was all just from competitors being jealous.

Lesnick couldn't help feeling concerned for Myron. He wanted to help. He wanted to share his feelings, if possible. But he couldn't get anywhere with him. He was totally withdrawn: "I guess he was involved in whatever it was he was thinking."

David would call him anyway.

"Is everything all right? How are you? How are you feeling?"

"Don't worry, everything is fine. I'm busy. Don't worry, I'll take care of it, you'll see. You just do what you have to do."

Myron was on autopilot. He wasn't even listening to what he was saying. Sometimes Myron would answer Lesnick's questions by asking them right back at him:

"I'm fine. How are you doing? How do you feel? How is everything going?"

In desperation, Dave went to see Mordy. Mordy was very cool.

"Right now it's all being handled. We're taking care of it. Don't get involved. Just do what you have to do. It's all going to be straightened out. You'll see."

Dave Lesnick didn't see.

"Are you involved?"

"No."

On February 26, Myron resigned from OPM. At Andy Lawler's suggestion, OPM retained Anderson Russell Kill & Olick PC as bankruptcy counsel. To Anderson Russell, Myron and Mordy swore that Mordy knew nothing of the Rockwell fraud until the day the subpoenas arrived. After his resignation, Myron still kept a hand in running OPM. He spent most of his time at Anderson Russell. They lent him a desk.

The afternoon of the twenty-sixth, Robert Clare of White & Case called Gary Simon. There were a number of "discrepancies" in some Rockwell documents he wanted to discuss. He read Simon a list of about half a dozen Rockwell deals. Simon stopped him at a number he recognized. He asked Clare to repeat the number. Simon was stunned. He had closed that deal in-house. Simon raised his voice.

"What sort of discrepancies?"

"I'd rather not discuss the details over the phone."

Simon called Lawler's office. Lawler shared office space with Anderson Russell. He told Myron about the call from Clare. Myron did not seem surprised. Simon was going out of his mind. He went straight up to Lawler's.

"I want to know what is going on here, right now. This is it. I'd better know what is going on or I quit."

He might have seemed outwardly composed, but inside he felt like a tuning fork.

Myron was in another room. Lawler was going to have to confer with Myron and Mordy to see whether they would be willing to waive the privilege so he could tell Simon the whole story. Lawler left his office and went down the hall to a conference room where Myron and Mordy were working. He returned a few minutes later.

"I'm sorry, they have declined."

Simon was beside himself. Here he was still getting the runaround in a company where he was supposed to be the head lawyer.

Lawler: "I have been authorized to inform you that Myron has resigned, as of five o'clock this afternoon. I know how you're feeling right now but Mordy has asked that he be allowed to speak to you before you have time to react to the resignation."

Mordy stepped in.

"Gary, I'm as surprised as you are by what is going on."

He gave Gary a pep talk. He'd like him to stick with the company. Mordy was going to reorganize the company under Chapter Eleven and he would be needing Gary more than ever. He wanted to take part of Gary's salary and put it in a trust fund, "So in case we go out of business you'll have severance pay." He offered to pay Gary's legal fees if he needed a lawyer. He wanted Gary to consider committing himself to staying on another year.

Simon took Mordy up on his first offer, to handle the legal fees. On the second, the trust fund idea, he turned him down flat. On the third, the time commitment, there was no way he could do it. But, out of personal respect for Mordy, he would do his best to stay on as long as he could.

Myron came in.

"Gary, I'm sorry I've hurt you."

Myron started to cry. The whole painful scene, thank God, didn't last long.

On March 11, 1981, OPM filed a voluntary petition for reorganization under Chapter Eleven of the Bankruptcy Code.

Mordy stayed on as president and announced the retention of Philip J. Ryan, a former assistant U.S. attorney, as special counsel and manager of operations. Mordy hoped to avoid the appointment of a trustee by the bankruptcy court by hiring an outsider untainted by fraud or previous association with the company.

On March 17, Ryan fired Mannes Friedman, Steve Lichtman, and Allen Ganz, for refusing to cooperate with an investigation being conducted by Anderson Russell. Marty Shulman was fired for the same reason two days later. On March 20, counsel for a number of OPM creditors asked to examine Mordy on the record about the fraud. Though Mordy still claimed ignorance of the fraud before February 19, he resigned as president of OPM on March 20. On March 24, the bankruptcy court directed the United States trustee to appoint a trustee to manage the affairs of OPM. That same day, Myron and Mordy filed personal petitions of bankruptcy.

On March 19, Myron checked into a mental hospital on Long Island. He claimed to be suffering from "nervous collapse." He began a series of treatments designed to detoxify him from the enormous quantities of drugs he had been living on for so many months. He was interviewed by two psychiatrists, Edward R. Sodaro, M.D. and Curston D. Goldin, M.D. They concluded that Myron "perceived plots against him . . . and experienced other grandiose delusions." Specifically, Myron told Lichtman and Friedman that he had "convinced the doctors he was crazy by claiming there was a plot against Israel and the Jews and that Rockwell was behind it." Myron was clearly doing his best to put together a credible insanity defense.

At the hospital, Myron had his secretary, Ruth Holloway, take dictation at his bedside. He said he might have made "some decisions . . . that were questionable." After the word "questionable" he laughed. He said: "I wonder if they make solid gold handcuffs." Then he laughed some more.

Ruth could see Myron had lost a lot of weight and was easily tired. But he did not seem insane to her. His mind was as sharp as ever, and what he said seemed basically reasonable. He read newspaper articles about himself with considerable interest. After putting down one such article in *The Wall Street Journal,* he said:

"Well, if you're going to steal, you might as well steal big. I'm going to make Robert Vesco look like a comic-strip character."

He said it would take so many lawyers and accountants to figure out what he had done they'd never find out the whole story in a million years. He read in one of the papers that Sid Hasin "disavowed any intent to ever join forces with OPM."

Myron: "Sid Hasin is a liar."

Ruth wondered, idly, if Sid Hasin had been the one who "dropped the dime" on Myron.

The co-conspirators held cover-up meetings on successive Sundays. The first Sunday at Friedman's house, the second Sunday at Lichtman's house. Marty Shulman couldn't make it the second Sunday. Lichtman was asked to fill in.

From the beginning, they recognized Allen Ganz as a potential soft spot.

Ganz: "They always said I would be the first one to break because I was the youngest and scaredest. They were always worried I'd break under pressure and throw them all in the fire." From March 17, the day all of them were fired, life was a "living hell" for Allen: "Living the whole lie over again." But Ganz did his best to keep his cool: "I did have some allegiance to those guys . . . They made sure I visited them pretty frequently during the course of that period."

They had all hired their own attorneys by then, but they had all agreed to lie even to them about their involvement and knowledge. They also took specific steps to hide their roles in the fraud:

> (1) Marty Shulman asked Myron to tell his executive secretary, Toni Pierre, that only Goodman was involved in typing phoney bills of sale and false financial statements.
> (2) They told Jeff Resnick, still at OPM, to cover their tracks as best he could.

At the synagogue on Saturday nights Lichtman kept telling Resnick to "hang tough." On April 30, Resnick was interviewed by Audrey Strauss, the assistant U.S. attorney. Resnick lied about his knowledge of and involvement in the fraud, and at the end of that interview she told him she questioned his truthfulness. He should go home and think about whether it made sense to be lying to protect others.

On May 11, he went back to the U.S. attorney and further perjured himself, compounding the crime by lying again at a deposition taken by the trustee on July 15 and 21.

Lichtman had taken the Fifth. He lied to his attorney and his wife. Ganz had taken the Fifth. He lied to his attorney and his wife. Mannes was not coming clean to his attorney either.

They were all worried about Joel Klein, head of Equity. According to Myron, Klein drove home with him one night after a meeting with Rockwell toward the end of 1980. Myron: "He wanted to know why certain deals couldn't be sold into equity . . . he questioned Hoby Shapiro's leaving, John Clifton's leaving."

Myron: "Don't worry. It's all being taken care of. Forget about it."

Myron says Klein refused to leave well enough alone: "He bribed me to buy him a house." Steve Lichtman came to Myron's house during the cover-up period. He had been talking to Klein, and he was worried: "How are we going to keep Joel Klein down?" Myron said Klein wouldn't talk, he'd been taken care of. Myron: "Lichtman was the one who always threw his hands around. Friedman would tell Lichtman to shut up. He didn't know what he was talking about. Then Shulman would tell them all to shut up. He was the ringleader."

The first witness to be questioned by counsel for the trustee was Gary Simon, June 18. During his examination, Simon was shown a hand-written note discovered with the Rockwell version of a bad lease:

Fin. Docs sent to Rocky.

Simon identified the handwriting as that of Allen Ganz.

Jeff Resnick, still at OPM, told Allen Ganz they had found the note. They had somehow overlooked it during the document purge.

Ganz, sure enough, was the first to go.

He broke it to the conspirators early one morning in June. He met them in the road in front of his house.

"I've reached a decision to go forward and you're not going to be able to talk me out of it."

They tried but didn't get far.

Mannes told Allen he was going up to Grossinger's for a three-day midweek vacation with his in-laws, and they were paying for it. He didn't want to spoil his "last vacation." He begged Allen to hold off just a couple of days until he got back. Allen figured, "I've waited so long, what is three more days?" Mannes had his vacation.

Mannes got back from Grossinger's around eleven on a Wednesday night. He and Allen and Steve sat for a couple of hours in Lichtman's car in a parking lot off Rockaway Turnpike. Shulman wasn't there. None of them trusted Shulman. They figured he'd do better for himself on his own.

They all agreed that if Allen was going to go forward, they were all going to have to go forward. Lichtman said he would have to tell Shulman about this.

Shulman had been keeping his end up. A few days before, he had shown up to his grand jury examination wearing a bowling shirt, without counsel. There were over thirty separate instances of perjury in his grand jury testimony.

Allen Ganz had a talk with his attorney. Then he had a talk with the U.S. attorney. He told them everything except about Jeff Resnick. He signed a letter of understanding, that he was willing to cooperate with the investigation on the condition that no charges would be brought against his father.

On August 3, Allen went to see Myron at his house. He said he was going to be indicted if he refused to cooperate with the government. He was going to have to tell them about Mordy's involvement in the preparation of the first two IBM invoices. Myron was outraged; he had forgotten Mordy had anything to do with all that. He believed Allen was willing to finger anyone to protect himself and his father. He was going to hand Mordy over to them out of spite.

Myron begged him to wait two weeks. He was going into the hospital any day now to have his pacemaker "recalled." There was something dangerously wrong with it, and they were going to have to take it out and put in another. Allen said he couldn't wait, they were putting all sorts of pressure on him to come forward immediately with everything he had. Myron: "He had obviously made a deal with Audrey Strauss implicating Mordy."

The following Monday, Myron had his pacemaker taken out and exchanged for a new one. On Tuesday, Mordy came over late at night for "one of our continual discussions on the conspiracy." They started out in the bushes surrounding Myron's house. Eventually, they moved into the woods a few hundred yards away.

Myron: "Allen Ganz has lied to the U.S. Attorney about you. He says you helped forge an IBM invoice."

Mordy: "That's right."

Somewhere between the bushes and the woods, Mordy broke down. He admitted he had in fact typed up an IBM invoice on one of the very first Rockwell deals, that Allen Ganz had given him the serial numbers and the equipment descriptions, and that Allen Ganz had seen him do it.

A few days later, Allen Ganz, Mannes Friedman, and Steve Lichtman paid a visit together to the U.S. Attorney's Office. Shulman and Resnick knew nothing about it. Both Resnick and Shulman perjured themselves repeatedly during the summer in depositions taken before the trustee. After Resnick's perjury, Allen Ganz permitted himself to be wired. He coaxed Resnick into a conversation tailored to nail him. Resnick talked about creating documents used in the fraud, and about destroying the Vydec word-processing disk as part of the cover-up.

According to Myron, he and Andy Reinhard talked on the phone "nearly every day" from the moment the subpoenas arrived at OPM. He says the first person he called, after passing out at LAX, was Andy Reinhard. He asked Mordy to leave the room during their conversation.

They met three times after that. At the offices of Anderson Russell, OPM's bankruptcy lawyers, in March; in Myron's room at the mental hospital on Long Island in May; in Central Park in August 1981.

Myron had been to see his shrink on Madison and Sixty-eighth. He met Andy there, and they took a walk in the park. It was a bright, hot, summer day. Myron bought Andy an ice cream.

Andy accepted the ice cream. But he was worried about other favors. Myron says he was worried about having charged a plane ticket to Florida on his OPM Amex card to go to his grandfather's funeral. It could be construed by prosecutors as some sort of payoff. Myron: "I could have slugged him right then and there! With all I had to worry about, he was going on about a $400 plane ticket?"

Myron told him about Allen Ganz coming forward to cop a plea. He says Andy was very concerned about his role coming to light.

Myron: "You basically have nothing to worry about."

Reinhard recalls the walk in the park, which he admits he did not disclose in advance to his lawyers. He doesn't remember the concern over the plane ticket. Only a bizarre scheme Myron was hashing out in his mind to return to OPM as a consultant to the trustee.

Andy did not have to worry about Myron wearing a wire: "I was not wearing a wire and never would have worn a wire with Andy Reinhard."

A few months later, Myron and Mordy dropped the cover story. They agreed to cooperate with the U.S. attorney. Mordy gave in only after Audrey Strauss read his lawyer a long list of charges referring not only to his involvement in the Rockwell fraud, but to his much larger role in a whole string of pre-Rockwell frauds. As part of his deal with the U.S. attorney, Mordy allowed himself to be wired. He recorded conversations with Joseph Verner of Fireman's Fund, Harold Farkas of Jerry Silverman, Inc., Richard Monks, formerly of IBM, and Henry

Weiss of Montefiore Hospital. All four subsequently pleaded guilty to criminal tax charges relating to their receipt of commercial bribes.

December 17, 1981: Goodman, Weissman, Lichtman, Friedman, Shulman, Ganz, and Resnick all entered guilty pleas before the United States District Court for the Southern District of New York. The charges: fraud, conspiracy, mail fraud, wire fraud, and making false statements to a bank. Goodman, guilty on sixteen counts, Weissman on nine, Shulman on five, Ganz on four, Lichtman and Friedman on three, Resnick on two.

38

December 1982: Audrey Strauss, head of the Business Frauds Unit of the U.S. Attorney's Office for the Southern District of New York, submitted a government's sentencing memorandum to U.S. District Judge Charles S. Haight, Jr., one year after obtaining guilty pleas from the OPM defendants. It represented the culmination of a nearly two-year investigation of the fraud at OPM.

A year before, Myron Goodman pled guilty to one count of conspiracy, one count of mail fraud, and fourteen counts of wire fraud, with a cumulative exposure of eighty years of imprisonment and $25,000 in fines. Mordecai Wiessman pled guilty to one count of conspiracy, six counts of wire fraud, one count of mail fraud, and one count of making false statements to banks, carrying a cumulative exposure of forty-two years of imprisonment and $27,000 in fines.

Ganz, Lichtman, Friedman, Shulman, and Resnick all pled guilty to fewer and lesser charges. The cumulative penalties were as follows:

Ganz:	17 years, $8,000
Lichtman:	12 years, $7,000
Friedman:	12 years, $7,000
Shulman:	22 years, $9,000
Resnick:	7 years, $6,000

The sentencing memorandum sought to describe the crimes committed and assess the relative culpability of the conspirators.

> This is an extraordinary case in which a business was built and maintained for ten years on a foundation of pervasive fraud. During the ten year period, Myron Goodman and Mordecai Weissman . . . resorted to multi-million dollar frauds to meet cash flow problems . . . frequently did business through the payment of commercial bribes . . . and utilized false financial statements as suited their needs.
>
> This pattern of criminal activity culminated with the Rockwell fraud, in which over nineteen lending institutions were fraudulently induced to lend OPM over $190,000,000. This crime, which standing alone would constitute one of the largest white collar frauds in the history of this country, was instigated, supervised and directed by Goodman, with active ongoing participation by Ganz, Lichtman, Friedman, and Shulman. Resnick joined in at the end. Weissman actively participated at the outset and then, knowing that the fraud was keeping his company alive, deliberately avoided active participation in an effort to protect himself from criminal prosecution.
>
> Finally, once an investigation began . . . all the defendants engaged in diverse and numerous acts of obstruction of justice. The primary goal of these efforts was to permit all the defendants to escape criminal accountability, except Goodman, who was prepared to accept the blame for all, but who hoped that his history of medical illnesses would cause the court to grant him lenient treatment.

In reviewing the check-kiting prosecution, the government found:

> In presentations to Assistant U.S. Attorney Pauline Hardin, OPM's lawyers represented that Goodman . . . was solely responsible for the scheme and was too gravely ill to be prosecuted. Indeed, the Assistant was explicitly told that Goodman's sarcoid would result in his death within a year or two. Based on these representations, the U.S. Attorney's Office did not prosecute Goodman individually and accepted a corporate plea . . . Goodman, who at that very moment was proceeding apace with the Rockwell fraud, cried to his attorneys in gratitude and swore that he would never go astray again.

The U.S. Attorney's Office was determined not to make the same mistake twice.

At this stage, the defense obviously seeks to have the Court place great weight on their presentation that Goodman was a physically and emotionally ill person whose judgment was severely affected by drugs . . . Several facts should be considered in the face of that contention.

It is evident that Goodman was repeatedly willing to do business by fraud for many years before 1978. Thus his criminal inclinations cannot be attributed to the use of drugs. There is evidence . . . that Goodman intended to use his illness to obtain leniency from the Court.

There is a question as to whether Goodman attempted to exaggerate or fabricate symptoms in order to escape punishment for his crimes . . . in the spring of 1981, when Goodman was hospitalized, he explicitly told one co-conspirator that he was playing games with his doctors . . . that he had convinced them he was crazy.

In sum . . . it should be recalled that notwithstanding his sarcoidosis and other ailments, Goodman found the physical and mental strength to commit the monumental crimes for which he stands convicted.

In assessing Weissman's guilt, the memo concluded that "Weissman's culpability in this case is less than that of Goodman's, and significantly greater than that of the other defendants in this case":

He was equally culpable with Goodman in all the pre-Rockwell frauds.

With respect to the Rockwell fraud, Weissman actively participated in at least two early fraudulent transactions. At the time of the bankruptcy in March of 1981, Weissman showed notable guile as he proclaimed to everyone who would listen his shock at learning of his partner's misdeeds . . . In this false pose, Weissman tried to convince the bankruptcy court to leave OPM in his trustworthy hands, promising to expel the culprit, Goodman.

His sentence should reflect his responsibility for these crimes.

The prosecutors grouped Ganz, Lichtman, Friedman, and Shulman in the second rank of guilt. Three motives for participation were established:

1. a desire to accede to Goodman's entreaties
2. a desire to be within the innermost circle at OPM
3. a desire to keep a well-paying job

Shulman may have been disappointed to find out that the government ranked him beneath Ganz and Lichtman as a Rockwell fraud team member, as a function of simple seniority. But Shulman was given extra credit for accepting $140,000 in payoffs from OPM while at American Express, and "for evading taxes on approximately half that sum." Shulman was also awarded points for "deeply aggravating" his guilt by perjuring himself repeatedly before the grand jury and the trustee. In the overall fraudulent scheme of things, Marty Shulman won hands down.

Allen Ganz at least placed: "His participation in the Rockwell fraud—from the first transaction to the last—is compounded by his knowledge of, and participation in payoffs and other pre-Rockwell frauds. Although to some extent this lengthy involvement in criminal activity is explained by his inability to stand up to his older brothers-in-law, a picture of long standing criminality nevertheless emerges."

Steve Lichtman merely showed. Unlike Shulman and Ganz, he did not commit any substantial crimes beyond the Rockwell fraud and the cover-up. He was also given additional "credit for efforts to alert non-co-conspirators to the fraud," namely, John Clifton, Mendy Weissman, and Andy Reinhard.

Friedman came in fourth. The duration of his participation was less than Lichtman's, and he did not have any other substantial crimes adding to his culpability. Resnick finished last, since he began participating only two months before the fraud ended. Still, he could hardly be viewed as altogether innocent, since he actively participated in the cover-up and in doing so committed wholesale perjury.

Under "Considerations Upon Sentencing of These Defendants," the government noted:

> This is a case involving . . . actual money losses to nineteen lending institutions totalling approximately $130,000,000. Although insurers may cover portions of some losses, for certain of the vic-

tims, such as The State of Wisconsin Investment Board, the losses were totally uninsured. Moreover, to the extent that insurance companies bear some of the losses, they and their shareholders become victims of the fraud.

Then there were further, far less tangible losses:

> Everyone who unwittingly participated in the fraudulent transactions—be they wholly innocent or perhaps even somewhat negligent—has been tainted by them. This includes numerous employees of OPM, investment bankers, accountants, officers of lending institutions, lawyers who represented banks, as well as lawyers and paralegals who represented OPM. Many of these people rightfully feel that they were among those defrauded by these defendants.

The government respectfully urged the court to consider the following:

> Many people touched by the events in this case . . . will be avid observers of the sentences imposed . . . the public at large, and the financial community in particular, will likewise observe and carefully note the sentences imposed. Most importantly, businessmen faced with problems which could be solved by resort to fraud may be affected—one way or the other—by the sentences imposed.

The government respectfully urged the court to answer three questions:

1. What sentences would be viewed by potential criminals, and the public, as adequate to deter the commission of a $200,000,000 fraud?
2. What sentences would be viewed by the defraud parties as just punishment for the fraud committed upon them?
3. What additional sentence is appropriate to adequately deter and punish the acts of obstruction of justice committed by each defendant?

December 20, 1982:

In a third-floor corridor of the Federal District Court on Manhattan's Foley Square . . . a tall, bespectacled man looking no more than his 36 years stood talking with his friends, nervously drawing

> on a cigarette . . . Just before 4:30, [Myron] Goodman stubbed out his cigarette and entered the cluttered, high-ceilinged courtroom, where he proceeded to promise the judge: "The wrongs I have done are behind me" . . . Goodman's promise . . . had a familiar ring for some in the courtroom.
>
> —From Stuart Taylor, "Ethics and the Law," New York *Times Magazine*, January 9, 1983.

Before the sentencing, Judge Haight recited a brief history of OPM for the benefit of those lacking the evident misfortune of firsthand knowledge. He did not buy Myron's promise to repent and repay, or the arguments of his lawyers that he deserved leniency because of his "devastating and life-threatening" sarcoidosis. Instead, he seized the opportunity to harshly chastise Goodman and Weissman from the bench: "I perceive in a fraud so massive and so prolonged an assault upon the integrity of the marketplace, upon those concepts of honesty and trust without which commerce cannot function, that it approximates a crime of violence."

Judge Haight gave some weight to Goodman's illness by making him eligible for parole should his condition deteriorate beyond the point that prison doctors could effectively safeguard his health. He gave some weight to assertions by Weissman's attorneys that he was "relatively less culpable" than Goodman, and that he helped the U.S. Attorney's Office conduct "undercover investigations" that resulted in a number of bribery convictions. But when it came time to hand out the sentences, the terms were tough: twelve years in prison for Myron, ten for Mordy.

> After hearing their sentences, Weissman and Goodman appeared grim, and refused to comment. Miss Strauss, who heads the business frauds unit for the Southern District of New York, also declined comment.
>
> —Paul Blustein, *The Wall Street Journal*, December 21, 1982.

Shulman was sentenced to four years, Ganz to three, Lichtman to two, Friedman to eighteen months, Resnick to three years' probation, three hundred hours of community service, and a fine of $5,000. For accepting commercial bribes and evading taxes, Richard Monks, formerly of IBM, got five months in prison, three years' probation, and a $5,000 fine. Joseph Verner, of Fireman's Fund received three years' probation and a $5,000 fine. Harold Farkas of Jerry Silverman, Inc. received two years' probation and a $10,000 fine. Henry Weiss of Montefiore Hospital got five years' probation, three hundred hours of community service, and a $10,000 fine. All those incarcerated were sent to Allenwood Federal Prison Camp in Montgomery, Pennsylvania. Where all good white-collar criminals go.

With the criminal investigation now concluded, the trustee's civil investigation into the fraud went on. On March 27, 1981, Judge Burton R. Lifland of the United States Bankruptcy Court, Southern District of New York, had appointed James P. Hassett as trustee of OPM's parent corporation, Cali Trading International, and all its myriad subsidiaries and affiliates. Hassett, a former computer-leasing executive, was instructed by the judge during a conference in chambers to recognize and emphasize the "examining" functions of his job: the in-depth investigation of management misconduct at OPM. The trustee promptly retained the prominent Washington law firm of Wilmer Cutler & Pickering as special counsel.

The purpose of the trustee's investigation was not to prosecute the principals, but to "develop facts relevant to whether the estate or any party in interest had actionable claims or defenses to claims arising out of the fraud at OPM." These "parties in interest," the defrauded institutions, pressed for a broad investigation to determine the role of "solvent third parties against whom they believed they might have actionable claims." The solvent third parties were Rockwell International, Lehman Brothers, Singer Hutner, Fox & Co., and Rashba & Pokart.

The sweeping investigation into the OPM fraud took nearly two years, with seventy-three witnesses testifying in formal examinations, producing over one million pages of documents for review by the trustee, yielding over sixty thousand pages of stenographic transcript. Fourteen law firms represented the interested parties, all of whom were permitted to examine witnesses with respect to their specific claims. Examination of witnesses by the trustee's counsel alone took two hundred days; examination of counsel for the other parties took an additional eighty.

The investigation was hindered from the outset by the very complexity of the fraud, the deliberate disarray of OPM's documents and records, and a prolonged delay in obtaining any useful information from the fraud team members. Though the cover-up was abandoned at the end of 1981 for the purposes of the criminal investigation, the defendants adamantly refused to consent to interviews by the trustee, and asserted the Fifth Amendment when asked to produce documents and testify to the details of the fraud. Andrew Reinhard personally pled the Fifth with relation to his role in the fraud, while Goodman and Weissman prevented Singer Hutner from coming forward by asserting the attorney-client privilege. It took a year of litigation through three levels of judicial review before the privilege issue was resolved in the trustee's favor, and Singer Hutner was permitted to produce documents and information relating to its decade-long representation of OPM.

The United States Attorney's Office rejected the trustee's appeal that any plea bargaining be conditioned on the conspirator's cooperation with his investigation. According to the trustee's report, "it was apparent that the guilty plea defendants believed they would displease the U.S. Attorney's Office if they testified on the record in the Trustee's investigation." The trustee's efforts to settle claims against the OPM estate were further hindered by the U.S. Attorney's Office's "consistent refusal to make relevant information available to the Trustee even when no legal or ethical rule prohibited it." In particular, when the trustee learned that Myron Goodman had purchased $250,000 worth of U.S. Treasury bearer bonds after the filing of his personal bankruptcy petition, the U.S. attorney had already entered into a plea bargain with Goodman granting him immunity from prosecution for bankruptcy crimes. "Needless to say, by the time the Trustee learned of the relevant facts, the $250,000 was no longer recoverable."

A year went by before Allen Ganz and Myron Goodman agreed to testify on the record, under a letter agreement restricting the use of their testimony until after their criminal sentencing in December of 1982. Immediately after the sentencing, the other OPM insiders agreed to testify, but the trustee determined that this additional questioning was "not likely to yield enough new information to warrant the time and expense required to develop it."

The investigation initially focused strictly on the Rockwell fraud. But as the pre-Rockwell frauds, bogus financial statements, commercial bribes, and illegal diversions of company funds came to light, the scope of the inquiry gradually widened. Finally, the investigation turned to the activities of the many outside professionals, including lawyers, accountants, management consultants, investment bankers, tax shelter promoters, bankers, and lessees without whom the ten-year fraud that was OPM could never have taken place, let alone succeeded over such a long period.

> The Trustee believes that one significant function of his Report is to help prevent frauds like the fraud at OPM from succeeding in the future. To this end, the Trustee considers it important to express . . . views on the standards of conduct to which accountants, management consultants, lawyers, investment bankers, tax shelter promoters, lessees, and financial institutions should adhere in their business dealings. Whether or not the law requires it, the Trustee believes that adherence to these standards will reduce the likelihood of recurrence of a fraud of the scope, magnitude, and duration of the fraud at OPM.

When the six-hundred-page trustee's report was finally filed with the Federal Bankruptcy Court in April of 1983, none of the above was let off lightly. The report faulted the "ignorance, carelessness, poor judgment, and self-interest" of the many outside professionals and businessmen who dealt with the company. "A variety of simple measures . . . could have or should have detected the fraud or prevented its continuation . . . Instead, in an 'After You, Alphonse' routine, all stood by in the mistaken belief that others were checking to verify that things were really as they seemed."

Accountants:

Without the aid of pliant accountants willing to certify OPM's financials, the fraud could never have succeeded, because OPM could never have remained in business. Accountants were OPM's primary tools of fraud, because without them the company could never have so painstakingly maintained the "illusion of success" and so remarkably disguised the harsh fact that the company was insolvent from inception.

Rashba & Pokart was commended by the trustee for refusing to bow to pressure from Myron to certify OPM as a going concern. But its 1973 financial statements were nevertheless "false and misleading . . . because they did not disclose the double and triple discounting.":

> Whether Rashba & Pokart learned of the double discounting before it reported on the 1973 financials is uncertain. If it did, its failure to disclose . . . [this] was clearly improper . . . On the other hand, if the firm refused to certify the 1974 and 1975 financials because of the double discounting problem, it deserves credit for steadfastness . . . Rashba & Pokart also deserves credit for ensuring that the unaudited financials it assisted in preparing showed the increasing losses and deficits OPM was in fact suffering.

Both John Clifton and Marvin Weissman were rather gently faulted for not doing more to stop the Rockwell fraud once they learned about it.

> By the spring of 1980 Rashba & Pokart and Clifton knew Goodman was engaged in massive lease fraud. Both sought to pass the buck for doing something about it to Singer Hutner . . . Perhaps they had no legal duty to make disclosure to government authorities or affected third parties. But there does not appear to have been any legal or ethical rule that prevented them from doing so. Surely it would have been better if they had. Although the law may not require a bystander to inform the police of an ongoing crime, basic moral precepts do not permit him to simply walk away. And Rashba & Pokart and Clifton were not mere bystanders.

The report reserved most of its ire on the financial front for Fox & Co.:

> Although OPM was never a public company, certified financial statements were important to it, especially in its later years. The OPM financials certified by Fox from 1976 through 1978 were materially false and misleading . . . At the most fundamental level, they misstated the financial condition of OPM by representing it as a profitable enterprise when in reality it was losing money hand over fist.

Even if Fox could be excused for certifying OPM's financials prior to 1978, the trustee found that "the Fox 1978 Cali/OPM financial statements were materially false and misleading . . . Given marketplace developments, Fox's failure to at least qualify its opinion on a going concern basis, or otherwise suggest OPM's precarious financial condition was indefensible."

The real culprit here, of course, was the Kutz method:

> [This] permitted OPM to record the cash received from sales of equity participations as income in the year those sales occurred . . . ignoring the contingency that exercise of early termination options could turn the booked profits into disastrous losses. Use of the Kutz Method allowed OPM to recognize prematurely over $13.6 million . . . in 1977 and over $20.5 million in 1978. As a result of the Kutz Method and other "creative" accounting techniques developed under intense pressure from Goodman, the Fox certified financials . . . falsely represented Cali's income and net worth as positive . . . when OPM probably was not even a going concern.

According to Price Waterhouse, retained by the trustee to examine the Fox financials, "application of generally accepted accounting principles in lieu of the Kutz Method would have resulted in a net loss in 1978 of over $17.8 million and a negative net worth of almost $31.5 million."

The trustee further noted that even after he left Fox to start his own accounting firm, Kutz continued to work with OPM in preparing 1980 financial statements for filing with OPM's bankruptcy petition: ". . . Kutz was accommodating to the end . . . a few days before OPM filed its bankruptcy petition, Kutz told Goodman he had a way 'to make OPM look good on its financial statements.' "

Fox financials were Myron's key element in casting an illusion of prosperity over a failing enterprise:

> Lehman and the First National Bank of St. Paul . . . relied on Fox's unqualified opinion . . . in determining to do business with OPM. Had these two institutions refused to deal with OPM, it is doubtful whether Goodman could have carried off the Rockwell fraud.

In June of 1983, the Denver-based Fox & Co., the nation's twelfth largest accounting firm, signed a consent agreement with the SEC restricting it from performing audits of publicly owned companies, as a result of actions brought against it by the SEC regarding its audits of OPM, Saxon Industries, and Flight Transportation, three of the largest corporate scandals of the 1980s.

Saxon Industries and a number of bank creditors sued Fox, Morton Berger, head of Fox's New York office and the partner in charge of OPM, as well as Arthur Rogovin, the former Fox partner who went into partnership with Steve Kutz after he left OPM. The suits charged Fox with auditing Saxon's copper division without personally checking inventories or even visiting the plant. Saxon examiner Arthur England reported that Saxon employees referred to the Fox audits as "a joke."

When Fox bought Morton Berger's New York-based accounting firm of Westheimer, Fine, Berger & Co., it established a presence in New York. Stanley Lurie, a former partner in Berger's firm who became CEO of Saxon, was named by Saxon employees as "the chef" in the cooking of Saxon's books, according to *Forbes* magazine.

The SEC charged Fox with overstating revenues for Flight Transportation on Fox-certified 1981 financials by "at least $14 million." Cash and short-term investments were overstated by "at least $2 million." Sworn affidavits by Flight employees as-

serted that the company never handled the volume of charters that could have produced anything close to those revenues.
Forbes quoted Norman Klein, managing partner of Fox: "Accountants cannot be the policemen of corporate America."

39

Lawyers:

OPM's trusty lawyers were not portrayed heroically in the trustee's report.

> Beginning in 1975 lawyers for OPM played an essential role in OPM lease financing transactions . . . Financing institutions naturally took comfort from the participation of independent lawyers in OPM transactions. But the lawyers never checked to make certain that the leases financed by OPM were legitimate, or that underlying equipment existed, even when circumstances strongly suggested that something was amiss. In relying uncritically on Goodman's representations, OPM's lawyers proved to be easy tools of fraud.

When Singer Hutner first learned in the spring of 1980 that Goodman had perpetrated a massive fraud, the firm "commendably retained reputable and independent counsel to advise it." But, in the opinion of the trustee, the firm's good judgment went straight downhill from there. Instead of acting in a way that might have stopped the fraud, the firm "acted in a way that helped Goodman continue the fraud for eight additional months, during which financial institutions were bilked out of more than $85 million."

Singer Hutner's first mistake was in relying on Goodman's claim that the fraud was over. In doing so, the firm ignored substantial evidence that it was not. The evidence cited: Clifton's prediction that OPM could not survive without continued wrongdoing; questions about the forged title documents raised by Eli Matiolli during the summer; the firm's own knowledge of Goodman's past misdeeds and OPM's precarious financial condition. A willful and reckless acceptance of Myron's unsupported claim that the fraud was over irrevocably determined their course of action. "By June 25 . . . Singer Hutner determined it would continue to close OPM's lease financings in reliance on Goodman's certification of their legitimacy . . . and keep Goodman's misdeed's secret." Neither would have been permissable in the knowledge of an ongoing fraud.

Even accepting Putzel's questionable assertion that "the firm was in no possession of any fact which in any way indicated the commission of an ongoing fraud" (a statement the trustee labeled "plainly false"), professional ethics would still have allowed Singer Hutner to follow certain other courses:

1. resigning as OPM's counsel immediately
2. declining to close OPM transactions unless shown the Clifton letter and full disclosure of the particulars of the fraud
3. acceding to Rubino's urgings to implement a system of third-party verification
4. turning to other OPM officers to prevent Goodman from continuing the fraud

In failing to advise Singer Hutner that the firm could have ethically considered these options, the trustee found Putzel and McLaughlin's costly advice to the firm "the worst possible advice from the point of view of OPM, the third parties with which it dealt, Singer Hutner's successor counsel, and Singer Hutner itself."

Even more egregious was Singer Hutner's failure to react effectively to Goodman's belated revelations in the fall of 1980. In seeking to prevent Goodman from defrauding successor counsel and Lehman Brothers, the steps taken were "shockingly inadequate," including the so-called due diligence memo to Gary Simon and the nondelivered "warning" letter to Lehman Brothers. The "due diligence" memo did not alert Simon or Kaye Scholer "to the need for extraordinary care in handling Rockwell lease financings." The firm failed to stop Goodman from fraudulently rolling over the three bridge financings by sending a letter to Lehman Brothers two weeks too late; by falsely assuming that the letter had been received by Lehman; by falsely assuming that Myron needed Lehman's participation to renew the bogus notes.

Finally, "Singer Hutner's acquiescence in the false characterization of its resignation as a 'mutual determination to terminate' permitted the fraud to continue because it misled OPM's in-house lawyers, Kaye Scholer, investment bankers, financing institutions, and others into believing they could safely deal with OPM . . . Singer Hutner's failure to deal effectively with Goodman's confessions of massive fraud recklessly and inexcusably resulted in approximately $85 million in further losses to the fraud victims."

What about the "Reinhard Question"?

"One of the most difficult issues encountered in the Trustee's investigation was whether Reinhard knowingly participated in any of the fraudulent activities at OPM. The United States Attorney's Office investigated Reinhard's conduct and in the fall of 1982 determined not to seek a grand jury indictment against him. But the decision of the United States Attorney's Office not to prosecute is not dispositive."

Reinhard denies any knowledge of the fraud before June of 1980, when the firm as a whole first learned about it. But, "Reinhard refused personally to respond to any questions by the Trustee . . . on a claim of Fifth Amendment privilege. Although judges and juries in criminal cases constitutionally may not infer guilt from a defendant's silence, civil courts—and the Trustee—are not so constrained."

The principle witness against Reinhard is Myron Goodman. But statements by other members of the OPM fraud team and Marvin Weissman tend to corroborate Goodman's testimony. Goodman testified that he told Reinhard "everything," about payoffs to vendor salesmen, double discounting, "taking care" of lessee employees, and finally, and "unfortunately," about the Rockwell fraud.

In finding "Goodman's testimony that Reinhard knew of the Rockwell fraud from the outset [to be] supported by other evidence," the trustee cited Lichtman's recollection of seeking Reinhard's assistance in stopping Myron from going ahead with the first bad deals; Allen Ganz's unshakable belief that Reinhard knew, both from Steve Lichtman's remarks to that effect and from the way Goodman instructed him and Lichtman not to discuss the fraud with Reinhard; and from Marvin Weissman's clear recollection that Lichtman told him he had discussed the matter with Reinhard. When Myron confessed to Weissman, Weissman received the distinct impression Reinhard knew all about the fraud, an impression not at all dispelled at lunch with Reinhard a few days later.

Myron considered Reinhard his staunchest ally at Singer Hutner: he could influence his partners to stick by Myron "come hell or high water"; he says Reinhard funneled information to him concerning the deliberations going on at the firm over the question of resignation; that while the firm was pressuring Goodman for disclosure, Reinhard provided them with none of the information he had at his disposal about the fraud.

Andy wrote to Myron after the firm's resignation, when there were no more secrets left to guard:

> I know pretty much what you have been going through lately. But I can only hope that somehow this will all be "history" in a short while & you will be able to chuckle about it.

The trustee's conclusion:

> The question whether Reinhard knowingly participated in the Rockwell fraud is by no means free from doubt. The Trustee nevertheless believes that there is substantial evidence . . . that Goodman led Reinhard to become a knowing, however reluctant, participant in the fraud.

In the wake of the OPM bankruptcy, Singer Hutner Levine & Seeman reconstituted itself as a far smaller corporate entity under the name of Singer & Chase. Joseph Hutner remained a partner, as did Andy Reinhard, in the notable absence of any official action to disbar, censure, or otherwise limit him in his practice of the law.

On August 2, 1983, the American Bar Association adopted a comprehensive new model code of legal ethics that prohibited lawyers from disclosing continuing fraudulent activities by their clients. The rule did adopt a number of official comments by which lawyers could signal to prospective victims and to successor counsel that their withdrawal from a representation was caused by "something amiss." This compromise code was adopted by the association's 383-member house of delegates after a rancorous debate reflecting a dismal lack of consensus over the confidentiality issue.

A special commission appointed in 1977 to propose new ethical rules was bitterly opposed in its efforts to encourage lawyers to disclose client secrets if needed to rectify illegal activities in which the lawyer's services had been used. The American College of Trial Lawyers was particularly upset by a proposed provision requiring disclosure of continuing, ongoing fraud. The fearful spectre of staggering damage actions if a lawyer did not disclose was enough to sway the Bar Association away from the new rule. Instead, the association attempted to give itself immunity from any such irritating litigation by adopting a model code requiring absolute secrecy, even when a lawyer learns he has been used as a tool of fraud.

The new code of ethics is only a model on which state courts and legislatures may base their own ethical standards. The New York State Bar Association was joined by the Florida bar in denouncing the new code for failing to even require that lawyers disclose a client's plan to commit murder. The president of the Federation of New York State Judges promptly blasted the new code for protecting "a regiment of criminals." The New Jersey bar committee branded it "totally unacceptable," while the Pennsylvania bar approved the code as "a great leap forward."

Senator Arlen Specter, a former Philadelphia district attorney, introduced a bill within a month of the ABA's controversial decision that would make it a federal crime for a lawyer not to blow the whistle on a client who is committing, or intends to commit, a criminal or fraudulent act. "The client ought not to have a right to use a lawyer's advice to cheat people," Specter explained. Such a binding, simple, sweeping law would at least have the effect of preventing a conflict-of-laws situation, in which a lawyer could be required to blow the whistle in one state and seal his lips in another.

From the trustee's report:

> The Trustee considers the ABA's action outrageous and irresponsible. The Trustee hopes that the ABA will reconsider the issue and that state bar authorities will reject the rule in favor of one that goes at least as far as the proposed rule, in permitting lawyers to prevent their clients from committing future frauds and from using lawyers as instruments in fraudulent schemes . . . No rules of professional ethics can or should exempt lawyers from the general legal proscription against willful blindness to their clients' crimes, or reckless participation in them.

Investment Bankers:

None of the investment bankers working with OPM knew that OPM was forging fake leases. But the trustee's report advances the notion that "the willingness of Goldman Sachs and Lehman Brothers to serve as OPM's investment bankers carried with it . . . a clear implication of sponsorship." The relationship of the investment banker to the company it sponsors "carried with it broader responsibilities than simply arranging financing on particular transactions." This obligation of due diligence did not extend to verification of the bogus leases because the investment bankers "never suspected a lease fraud and they assumed that the financing institutions and their counsel would never close a transaction without obtaining whatever verification was appropriate."

Even if the obligation to check the facts beneath a transaction is not assumed, Lehman Brothers failed to grasp the underlying facts behind OPM and disclose them to the financing institutions. The basic fact was that OPM was a hopelessly insolvent enterprise. The evidence was staring them right in the face: the enormous gap between lease receivables and equipment purchase obligations; the sevenfold buildup of equipment in inventory between 1977 and 1978; the continual cash-flow crises; the check kiting caused by the need to generate cash; the chaotic condition of OPM's accounting department; and the sure signs that early terminations and declining equipment values were driving OPM straight down the road to ruin.

OPM's financial condition was not "irrelevant" to the lease transactions, as both Lehman Brothers and Goldman Sachs insist. If Lehman Brothers had forced Goodman to supply them with a complete analysis of OPM's long-term profitability, the inevitable result would have been Lehman's earlier resignation: "Without Lehman's implicit imprimatur . . . other institutions would have shied away from OPM, with the result that OPM's collapse . . . would have occurred earlier and resulted in significantly smaller losses to the financing institutions."

Bankers:
Not that the bankers were blameless. They assumed Lehman Brothers was doing the checking and neglected to do any themselves. Of the nineteen institutions that extended $188 million in loans on bogus Rockwell leases, none bothered to "undertake even the most rudimentary efforts to verify the facts underlying the transactions they financed. Had they done so, they could have stopped the fraud at OPM dead in its tracks."

The St. Paul bank was certainly well aware of OPM's chaotic business practices, Goodman's personal peculiarities, and ominous trends in the leasing business as a whole. But lured by high interest rates and lulled by Lehman's assurances, St. Paul went ahead and extended bridge loan after bridge loan while doing nothing to verify transactions, not even bothering to send a representative to lease closings. Though St. Paul claims to have relied on Lehman as its "eyes and ears" on OPM, Lehman Brothers never claimed responsibility for verifying transactions. For St. Paul to blithely loan so much loosely secured cash to an obviously tottering enterprise, flying straight in the face of what it knew, was at best naïve, at worst deluded.

At least St. Paul, as a bridge lender, enjoyed the luxury of reviewing OPM's financials. Permanent lenders were not quite so privileged. Some institutions did not ask to see OPM statements on the grounds that OPM's financial condition was irrelevant. Others asked but were rebuffed on the grounds that OPM was a private company, and that its financial statements were confidential.

The banks found a full flurry of excuses for failing to verify leases, after the fact: there was no reason to contact a lessee as solid as Rockwell; they thought Singer Hutner, Lehman Brothers, or their closing counsel did it as a matter of course; they thought St. Paul had done it if the deal came off a bridge loan; they thought IBM attended closings and that was enough. The amazing fact was that one simple phone call by any of these institutions at any time would have blown the fraud, although too late to save the $200 million already dropped down the drain, as Robert Clare's efforts on behalf of Bankers Trust eventually showed.

Lessees:
Then there was Rockwell.

> "It is clear that a number of Rockwell's practices facilitated the fraud. One was the concentration of substantial responsibility . . . in Hasin's office . . . Other Rockwell practices that played into Goodman's hands were Rockwell's incomplete lease files, careless execution of closing documents, absence from closings, and disregard of the contractual obligation to pay rent directly to the financing institutions."

The Hasin Question:
None of the above might have mattered much, except for Sid Hasin. The trustee's investigation expended considerable effort in trying to determine Hasin's role in the fraud. Hasin himself denied complicity, a claim confirmed by Myron and the rest of the fraud team. But "the question remains whether he was aware of the fraud but chose not to speak . . . a welter of circumstantial evidence suggests the possibility of silent complicity."

The trustee concluded that the very nature of Goodman and Hasin's relationship "raises doubts concerning Hasin's loyalties and whether he dealt with OPM in an appropriate arm's length manner." Hasin has acknowledged making lease awards to OPM without competitive bidding. When Rockwell senior management instituted a "freeze" on dealing with OPM in the wake of the check-kiting scandal, Hasin so successfully "circumvented" and "vitiated" the effects of the freeze that "Lichtman was only vaguely aware of its existence."

There can be no forgetting the Black Book. Whether spurious, capricious, or altogether imaginary, the name itself nevertheless suggested a private arrangement verging on the illicit. Hasin on more than one occasion knowingly and improperly signed leases in the absence of approval from above or even an underlying piece of equipment; at one point he caused Rockwell to execute leases for two pieces of equipment, knowing that Rockwell wanted only one; he was even sent copies of financing documents on a number of fraudulent "bridges to nowhere." Goodman claims Hasin knew what they were about; Hasin is not able to recall even having seen them, let alone realizing what they were for.

There can be no avoiding the Smoking Gun: a three-ring binder sent by Goodman to Hasin in the summer of 1980, containing a chart reflecting twelve phantom and two altered leases. Hasin claims not to have noticed the numbers when he glanced at the chart in October of 1980. When cleaning up his office in January of 1981 he took the binder and the chart home with him, intending to "look at it at some later point in time." He is not able to explain why he selected this particular document out of the many thousands he left behind. He claims not to have even bothered to review it until March of 1981, after the fraud surfaced. At the suggestion of others at Rockwell he noted in the top right-hand corner: "Not reviewed until 3/25/81."

The trustee even provides a reasonable motive for Hasin's "silent complicity": by creating a situation in which Rockwell had exposed itself to enormous losses in the event of an OPM default, Hasin had a considerable investment in keeping OPM afloat. "If OPM defaulted, Hasin knew who would be blamed." Even a massive fraud would be better for him than a bankruptcy: "If the fraud ultimately came to light, he could successfully deny knowledge or participation."

> Hasin's unerring pattern in doing just the right thing in each instance to avoid uncovering the fraud creates a strong basis for inferring that Hasin knew Goodman was fraudulently financing Rockwell leases . . . Assuming Hasin had knowledge that Goodman was engaged in fraud, Hasin had a strong motive not to disclose it . . . Hasin made his career at Rockwell dependent on OPM's survival . . . If Hasin did not have knowledge of the fraud . . . given the number and quality of opportunities to discover it, his failure to do so amounted to reckless disregard of the interests of the financing institutions and of Rockwell itself.

Despite the Trustee's suspicions, however, no criminal action was taken against Hasin by any of the interested parties, and Rockwell even rehired him to serve as a consultant, primarily on matters concerning the OPM case and its aftermath.

On March 1, 1983, a "global settlement" was concluded among the various parties involved in civil actions arising from the fraud. The damages to Rockwell, Lehman Brothers, Singer Hutner, Fox & Co., and Rashba & Pokart could well have reached over $600,000,000. The settlement, for an undisclosed amount, has been widely reported as totaling $65 million, with the bulk of the damages borne by Rockwell. Industry sources have placed the figure at somewhere between $30 and $40 million.

Rockwell did not charge any of these fraud-related losses against earnings, referring to them as "immaterial." A spokesman for Rockwell's outside accountants noted that losses amounting to less than 10 percent of the company's $2.2 billion shareholder equity "might properly be considered not material."

In March of 1984, Rockwell submitted a claim for unspecified fraud-related losses to the Air Force. Since Rockwell used OPM computers mainly on military projects such as the B-1 Bomber, the MX Missile, and the Space Shuttle, the company asserted its entitlement to reimbursement for losses suffered fulfilling those contracts. Negotiations on the claim were to be conducted between a Rockwell assistant controller and the Air Force civilian contract officer assigned to Rockwell's assembly plant in Palmdale, California.

The Wall Street Journal, March 23, 1984: "An Air Force spokesman said it wasn't clear when the negotiations would begin or how long they would take . . . The Air Force declined to specify how much Rockwell was seeking; the spokesman said publication of details could jeopardize the Air Force's negotiating position. Rockwell declined to comment."

In 1982 government contracts accounted for 52 percent of Rockwell's $7.4 billion in revenue. In that year it jumped from sixteenth to eighth place among the nation's defense contractors.

OPM is now operating under a voluntary reorganization petition under Chapter Eleven of the Bankruptcy Code. Its remaining assets are its computers still on lease; its revenues are the lease payments still flowing in; all early-termination provisions were canceled by the court; any profits are to be disbursed to the creditors in proper order.

In January of 1984, OPM moved from 71 Broadway to smaller, cheaper offices in Stamford, Connecticut.

The final phase of the trustee's investigation was to find out where all the rotten money went. The total of all funds bilked by OPM over its ten-year operation came to well over $228 million, a sum described by the federal judge in New York as "without parallel in the annals of this court."

Pre-Rockwell frauds grossed over $40 million. By 1978 nearly all of that money had been repaid. The Rockwell fraud grossed over $188 million, with a net of $106 million, representing the total take minus payments on the "good" versions of the "bad" leases and other expenses.

In attempting to trace any diversions of funds to foreign bank accounts or other hiding places, the trustee found no "large, suspicious disbursements . . . unexplained." After totaling all "extraordinary cash outlays" from the beginning of 1978, only a $3.5-million gap remained between the total outlay and the net proceeds from the fraud. Another $4.4 million was traceable to "misuse of funds by Goodman and Weissman."

The finding that substantially all the proceeds of the Rockwell fraud were consumed in OPM's hopelessly losing operations tends to support the assertions of the fraud participants that no fraud proceeds were diverted into secret accounts.

Of the approximately $4 million skimmed by Goodman and Weissman off the top of OPM's cash pool, $3,392,935 could be traced to various charities. In 1981 alone, as the company was going rapidly under, corporate and personal charitable contributions reached their peak: $1,927,750.

Myron and Mordy donated primarily to Orthodox Jewish organizations in the United States and in Israel, but they also contributed handsomely to the United Way, the Metropolitan Museum, to an old woman Myron found picking through garbage for food, and a boy with cancer whose plight Myron read about in the New York *Post*. Myron's favorite charity was The Hebrew Academy of the Five Towns and Rockaway, to which he gave a total of $1,043,128. To Yeshiva University, over the same period, he gave $876,043 as partial payment on a pledge of $10,000,000. In recognition for his services, Myron Goodman was elected the youngest member of the board of trustees in the Yeshiva's history.

Myron gave a little speech at Yeshiva at the time of the pledge.

"I'm a firm believer in God. We do God's work. We are put here to do what he wants. God wanted me to do this. My thought processes were really not my own here. I'm here for a purpose."

Fulfilled in mysterious ways.

AUTHOR'S NOTE

Much of the factual material in this book is drawn from transcript deposition testimony by the principle participants, taken before the OPM trustee. This testimony served as the primary basis for the *Report of the Trustee Concerning Fraud and Other Misconduct in the Management of the Affairs of the Debtor,* as submitted by the trustee and his special counsel, Wilmer, Cutler & Pickering, to the United States Bankruptcy Court, Southern District of New York. Thousands of pages of deposition testimony were supplemented with interviews by the author of a number of the participants, among whom John Clifton, Joseph Hutner, and Martin Zelbow were particularly forthcoming. Dialogue was reconstructed from the best recollections of all available sources, as reconciled by the author to form a reliable composite. In instances where testimony concerning events differs substantially among various parties, such discrepancies are noted in the text.